American Culture
and the Quest for Christ

American Culture and the Quest for Christ

by Anthony T. Padovano

SHEED & WARD   NEW YORK

For those who wait and hope . . .

© *Sheed and Ward, Inc.*, 1970
Library of Congress No. 77–82597
Standard Book No. 8362–1315–7

Manufactured in the United States of America

Preface

Theology is a search for reality. Since reality cannot be met exclusively in Scripture or totally in the Church, theology must take seriously that which really happens beyond the periphery of these realities. The task of a theologian is not the creation but the discovery and the proclamation of the real. Hence, a theologian must be sensitive to life whenever it is happening if he hopes to give life an ultimate and persuasive interpretation.

Of the many questions concerning life, few are more urgent than the need to know whether life has a meaning to be preserved. In traditional terminology, we call this salvation. The foreverness of life which faith confesses demands that death not terminate life and, furthermore, that absurdity never eliminate life's essential intelligibility. Salvation requires that man always have a life to live and that he be given endless and infinite opportunities to give life further meaning. Immortality without purpose or without dynamic growth is merely another form of death.

Whether Jesus Christ is able to save man's humanity is the point of this present book and its forthcoming complement. To answer this inquiry one must know something of what it means to be human and what precisely is worth saving in human experience.

It is my hope to offer in this study a Christology that is both contemporary and American. To do this, a distinctive methodology is imperative.

The articulation of a Christology in an American context will require two books. Each of these will be a self-contained unit and yet one will complement the other. In this first book, it will be my intention to delineate what may be called pretheological data. It is pretheological not because it is not theology, but because it is not formal theology. A second book will develop explicit theological conclusions from this data.

There are three features which should be incorporated into a contemporary study of salvation and Christ. The first of these concerns the "reality" of a need for salvation. One must not presuppose that salvation is a category in which man wishes to interpret himself. This must be demonstrated. The first book, therefore, will explore contemporary philosophy, world religion, American culture, and American literature in an effort to determine whether modern man, and especially the modern American, is interested any longer in a search for salvation. If theology is involved with the real, it must ask itself what is real about man and whether man really wants to be saved.

A second feature of this inquiry into the mystery of Christ is a synthesis of the teaching of the Scriptures and the Church on who Christ is and what he is for. In the past, we may have diminished the impact of Christology by limiting this study to questions concerning the nature and redemptive mission of Christ. A more effective approach would explore, in addition to this, the Christological import of Creation and Revelation.

A final feature of this study will be an attempt to draw from the whole range of questions which confront us a contemporary spirituality. Beneath the surface agnosticism, the sometimes hostile atheism, and even the artificial faith some may profess, there is an anxious desire for something to believe in and affirm. Our age is especially attuned to religious values and suffers from the lack of a viable spirituality.

It is my hope that this book and its sequel will make those who read it conscious anew of how God chooses human life to reveal himself and redeem us. So worthy a value is human life that even he who "was by nature God did not consider being equal to God a thing to be clung to" and therefore emptied himself and stood by our side.

Anthony T. Padovano
Immaculate Conception Seminary
Darlington, New Jersey
December 20, 1969

Contents

Introduction

Man, the Unanswered Question

Something along the way went wrong. What it was or when it happened is difficult to say. This we do know: something went wrong. There is hardly a serious thinker who doubts this. At times, most people sense the same experience. There is a vague, indefinable problem involved with being a human being. Most people, sooner or later, feel strangely responsible for this condition, somehow guilty about it, and yet not certain they should be. If something has actually gone wrong, can we recover? Is there a real possibility that someone may reveal to us the nature of this malady in our very nature? Is salvation an unfounded wish for the impossible or is it a realistic hope?

Pessimists maintain that the severity of the deformity which afflicts the human family precludes healing. At best, man is condemned to live out his tragic existence; at worst, he is destined to suffer ever-increasing absurdity until he is extinct. The forces which set man on this path to destruction were set in motion long before anyone can recall. One day, as a result of this, the planet will contain no human life and there shall not remain a memory of man. The courageous pessimist accepts this situation and vows to do what he can to hold off the darkness as long as possible. The fearful pessimist decides that to struggle is to prolong suffering and to postpone the inevitable.

Optimists recognize human distress but insist it is curable if men do the right thing long enough, looking neither to heaven for help nor to hell with misgiving. They argue that the existential sickness we suffer is not terminal and that man has it in his power to save himself. Salvation may require an act of the will (Schopenhauer) or the greatest pleasure for the largest number (Mill). It may come about if there is economic equity (Marx), or if we can achieve maximum awareness in a situation which may be therapeutically painful but is at least clinically objective and scientifically precise (Freud).

Even if such "optimists" despair of man's saving himself, they know how he can be saved; they declare salvation possible, and they offer a program for its accomplishment.

At the risk of appearing biased, we list Christians among the realists rather than among the pessimists or the optimists. Christians seek a middle course. Man is a creature who does, indeed, suffer a malady. As long as he lives, he will never be all he should be. He lives hardly a day without sin. He verges on despair and sometimes collapses before it. Man is able to destroy those who love him, to corrupt the innocent, to revel in the death of his enemies and even of those friends whose competition he feels too keenly. Every evil the human imagination was able to devise has come to pass.

Something did go wrong along the way. Christians are "pessimistic" enough to insist that the solution to the human predicament is not in our power; they are "optimistic" enough to proclaim that a solution is nonetheless forthcoming.

The human family knows it needs saving. We may differ as to who can save, or what saves, or how salvation comes about, or whether a Savior is necessary for salvation. We sense, however, our need. The need is so keen that our philosophy and our literature are often a cry for help or a muffled moan which tell those who listen attentively that we fear we have nowhere to turn.

The need for salvation is the fundamental factor in man's religious experience. The difference between philosophy and religion occurs when men no longer speculate about an answer to the question of man but add to this speculation a prayer for help and light for further comprehension. This turning to religion does not exonerate man from his responsibilities, or demean him, or make him dependent. Instead, it releases him for freedom and inspires him with some awareness of who he is and why he is. So basic is the need for salvation that it would have been there even if sin or death had never touched us. Man was made to turn for help. He has required rescuing for as long as he has been. The nature and depth of this need changed with sin, but the fact that he needed something or someone to save him did not change.

The present age has become aware of how infinite human need is. This awareness predisposes our age toward a religious interpretation of life. Self-satisfied eras are further from God than self-questioning eras. We have become nonconformists about how our religious expression will take form and even about whether we wish to call these needs "religious" any longer. We are not, however, nonconformists about whether we shall be religious. Religious awareness of life is present in our literature, our philosophy, our music, our protest against the scientism, materialism, or historicism of much nineteenth century thought. The twentieth century, to the surprise of many, will be recorded in history as a time when men understood how much they needed a Savior and how impossible it was for men to save themselves. Precisely because men have tried most of the salvation substitutes for God, they are able to recognize more clearly the truth of the statement that God is man's only hope. Even our fascination with declaring God dead came from a hope so real and yet so uncertain of itself that it feared God was not there or could not be reached.

When Nietzsche said God was dead it was a triumphant proclamation meant to usher in man as his own Savior. When we said God was dead, it was a cry of despair, a plea for help, an end of all our hopes and the beginning of cosmic despair. When Nietzsche said God was dead, he was happy at the thought. When we said God was dead, it was because we were terrified. Even as we said it, we hoped it was not true.

This century has been marked with a hunger and a hope for God. It made so many mistakes, even about God, that it feared it might make others and misplace its trust. Hence our century, let it be noted, was a century of waiting, not sterile waiting but expectant waiting, waiting for Godot, waiting because it believed, almost in spite of itself, that God would come this way again and speak so that we might hear. History will say of us that we wanted God and waited for him, sometimes faithlessly, perhaps, too often without hope, but we waited. We were not a century which knew God would not come or which wanted him to go away.

This first book will attempt to demonstrate how we waited, the mistakes we may have made while waiting, and the substitutes we offered for God, more particularly for Christ, as we became impatient. The object of this book is more than the transmission of data. It will try to communicate an experience of our needs and an awareness of our openness to some form of salvation.

Christianity and Christ always happen in an experience, never in the mere articulation and repetition of truths. This is not to say that doctrine is unimportant. Quite the contrary. Doctrine, however, is only conceptual knowledge rather than personal affirmation unless, of course, it issues from, accompanies, and tends toward experience. Doctrine matters, not because it is an end in itself, but because experience is too polyvalent and too individualistic for community to grow from it alone.

The approach we take will utilize Scripture and will even consider it central. Much of this will be more apparent in the related book which will follow this one. We must not, however, limit ourselves to Scripture. Even Scripture is not enough when we seek to know whether we have felt the need for a Savior. Nor does it tell us completely who Christ is.

All men, we believe, tend toward Christ. They do not always seek him in biblical categories. The way men most often seek Christ is in their need for salvation. Biblical categories clarify this need and declare a normative explanation of the origins and destiny of this need. Men seldom begin and never end their search for salvation in biblical categories.

The methodology we employ is one which, we believe, is suited to our times. We wish to know whether God or Christ, faith or salvation are real concerns. Does man care to be saved? Or is salvation something religions engender in order to perpetuate themselves? Is salvation a category one uses to explain primitive man but a category unfamiliar to modern man?

An effective way to test the genuineness of this concern is to consider what man says about this need when he is not a believer or a theologian. Christians should welcome such an approach since they ought to be optimistic enough to insist that reason retains its validity even after sin and that at the basis of valid human experience is a religious concern. It is not as though Christ must be encountered in terms easily recognizable to a Christian as distinctively Christian terms.

The connections between and among the topics we discuss or the evidence we offer will not be always logical. The universality and multiformity of the subject we consider do not permit logical clarity in every case. The viability of these connections must manifest itself in their cohesiveness with life situations rather than in their strict syllogistic consistency.

This book is meant for an age which has questioned

radically the validity of the religious endeavor. We believe
that it has raised this question, not because it wishes to
dismiss faith, but because it feels it must be religious in a new
way.

1

Salvation Themes
in Modern Philosophy

Arthur Schopenhauer

In this opening chapter, we shall consider the life and thought of five major philosophers in an effort to discover whether philosophy in its analysis of man and its reflection on being is conscious of a need for salvation. The first of these philosophers is Arthur Schopenhauer.

Schopenhauer was born in Danzig in 1788 and died in 1860. Both the life he lived and the philosophy he wrote were marked by pessimism. He tended to be paranoic, egotistical, and lonely. He reacted neurotically to noise and was capable of completely rejecting those who did not accept him as he wished to be accepted.

There were three significant influences upon his thought: the *Upanishads*, Immanuel Kant, and Hegel. Two of these influences shaped his philosophy by their positive contributions; the last influenced him by his negative reaction to it.

The influence of the *Upanishads* will become evident when we discuss Schopenhauer's concept of the good man but more especially in his approach to salvation by means of self-negation in asceticism.

Kant was a further positive influence on Schopenhauer. Kant maintained that human knowledge was a synthesis between things-in-themselves (noumena) and the mind's complex structure (phenomena). It was only through his mind that the world existed for man. Knowledge resulted from the interaction of things-in-themselves and our mental processes. Although Schopenhauer would not accept the entire Kantian theory, he agreed with its essentials.

Hegel was an occasion for Schopenhauer's negative reaction. Hegel reasoned that Absolute Reality explained everything even though it needed no explanation itself. Absolute Reality was concretized in nature and strove constantly to harmonize its inner reality with its manifest reality in nature. The "Spirit" is the name Hegel gave to the energy of the Absolute which was at work in completing nature.

Schopenhauer rejected Hegel's optimistic view of history and life. For Schopenhauer, it was intolerable that Spirit or even Reason influence Nature. It was even more unthinkable that everything which happened in Nature happened for the best. Schopenhauer argued that Hegel seemed unaware of evil and suffering and that he was naive in his assumption that evil and suffering serve a useful purpose.

The substance of Schopenhauer's view of the world is contained in his three-volume work, *The World as Will and Idea*. The first volume of this work was published in 1819, the last two in 1844.

Schopenhauer is a voluntarist who had an admitted influence on Nietzsche and Freud. Freud and Schopenhauer agree in their pessimistic outlook on life, a pessimism derivative from their respective voluntaristic positions. Nietzsche is more optimistic, emphasizing instead the creative power of man's will.

THE WORLD IS MY IDEA

Schopenhauer maintains that without a subject to perceive it, there is no world. He begins his philosophical work with the famous sentence: "The world is my idea." By this, Schopenhauer means that the world is an illusion which begins to be what it is only when a subject is present. We cannot make a statement about the world unless we presume first our presence in it as a perceiving subject. In the world, the subject knows, but the subject is not known.

In spite of this concentration on the experiencing subject, Schopenhauer is not a radical Idealist. The substance of the world, he argues, is neither the object-in-itself nor even the subject-in-itself but the Will-in-itself.

The human subject for Schopenhauer is more than an observer of the world. He is rooted in the world. The source of his being rooted in the world is the body which always exists with a will. To be an individual, in fact, is to be rooted in the world as the body of a ceaselessly striving will.

Thus, Schopenhauer rejects Kant's interpretation of thing-in-itself. He accepts Kant's insistence on some reality independent of the human mind, and he calls this "Will." The whole world is nothing more than a manifestation of Will-in-itself though, of course, not a perfect manifestation of this. The world itself is the result of an endlessly-striving Will which objectifies itself as world, without itself being moved or changed thereby. The force by which the world proceeds and of which the world is a manifestation is Will. This Will is beyond time and space, unique in itself, distinct from the world. It is without cause, the ground of all reality and, hence, Absolute.

This Will is at work in all physical force and in all animal instinct. It is the life of the world and the substance of all we experience.

The clearest insight we have into the nature of Will-in-itself is the human will. Will-in-itself is beyond man's will but nonetheless it is experienced most immediately in man. In man, Will becomes aware of its own willing and conscious of what it wills.

In man, then, the Will struggling in the world achieves consciousness and knows it is suffering. Thus suffering is man's inescapable fate. He is condemned to suffer with, as we shall see, a limited hope of deliverance in aesthetic creation and a victory, of sorts, in asceticism.

The individual man touches the reality of Will-in-itself when he experiences his own individuality. He comes to realize, however, that all willing in man comes from his deficiency. He learns that life is a succession of wishes satisfied and new wishes desired. This undying desire condemns man to restlessness and unhappiness. The influence of the *Upanishads* is evident in Schopenhauer's analysis of the source of human distress.

Salvation from this endless cycle of wishes, fulfillment and more wishes lies in a surrender of our self-interest by absorption in artistic endeavors or ascetical living.

Art delivers us from the servitude of human desire. It makes us self-forgetful and renders us timeless. Art does this because it expresses a reality outside the categories of space and time. It seeks that reality which is subject to no change, that is, the Will. An artistic work possesses, therefore, the ability to reveal to us not moment-to-moment existence but the eternal in the temporal process. Art realizes its fullest potential in its presentation of tragedy. In tragedy, the struggle of the Will-in-itself in the temporal world becomes visible. Tragedy is especially forceful when the hero suffers, not because of his own sins, but because of the original sin of existence itself. In this case, one suffers merely because he is alive.

SUFFERING AND FREEDOM FROM IT

The reason why men fear death is because they fear the loss of their individuality. This is vanity. Men should realize that unless they lose their individuality, they never achieve timelessness. Death does not destroy anything real. It merely dispels the illusion that made us assume we were self-sufficient individuals or independent creatures. Thus, in death, we pass away, not substantially, but only in terms of our illusory spatial-temporal existence.

Death, then, is an appearance in which a man loses his individuality but retains his reality. To understand this one must realize that for Schopenhauer the reality of man is not found in himself but in the eternal reality of Will-in-itself. Our illusions are so deceptive that some may think death returns us to the Will. In actual fact, it does not since we were never separate from the Will. Death changes nothing. It makes us aware of something which was always true although we failed to recognize it. Man is one form Will takes. He is nothing in himself.

The Will which makes man be what he is endlessly strives in us since struggle is the Will's nature. In nature, every being, living and nonliving must struggle to survive. Man is no exception to the universal suffering of nature. In fact, he suffers more since he is conscious that he suffers and becomes conscious that suffering cannot end.

Indeed, all efforts to bring suffering to an end are futile since suffering does not cease. It merely assumes new forms. We know this from our own experience. Everything we hope for dissatisfies us when we have it. For man, to live is to suffer.

Schopenhauer offers one way to salvation, but it is an arduous way. Salvation lies in a denial of the will to live. Every assertion of the will is a dedication to life as it is or has been. To will something is, therefore, to intensify egoism. It leads us to imagine we are something real, and it tends to make us treat people as objects. It is better to will nothing, not even life.

The source of evil, properly so-called, in life is every unnecessary infringement upon another person. This occurs and evil, consequently, endures because men have an excessive will to live. A person who greedily clings to the illusion of his individuality, and who, therefore, imagines he is something real refuses to allow other persons their place. He makes everyone except himself an object.

Goodness occurs when this situation is counteracted by justice or by virtue. The just man is the person who does not have an excessive will to live. He instinctively recognizes a rightness and wrongness about things even though there are no laws or commandments which force him to do this.

The virtuous or good man goes beyond this: he does not merely restrict what is excessive about his will to live. He denies that will altogether. As he does this, he is able to see all men as he sees himself. He regards their well-being as his well-being; he enters into and shares their suffering; he loves them for what they are and for who they are; he does not value them or serve them because they are objects or because they may reinforce his selfish need to live.

The good man rejects pleasure, pursues voluntary renunciation, becomes indifferent to life, and achieves perfect willlessness. Though he will not commit suicide, he refuses to reproduce life or to live in luxury. Suicide is not, as it might at first appear, a denial of the will to live. It is rather an assertion of one's individuality. This observation of Schopenhauer is borne out by Dostoevsky who, in *The Possessed*, has Kirillov commit suicide to prove that he, like God, has life at his disposal. Kirillov affirms the uniqueness and supremacy of his individuality by taking his life.

The person who commits suicide, Schopenhauer observes, is dissatisfied with life rather than indifferent to it. The suicide underscores his individuality and intensifies his egotism by a dramatic, almost theatrical, gesture. This is wrong. The good man awaits death and denies his will to live by actions which are less ostentatious. When his death does come, he welcomes it as a decisive end to his remaining egoism.

The sole hope for salvation comes, then, as a person resigns himself to suffering. It is true that artistic endeavors, as we have seen, offer a momentary relief from the suffering of life, but this relief is not lasting. Man is soon drawn back to the cares and pain of everyday living. Only an ascetical life leads to enduring salvation. The real cause of all suffering is individuality. Once again, the influence of the *Upanishads* on Schopenhauer is evident. Salvation demands a rejection of self. In this rejection, the good man finds relief from pointless suffering and resigns himself to the suffering of existence or of the Will-in-itself. He becomes a person who has nothing to do with evil. He has renounced himself, accepted reality, and awaits death with joy.

CRITIQUE

The search for permanence, for something durable, is the most noteworthy element in Schopenhauer's thought. Man is saved because he recognizes that more than himself is at issue in living. He is saved because he refuses to see himself as an absolute.

There are further aspects of Schopenhauer's synthesis which leave much to be desired. His rejection of the world as really real disturbs a Christian. His thought leads, it seems, more to individual salvation than to a concern for the salvation of others. While it is true that one does not inflict evil on others, it is also true that a community relationship with others in the process of salvation is rendered impossible.

In fact, it can be said that this search for one's own salvation seems hardly to be a salvation. One wonders if there is not an antihumanism at work in Schopenhauer's salvation, a severity about life and salvation which may be untrue or, even if it be true, make salvation undesirable. Schopenhauer asks us, in effect, to achieve salvation by rising above the human condition and by renouncing human nature. We think it is possible to save others and ourselves by accepting their reality and our own. Such a salvation takes the human condition seriously and passes through it, never relinquishing its reality, as transformation is achieved.

Auguste Comte

Auguste Comte developed the philosophical system called Positivism by his strenuous efforts to reconcile science and religion. This reconciliation was a secular religion or a religious secularity rather than an encounter between two mighty forces. Comte's syncretism was the result of a tendency, continuing into the present, which seeks the fusion of the secular and the sacred.

The age in which Comte lived prized concordism, or when it did not, pitted science and religion against each other. The idea of a higher synthesis toward which both science and religion aspired and in which each played its part was not a popular notion. This was a time when the conflict between science and religion sharpened because each was insensitive to what the other was doing; each suspected the other of error; and, hence, both felt threatened.

The world of science was electrified with the discovery of the scientific method, and it was emboldened by its remarkable successes. Science wondered whether this new method might bring the human family a salvation which had eluded it for centuries. In all eagerness scientists called for the vigorous application of the scientific method to human affairs. It was a method, of course, neither used by religion nor, as we know today, able to solve religious questions. In fact, men would discover that there is more to human affairs than the scientific method could control.

The world of religion had not yet realized the scope or depth of this new age. Contrary to what many may think, this was not as easy for religion to accomplish as it might seem at first sight. Christianity was convinced it had something of value to offer men in its Scripture, its worship, and its style of life. There was, furthermore, a conviction that there were truths about man and about life which had to be spoken, even though some men might not care to hear them, and others might articulate them poorly. It was not yet clear how these values could be preserved in the light of a new scientific age which, at best, could not, it seemed, support religious claims and, at worst, denied their validity.

The arduous contest between science and religion was neither futile nor unnecessary. It was not futile because, as each side was seasoned in the controversy, each learned better what it had to offer man and what it could not do for him. Both science and religion had to understand that neither was a total answer to life, and that human history would hereafter need both of them.

It was not an unnecessary conflict because the issues involved were too turbulent and too vast for either side to know exactly how to proceed. Science, for example, was certain that the earth circled the sun; religion was certain that the Scriptures were true. The effort to define the "true" for either side was bound to be painful. At stake in the controversy was not only the objective truth of this or that proposition but the validity of a whole way of looking at life and reality. It took many years and considerable contention for science to know that even when we knew the earth circled the sun we had not helped man live a more human life in the deepest sense of that term. We had more data with which to operate, and this knowledge was progress. Whether or not this knowledge was wisdom was another question.

Religion, likewise, had to learn that its message said less about the physical universe than it had imagined. Religious truth, furthermore, was less empirically verifiable than many religious men had hoped it might be. Today it is fair to maintain that we are more aware of the power and promise of science. We are also more conscious of the nature of faith and of the need men have for a hope more ultimate than their knowledge. The clash of opinions proved to be, as Whitehead observed, not a disaster but an opportunity. The contest was, therefore, neither futile nor unnecessary. We are the inheritors of its resulting benefits.

POSITIVISM

The most ambitious structure for expressing the scientific reinterpretation of all religious categories was devised by Auguste Comte. In essence, his approach does not preserve a constructive tension between science and religion but attempts the resolution of that tension in an unwieldy artifact. Comte was not aware that the solution of this tension was unfortunate because without the tension science and religion could no longer serve as a mutual corrective to each other. The effort to solve this tension gives us, however, another insight into the unending search for salvation which characterizes the thinking of many major philosophers.

Auguste Comte labored to create a religion of humanity. His major work in this endeavor began with the six volumes of his *Course in Positive Philosophy* (1830–1842) and went on to include his plan for an ideal society in his *System of Positive Policy* (1851–1854). He became so specific about his new religion of humanity that he wrote a book entitled *A Positive Calendar* (1849) and even *A Positive Catechism* (1852).

There were a number of important influences on the thinking of Comte. From Saint- Simon, he learned that a social science was needed to explain and guide human planning; this science, which would later develop into sociology, would reduce social phenomena to laws and create a secularized spiritual order which would take the place of religion. With de Maistre and de Bonald, Comte decided that social organization required a religious framework. From the French Revolution and its exaltation of reason, he derived the thought that religion must be secular. The French Encyclopedists of the eighteenth century taught him that a history of the progress of the human mind was useful for interpreting the nature and social significance of the sciences.

The "Positivism" begun by Comte has occupied a leading place in modern thought. The specifics Comte developed were less significant than the spirit he set in motion. The positivistic spirit is suspicious of theology or metaphysics. It prefers to limit thought to those areas where definite, rational, empirical answers can be given. John Stuart Mill, Karl Marx and Sigmund Freud, all of whom we shall discuss in this chapter, were influenced by this spirit. American culture and the pragmatic philosophy of John Dewey, which we shall consider in the third chapter of this book, were also in favor of this spirit.

Positivism proposes a problem-solving approach to life. It is practical rather than contemplative, choosing to solve concrete difficulties one by one rather than to present a universal worldview. As a means to this end, it applies the empirical sciences to every aspect of human life. Positivism intends to give a total answer to life. It does this, in effect, although it explicitly denies this objective when it assumes that a total meaning comes about by a solution of particular problems and when it insists dogmatically that the scientific method can answer infallibly all the legitimate questions man raises. Positivism is more rigorous than religion in its contention that certain questions cannot be honored by intelligent men and that the posing of them is as fatuous as the attempt to answer them.

Comte's most enduring influence came from the scientific orientation he gave philosophy. His least viable proposal was his creation of a religion of humanity.

A RELIGION OF HUMANITY

Comte declared in his *System of Positive Polity:* "Today, there are only two camps: the one is retrograde and anarchical, where God confusedly presides; the other is organic and progressive, being systematically devoted to humanity."

Before we consider the religion of humanity which Comte develops, we should say a word about his outline of the law of scientific progress since this insight is pivotal to an understanding of his thought. For Comte, each science and, hence, all human knowing passes through three distinct stages of growth. This progression is not only inevitable; it is also irreversible. These stages include the theological, the metaphysical and the scientific.

Each of these stages brings with it a concomitant and representative social organization of life. In the theological stage of knowledge, for example, human emotions are projected into the physical environment, and events are explained in terms of gods and spirits. The society which results from this outlook is military and aggressive. In the metaphysical stage of knowing, man empties his environment of gods and spirits and explains reality in terms of abstract essences. Abstraction is substituted for the excessive personalism which saw divine persons and powers everywhere. The societal form which follows upon this view is legal and juridical. The scientific state of human knowing is final and perfect. It rejects all appeal to unobservable beings, and it accepts the impossibility of achieving absolute knowledge. This leads to an industrial society.

Unfortunately, all men in the same society do not move forward into the successive stages of knowledge at the same rate. The metaphysical stage, for example, has remained longer than it should have because many seek a compromise between the discredited theological approach to life and the positivistic spirit. This second stage will endure until the positivistic spirit prevails.

We shall see later that Karl Marx will be sympathetic to the basic principles in Comte's system although he will have little patience with the form in which Comte situated his thought.

Of more interest to us is Comte's delineation of a religion of humanity. He called for the ordering of society by a new elite. He himself was to be the high priest and the supreme social planner of this society. There would be a priesthood and a clergy whose numbers would include secular sociologists, men who would preach a positivistic gospel, be available for counsel, arbitrate disputes and control education and public morality. Women would influence private morality by the example of their dignity, discipline and austerity. They would assure monogamous marriage and live out lives of perpetual widowhood if their husbands should die. Society, then, was to be rigidly ordered. There was to be not only a priesthood but ritual, holydays and worship.

Comte's eagerness for this endeavor came from his belief that social improvement required moral transformation. Since religion could no longer provide the energy for ethical conversion, science must carry on this mission. The religion of humanity would be nontheistic but it would not be permissive or immoral. It would worship, in place of God, the Great Being which is humanity past, present and future. Its moral imperative would compel man to "live for others." The tonality and temper of this new society would be governed by the cult of reason. Reason would be the norm for its faith and its morality.

Comte aimed at nothing less than a complete system. The individual, he argued, is not significant apart from the collective organism in which he achieves existence, salvation and immortality. A religion which teaches an immortality apart from the collective social organism in which we live is erroneous and harmful. It is erroneous because it presupposes that there is an immaterial principle in man. It is harmful because it draws man's attention away from his social tasks. The only genuine immortality man may be promised is in the inspiring example he gives his fellowmen and in the social forces he helps set in motion. This new man Comte dreamed of would live for others in the service of the Great Being of humanity, and he would substitute a love for the human race in place of his former love for God.

The specifics of Comte's vision included a new calendar which would commemorate the great men in history who furthered the progress of humanity. Christian saints were supplanted by philosophers, scientists, political and military leaders, poets. A catechism was also written in which Comte explains that the objective of this religion of humanity is not affluence but a universal moral and human order.

CRITIQUE

There were a number of advantages to what Comte was trying to do. He sought to give modern science a human dimension and a human commitment. He saw more clearly than many of his contemporaries the unity between and among the sciences and their relationship to one another. He helped give rise to a new humanism which focused attention on self-less service of one's fellowmen in a series of concrete tasks.

Comte's work was serious enough, at least in its nonreligious aspects, to have had a considerable influence on John Stuart Mill. His writing accelerated in Germany that antimetaphysical, materialistic, and sociologically-oriented version of Hegelianism which culminated in the thought of Karl Marx. Nor are Comte and Marx far apart in their mutual belief that an ultimate state of society planned and governed by reason is possible.

Some have scoffed at the specifics Comte devised in his eagerness to create a new religion. To his credit it can be said he was a dreamer, a visionary who wanted humanity to be better than it was. He was a man of hope who thought he foresaw Utopia beyond the horizon and became impatient to reach it. Comte's ideal was apocalyptic and eschatological. For this he can hardly be faulted.

A Christian, nonetheless, takes exception to much that Comte attempted. He sees in Comte's synthesis the lengths some will go to in order to assure salvation. In Comte, there is a reemergence of the Pelagianism which never ceases to tempt us. Pelagianism is a search for salvation in manageable limits conducted under our control. Christianity counters that salvation cannot occur wholly within the resources of the human family. Christianity insists, furthermore, that men have every right to expect paradise even though they have here no lasting city. In Comte, the dream of an earthly paradise which never ceases to tempt us reappears. Karl Marx dreams the same dream and, as we shall see, so does American culture.

A Christian finds Comte's ultimate synthesis stale. There is a dreariness about an explanation of human life which limits itself to reason. There is a certain naivete about the reduction of the complexities of reality to simple components and practical projects. This may account for the fact that Comte is bland when compared to the Gospel his religion seeks to supplant. Apparently, the easier and more efficient way is not always the better way. In Comte suffering serves no purpose and, perhaps, because of this his synthesis lacks grandeur and sublimity.

The ultimate objective for Comte was service of one's fellowman. In a manner not comprehensible in Comte's system, Christ lived for others and did this so persuasively that he has inspired countless numbers to do the same. The explanation for this may lie in something not easily explainable. It may well be that one does more "for" others when he has a depth or faith "from" which he operates.

Comte hoped for salvation in a universe of reasonable laws which would regulate human behavior. In so doing, he created something more artificial than the religion he thought was so arbitrary. His search for salvation was real, even though his effort may not long be remembered.

John Stuart Mill

The term "utilitarianism" was first used in 1863 as the title of a book by John Stuart Mill. It refers to a theory which evaluates the morality of human conduct in relationship to its utility for humanity at large.

One of the more lasting influences on Stuart Mill was his own father, John, who was a famous English philosopher in his own right. Auguste Comte brought social science to the attention of Stuart Mill. Mill depended most immediately on the thought of Jeremy Bentham. Bentham worked out an equation between happiness and pleasure, and on this basis appealed to the principle of the greatest happiness for the greatest number as the ultimate moral norm. Mill differed from Bentham in his insistence on the qualitative content of pleasure rather than on its quantitative intensity as an ultimate norm. This refinement of Bentham's thought brought a measure of sophistication and subtlety to utilitarianism.

Mill wrote *System of Logic* in 1843. In 1863, he published his most famous work, *Utilitarianism*. His indebtedness to Comte was evident in a book he issued two years later, *Auguste Comte and Positivism*. He disagreed, however, with Comte's preoccupation with external structures and procedures in the search for happiness. Mill was convinced that a more introspective approach was needed, one better suited to the individual's pleasure.

THE PRINCIPLE OF UTILITARIANISM

Mill was eager to discover a norm which would help both the individual and society to judge accurately between right and wrong. The norm would be most effective if it were simple and practical. Mill's system, as we shall see, takes on wider implications than ethics alone, since the norm he seeks requires at least an implicit understanding of what man's purpose in life may be.

Mill states explicitly that he is looking for something clearer and more concrete than an instinctive awareness of what morality is. This awareness is too vague, too little subject to logic and too confusing. Men need a moral system which would be applicable in all individual cases and so convincing that a person would have no doubt as to how he should proceed at the moment when moral decisions had to be made. Utilitarianism, Mill reasoned, offered men both the ability to express their moral nature and to do this in the context of clarity and altruism.

Mill defines utilitarianism as a "creed which accepts as the foundation of morals, Utility, or the greatest happiness principle." Actions are right if they promote happiness, wrong if they produce the reverse. Happiness is "pleasure and the absence of pain"; unhappiness is "pain and the privation of pleasure."

The position Mill takes on human happiness is the direct opposite of Schopenhauer's. Schopenhauer thought that men were offered most in pain, renunciation and death. Mill required maximum pleasure for maximum happiness. There is more complexity in Mill's system than may appear at first sight. Actions are good, not only when pleasure is inherent in them, but even if they can eventually become a means of promoting happiness or preventing pain. Thus, one may be morally obliged to perform a less pleasurable action in the present so that more pleasure will accrue to more people in the future. There is need for sacrifice and charity in Mill's philosophy, but this sacrifice is lawful only if one is certain of the reasons why he sacrifices and only if this sacrifice is essentially linked with the promotion of happiness and the elimination of pain.

Utilitarianism, furthermore, is not expediency since it intends not the "agent's own happiness, but that of all concerned." The happiness of the greatest number is more important than the happiness of the individual. Hence, there is place for considerable self-sacrifice and no place for expediency. In fact, utilitarianism is fundamentally religious. It does not, of course, appeal to a transcendent principle, but even theists will admit that if God exists he would deserve the happiness of his creatures.

The effectiveness of utilitarianism, as Mill sees it, lies in the fact that it meets all situations and leaves no exceptions. There need be no circumstance in which the person does not know exactly what to do. To demonstrate this, Mill offers an example illustrating the superiority of his system over other moral theories dependent upon intuition or religious principles.

We may be instructed by other systems that lying is always wrong. This can lead us to err on some occasions and on others to know not what to do. Should a dying person, for example, be told a truth which will distress him and which serves no purpose, or should one lie in a way which will help a person die happy? If our moral norms derive from intuition, we will experience a conflict between an obligation to speak the truth and an obligation to comfort the dying. If our moral awareness depends upon religious principles, we will tell the truth even though we realize this serves no purpose and, indeed, worsens the situation. A utilitarian, on the contrary, knows exactly what to do. The truth will cause more pain and less happiness than a lie. One must always create the greatest happiness possible. Therefore, there is a moral imperative to lie.

This example manifests how the utilitarian principle makes one sensitive to others rather than to himself. One does not satisfy his own need to speak the truth at the expense of a dying man. In this manner, utilitarianism relates the person to the wider community of men. There is no conflict between personal happiness and social welfare. Happiness is maximum pleasure for the greatest number. This redounds to the favor of the individual person sooner or later.

In other moral systems the person may feel forced or compelled to make decisions he considers wrong. Utilitarianism, however, threatens no one. It urges people to do that which they prefer to do, namely to desire their happiness and that of others. Maximum happiness is assured when the maximum number can find their own happiness. Men know that this is the way things were meant to be.

There may be cases where some guidance will be required as to which specific choice is most productive of happiness for the greatest number. In these cases a committee of qualified experts will decide which pleasurable actions are to be preferred to other pleasurable actions. Sometimes the action to be preferred will be less intensively pleasurable than its opposite. This preference will be determined by a judgment of the quality, not the quantity, of the pleasure sought.

Mill concludes that utilitarianism is a positive force in moral behavior. Christianity is too negative in its moral judgments. Utilitarianism, furthermore, benefits man here and now. Christianity is excessively other-worldly and, therefore, cannot serve as an effective instrument for social reform or human betterment.

CRITIQUE

Comte and Mill both look upon human society as the ultimate goal of all striving. Right and wrong, life and death, meaning and absurdity are fundamentally rooted in our understanding of human improvement.

There are elements in this synthesis which are in agreement with Christian objectives. A Christian must be involved in love for his neighbor, or else he is no Christian. Christianity does not acknowledge salvation in isolation. Judgment and consequent salvation is based on what one did for the least of Christ's brethren.

Utilitarianism is valid as far as it goes. Christianity thinks it does not go far enough. It does not account for the religious concern and the question about something larger than human society which have preoccupied man from the beginning of his existence.

In spite of Mill's evaluation of his own system, it does not solve as many problems as he claims. Happiness depends less on maximum pleasure, even qualitatively, for one's fellowmen than it does on a more expansive vision of life than this and on a hope that something more permanent than human society exists. It is possible that one day human society will end; hence, durable as it is, it is a perishable value. Life may have a meaning deeper than this and offer happiness a sturdier guarantee than inevitable extinction. Christians believe that it is not illusion but truth which has caused man to seek something beyond himself and his social projects. This quest has been so persistent and so seriously considered by men in their history that it cannot be dismissed as easily as Mill dismisses it. Granting the cultural distortions and scientific ignorance which accompany much of human hope, there is a substantial content which remains valid. In this century, the Existentialists realized the need for a more sophisticated dismissal of the transcendent, as in the case of Jean Paul Sartre, or a more effective analysis of its force, as in the case of Martin Heidegger, Karl Jaspers, or Gabriel Marcel.

Mill's system lacks the ability to interpret and give meaning to that unhappiness which is as much a part of human life as happiness. The record of broken lives and shattered hopes is no less real than the record of success and fulfillment and no less human. Indeed, in its own way, the unhappiness is essentially linked to the achievement of happiness. A total system must have a meaningful word to declare about man's failure as well as his accomplishment. Does the evil man suffers, the tragedy he endures, the resistance he encounters, the good he wanted to do and never expressed, does all this have no meaning? Is such a life wasted? Were the unhappy hours we experienced useless? If they serve a purpose, can we know that purpose? The greatest happiness for the greatest number accounts for only one element in the human equation.

Mill's pleasure principle remains vague, a vagueness he himself recognizes in his requirement that a committee must decide which pleasures are to be preferred to others. One wonders which principles the committee would employ to make their judgments. Qualitative pleasure is an ambiguous and difficult criterion, more nebulous, in fact, than quantitative pleasure. If a committee must have recourse to a further principle, then Utilitarianism is not an ultimate principle.

Christianity suggests a principle more absolute and ultimate than the pleasure principle. This ultimate moral norm is love. Moral issues are confronted on a level deeper than utility, although even love, as such, is difficult to define. Even love needs direction, enlightenment, certification, purification. It needs this not because love is not ultimate but so that love may remain love. Christianity seeks not only the designation of love as absolute but proposes an interpretation of what love is and can be.

Mill's assignment of happiness as the goal of life is not the problem. The problem lies in discovering what it means to be happy. Pleasure, even qualitative pleasure, seems a superficial consideration in the definition of happiness. Even the case he offers of a dying man and of our difficulty with telling him the truth is solved more easily in terms of love and the dignity of the human person than it is in terms of utility, pleasure or happiness. Mill has no principle to appeal to beyond a consensus on happiness or pleasure which excludes infanticide or killing the aged or enslaving our fellowmen. It may happen that the majority will find any or all of these alternatives pleasurable when, in fact, they violate love and human dignity.

Wasn't the United States wrong about slavery even when that situation brought happiness or pleasure to greater numbers than freedom of the slaves did? Mill may claim that these were pleasures whose qualitative content was less desirable than their quantitative intensity. But how do men know that the qualitative content of these actions is immoral unless they utilize a higher principle, namely, that of love or the dignity of the person. Every evil we mentioned above is excluded by reason of the dignity of the person, regardless of the consequences for the majority; yet any of these alternatives can be deemed moral in virtue of the pleasure or happiness principle Mill proposes.

In a sense, Mill may be more of a logician about his morality than he is an ethician or a religious thinker. The ultimate norm of morality need not necessarily be the norm which covers the most cases, but it may be the norm which is most absolute. A morality which attempts the solution of every case may be more legalistic and less creative than a morality which speaks absolutely but which requires responsibility and decision on the part of the agent. Morality is intimately tied to an interpretation of life and may have to be, at times, as unclear as life is.

Mill admits that there is a distinction between what *is* desired, and what *ought* to be desired by the majority. He maintains, however, that the "ought" is derived from the "is." Furthermore, Mill does not explain why "ought" is not "is." Morality, than, requires a higher principle than utilitarianism. Evidently, human consensus, a society's decision or a committee's judgment are not sufficient norms for morality. In this century we have learned how painfully true this is.

Mill's search for salvation seems not unlike that of Auguste Comte. Both thinkers sought the greatest happiness of the greatest number in service of one's fellowmen. Christians find such an endeavor noble but yet uncertain, incomplete and transitory. It is, admittedly, a type of salvation, but Christians consider seriously another approach to salvation, one they judge more adequate to the human condition.

Karl Marx

Karl Marx was born of Jewish parents and was received into the Lutheran Church when he was six. His outlook on human society, which eventually became his outlook on the nature of man, was influenced by French socialism, English economics, and German philosophy, especially the thought of Hegel and Feuerbach.

From Hegel, Marx borrowed the dialectical method. He interpreted this method empirically, however, rather than idealistically. Hegel's thesis that history progresses by struggle also influenced Marx. Marx was convinced, furthermore, that Hegel had discovered a crucial insight into the dynamics of change by demonstrating that change occurs in a revolutionary and violent leap forward rather than gradually.

From Feuerbach, Marx borrowed the idea that man develops in his concrete environment rather than in abstract or speculative experiences, Man's situation in specific circumstances, Feuerbach argued, explains human knowledge. Karl Marx was not, however, a materialist. The materialism of Feuerbach was too unrefined for the more subtle mind of Marx. When one compares Marx with Feuerbach, he realizes how much Hegel did influence Marx and how inaccurate it is to describe Marx simply as a materialist. It is, perhaps, not so much Marxism but some forms of Communism which must be judged in terms of strict materialism. Lenin, and especially Stalin, made Communism what it is today. Admittedly, Marxism lends itself to the interpretation which Lenin and, more remotely, Stalin gave it. Our concern, however, is with Marx. In fact, it is conceivable that Marx would not have approved some of the forms Communism has taken.

Marx differed with Feuerbach because of the totally materialistic and deterministic way Feuerbach explained man's relationship to his environment. Man's environment, Marx argued, is not a human evironment if we limit our definition of man to his relationship to physical labor. A truly human environment is one which includes another essential element, namely the social relationships in human living which lead men to interact with one another as well as with their material surroundings.

Two of the most important of Marx's works are *The Communist Manifesto* (1848) which he wrote with Frederick Engels and *Das Kapital*, the first volume of which was published in Marx's lifetime (1867) and the other two volumes after his death (1885 and 1894).

ALIENATION

Hegel convinced Marx that the phenomenon of alienation was essential to any definition of man. The concept of alienation (*Entfremdung*) or self-alienation was, of course, handled differently by Hegel. The root idea, however, intrigued Marx who felt that alienation had to be explained in empirical and economic categories rather than in terms of the Hegelian system.

This concept of alienation was developed in another manner by contemporary existentialism. It is evident in the writings of Dostoevsky (especially in the figures of Raskolnikov, Stavrogin, and Ivan Karamazov), in the novels of Albert

Camus (especially exemplified in Meursault, the chief character of *The Stranger*, but also in *The Plague* and *The Fall*), and in the philosophy of Jean Paul Sartre (*Nausea*) and Martin Heidegger (*Being and Time*).[1]

Marx, however, was neither a Hegelian nor an existentialist. The source of alienation was not due to the nature of reality nor to the nature of human existence. Marx considered alienation an economic phenomenon.

The laborer has nothing to sell except himself. His worth is measured, not by values which are truly human, but by the impersonal conditions of exchange which are beyond his ability to control or to humanize. The product the worker creates is thus separated from his life situation in a way which violates his human nature and dignity. In this manner the worker is alienated. He is alienated from the means and machinery of production which he no longer possesses; he is alienated from every human relationship which should give a human meaning to the process of production; and he is alienated from identification with the product he himself creates. This three-fold alienation from production, human relationships and product has made the modern worker an object who is used and degraded by those who gain profit from his misery. A more complete understanding of this alienation requires an insight into Marx's almost mystical concept of a product and the worker's relationship to it. We shall consider this in a moment.

Capitalism has been responsible for the tragic alienation of which Marx speaks. A new economic and social order was envisioned by Marx, an order which would put an end to man's alienation and render him, not only economically, but even humanly satisfied. Marx demanded the destruction of Capitalism and the substitution of a new society. The goal of this revolution would be complete human happiness and total fulfillment.

Capitalism robs man not only of his economic value but

even of his human value. There is no salvation from alienation and degradation as long as Capitalism exists. Human selfhood cannot develop because Capitalism creates a situation of *Verdinglichung* (wherein men are made things) which is the antithesis of humanness. Marx was eloquent on this point:

The devaluation of the world of men is in direct proportion to the increased utilization of the world of things. Work produces not only commodities; it produces itself and the worker as a commodity. . . . The object which labor produces . . . is opposed to it as an alien essence, as a power independent of the one who produced it. . . . In this economic condition the reality of labor emerges as the loss of the worker's reality . . . as alienation, estrangement. . . . The reality of labor becomes so much the loss of reality that the worker is depersonalized even to the point of starvation.[2]

Marx's concept of the alienation of labor depends, as we said above, upon his remarkable insight into the mystical character of the commodity:

A commodity is therefore a mysterious thing, simply because in it the social character of men's labor appears to them as an objective character stamped upon the product of labor; because the relation of the producers to the sum total of their own labor is presented to them as a social relation, existing not between themselves, but between the products of their labor. This is the reason why the products of labor become commodities, social things whose qualities are at the same time perceptible and imperceptible by the senses.[3]

Labor itself becomes a commodity in this economic system and the lives of men are bartered on a competitive and impersonal market. Marx's concept of human dignity was too noble for him to stand by silently while his fellowmen were exploited. In the name of man and for his sake, Marx protests:

The bourgeoisie, wherever it has the upper hand . . . has piteously torn asunder the network of feudal ties which bound man to his 'natural superiors,' and has left no other bond between man and man than naked self-interest and callous 'cash payment.' It has drowned . . . chivalrous enthusiasm . . . in the icy waters of egotistical calculation. It has resolved personal worth into exchange value and . . . set up that single unconscionable freedom—free trade. In this one term for exploitation, veiled by religious and political illusions, it has substituted naked, shame-less, direct, brutal exploitation.[4]

Marx's writing is further indication of the lack of crass materialism in his philosophy. He felt it was his obligation to make the proletariat aware of how its labor was being used as a mere commodity and of how the capitalistic relationship of employer and employee was devoid of human or moral content. This awareness would lead to a violent class struggle and a victorious revolution which would assure man permanently of his human dignity in a situation where harmony prevailed and alienation was overcome. Paradise was in the making and within reach. It would inevitably come about because Capitalism would dialectically create the conditions precipitating its own destruction. It was urgent, however, that the inevitable be hastened so that men not suffer longer than necessary.

TRANSFORMATION

Marx believed that the key to the transformation of man and society lay in the restructuring of material conditions and social relations. If this could be accomplished, philosophies, cultures and religions would also be changed. This would happen because all these phenomena depend upon the material order. This insight might lead some to suppose that Marx was a materialist. Marx's thought, however, was more complicated.

He believed that ideas themselves were able to change the material order which, in turn, would change ideas. When Marx reasons that the inevitable dialectical antithesis leading to the destruction of Capitalism can be hastened, he leaves no doubt about the fact that ideas, his ideas, can accomplish this. If ideas can accelerate the inevitable, they can change the material order.

Marx affirms the power of ideas over materialistic determinism. He presents his ideas, furthermore, not as a thinker mechanistically describing reality, but as a man who speaks from moral conviction and ethical outrage. Marx proclaims the class struggle and denounces oppression with the power of a prophet who sees in man someone superior to material conditions and preeminent over the economic systems which enslave him.

The transformation of society required, as we said above, a change of the material order. This change could be influenced by ideas and by a vision of man which transcended the material conditions in which he was rooted. A combination of correct thinking and effective human action could give men the capacity to predict, predetermine and realize the future. Thus, once again, it is *human* action and not impersonal material forces which could save man.

Marx's dialectical materialism presupposed, it is true, a certain economic determinism. In a sense, the future of man was fated. The bourgeoisie was even now unwittingly creating the conditions which would necessitate its negation and demise. Although this would happen even without human interference, a program of revolutionary thought and action could bring this inevitable event into history sooner, and it could do so by human effort.

A sense of fairness to Karl Marx's thought and hope for progressive Marxist-Christian dialogue require that due attention be given to the nonmaterialistic direction of Marxism. As Marx speaks of economic determinism and neglects man's spiritual potential, he also provides for the dominion of ideas over matter, the possibility of an ethical vision of human life, and the power of human action in a revolutionary cause.

Feuerbach would not have countenanced such independence from matter in the interpretation of man. The difference between the two thinkers lies in the fact that Feuerbach is a materialist and Marx is a *dialectical* materialist. Although Christians cannot accept even this outlook on life uncritically, dialogue may prove fruitful if the adjective rather than the noun is emphasized in discussing Marx's dialectical materialism.

Christians are also sympathetic to Marx's call for a brotherhood among men in deed as well as in name. Auguste Comte dreamed of a religion of humanity supervised by a priesthood drawn from a scientific fraternity. Marx is not totally removed from Comte's thoughts. His concept of human fraternity is deeper than that of Comte. Marxism would permit no endeavor which would not benefit the proletariat or the human community as a whole. Marx may well have turned in the direction of materialism for the ultimate construction of his dialectic, not because of an exaggerated concern with matter, but from an anxiety for man's transformation. Marxism was empirical for the sake of man, not for the sake of matter. He was weary of that speculation which devised theories for human reform and wrote theses on human dignity while men were being degraded and exploited. He said as much in his "Theses on Feuerbach": "The philosophers have interpreted the world in various ways; the point, however, is to *change* it."

DIALECTICAL MATERIALISM

Can it be said, then, that Karl Marx was in any way a materialist? The answer to this question is affirmative, but one must add that Marx was a materialist in Marx's way, that is, dialectically. In dialectical materialism, Marx claimed to have uncovered reality's ultimate meaning. Through this process, Marx argued, a new order, indeed an ultimate order, would come about. In this process, history would achieve its perfection.

Christians recognize in Marxism a hope for that definitively eschatological community which is also their hope. This community will be immune from exploitation and alienation. We shall consider this point further in our critique.

Marx looked upon history both optimistically and deterministically. His outlook was optimistic because he believed history was tending in the direction he envisioned. History would one day provide for a utopia by means of the inexorable laws of dialectical progress. His viewpoint was also deterministic because he thought history was governed by laws which transcend human resistance to them, laws which the human mind could with effort, recognize. When these laws were known, the future itself could be predicted with certainty.

Marx steers a course between the idealism of Hegel and the materialism of Feuerbach in the elaboration of his dialectical synthesis. His system clearly seeks more than new economic structures and more humane sociological conditions. His philosophy intends nothing less than a final solution to the mystery of reality which includes a practical program for the salvation of man.

In developing his materialism, Marx moves beyond Feuerbach as we have said. Man is not only made by his environment; he makes his environment. Man is a relational creature in Marx's thought, one destined to live with his fellowmen in fraternity rather than merely contending with matter to survive. Man is not a pawn of physical forces which manage and manipulate him but a history-making creature who can forestall or precipitate his own destiny.

Feuerbach had made man entirely passive before a world which shaped him far more than he shaped it. Marx, however, linked man to a history which could be truly human and enabled man to produce his world rather than being but a product of it. Marx sought a place for man in a world where man himself was active, where he was an effective human agent, a creature sufficiently independent of matter to exist in tension with it. For Feuerbach, man was an outgrowth or a consequence of matter rather than someone who realized himself in creative antithesis to matter.

Marx set man in a true relationship with matter and hence distinguished man from matter. Man could have ideas which controlled matter. Human consciousness opposed itself to matter and in virtue of this opposition made dialectical materialism possible and defined the phenomenon of man. Consciousness, obviously, had to resist matter for the dialectic to operate on an anthropological level. In Marxism the rational and conscious dimensions of man were real enough for there to be a dialectic between man and matter. This dialectical relationship was, however, in no way a transcendental relationship. Man and matter opposed each other and developed. But man in no area of his life transcended or overcame matter.

Marx felt that his dialectic eliminated the disadvantages of Hegel's exclusively idealistic anthropology and Feuerbach's exclusively materialistic anthropology.

Marx's philosophy, then, is more subtle and ingenious than Comte's Positivism. It is more idealistic and spiritual than Feuerbach's materialism and physical determinism. It envisions a history which is determined but not so mechanistically determined that man cannot make a difference. Dialectic materialism provides for the impact of human consciousness on physical forces and even on economic forces which are not so inflexibly inevitable that man cannot make reform happen when he wants reform to happen.

CRITIQUE

John Dewey once described Marx's philosophy as an oversimplification of reality which nonetheless combines "the romantic idealism of earlier social revolutionaries with what purports to be a thoroughly objective scientific analysis, expressed in . . . a single, all-embracing law."[5]

Christians are sensitive to both the romantic idealism and the objectivity of the Marxist outlook on life. The area of disagreement with Marxism is concerned with the oversimplification to which Dewey refers. Marx considers profoundly that which he chooses to consider. There are, however, aspects of life which his system ignores and realities of history which his philosophy cannot interpret.

Marxism functions best in a nineteenth-century environment and depends for its cogency on an exploitative capitalistic system. The ability of a society to modify its Capitalism in a socialization process without notable class conflict and with no revolution was neither forseen by Marx nor explainable in terms of his theory. This capacity did not remain a possibility but became an historical fact. In the United States, the chief capitalistic country, a society has evolved which tempered the inhuman aspects of Capitalism with some of the most enlightened social thinking of the nineteenth and twentieth centuries.

The fact that the U.S.S.R. has not been able to create a social situation which either ends alienation or creates a new man is concrete proof that the problems which beset the human spirit are more complex than economic systems. The Soviet Union, in an imaginatively experimental fashion, has put the theories of Marx into operation and has, furthermore, experienced a generation born and brought to maturity in an exclusively Marxist environment.

Few objective observers would agree that Soviet man has not felt as keenly as non-Soviet man the burden of the human condition, the estrangement of man from himself, or the need to be renewed more deeply than the "newness" Marxism provides. Nor would many affirm that exploitation is absent in the Soviet Union. The perversity of the human spirit which tempts man to make an object of his fellow man or to "use" him is not eliminated when economic structures are radically and even idealistically reformed. It is not what Marx saw or even his economic theories to which Christians take exception. It is the application of his thinking to the solution of ultimate questions which seems deficient.

If Christianity seemed antithetical to science in Marx's day, it must also be said that science often pretended to be a religion. Marxist-Christian dialogue must consider, however, not the situation of the nineteenth century but the present moment in which we live. Christianity has demonstrated its respect for science and its need for science during the present century. The redemption of man involves the redemption of his heart and his inner being which religion considers. It includes, also, that other redemption which seeks the cure of man's ignorance of the empirical order and the healing of his body, his emotions, and his social structures. This is the province of science and science has done its work well. No humanist today, Christian or otherwise, would withhold from his fellowmen the benefits of science.

It must become clear to science and religion that they are partners in the discovery of truth and that error is their common enemy. If the truth science seeks is different from the truth religion seeks, this is no indication that it is not total truth both desire. If science can help religious systems purify themselves further, then religious systems become even more ultimate and more appropriately religious in their concerns. If religion convinces science of its inability to do more for man than its method or capabilities permit, then science is even more humanistically serviceable because it seeks to do what it can do, and it avoids the pretension which makes it suppose that it can do everything for man. It is not science's claim to do everything to which Christianity objects. It is science's inability to realize that claim. If science could do everything for men, religion would be superfluous and honest religious men would be obliged to cooperate with science in the destruction of all religious systems.

A concern for truth and a conviction that science is in error when it attempts a total answer lead some religious men to oppose scientism. Although Christians must pledge in any society noninterference in its totally secular and scientific concerns, Marxists must guarantee that men will no longer be persecuted for their faith. The State has no right to impose upon his citizens a monolithic interpretation of truth univocally interpreting not only the civic order but the cultural, religious and philosophical orders as well. If Marx claims Christianity denied freedom to science, it must also be said that Communist society denies freedom for faith. One of the objectives of dialogue is the achievement of a situation wherein science and religion live together, not in grudging coexistence but in the realization that each has need of the other.

PRINCIPLES FOR DIALOGUE

Significant changes have come about in Communism during the last decade and likewise in Christianity which has inaugurated an ecumenical age and considered a theology of the secular. Granted this, are there areas, we might ask, where Christians and Marxists might initiate dialogue with each other without either party feeling it must be untrue to its valid insights? It is possible for Marxists and Christians to agree that there are many objectives which they are passionate about and which together they can implement more effectively.

Christians are willing to admit that religion, as conceived by Marx, should have no place in the realm of human affairs. Marxists, however, must be open to the fact that Christianity was not fairly and fully presented by Marx. The present possibility of serious dialogue is already an indication that Christianity has available to it resources which Marx himself did not understand.

Christians wonder, for example, if the antithesis of human consciousness to the world around it might not be worthy of exploration. If there is an antithesis, as Marx permits, then this consciousness must have some originality and a certain a priori. If consciousness is little more than an outgrowth of matter, there would be no antithesis nor would the human spirit become dissatisfied with materialism. If consciousness is more than an outgrowth of matter, what is the nature of this "more"? Why does human consciousness persist in its transcendental search even when ideal economic or social conditions exist, as they do in areas of the United States and the U.S.S.R.? What is it in human consciousness which seeks transformation even after society has been transformed in every possible way? Why is it that society's transformation does not necessitate man's transformation and terminate his quest for "newness," "difference," "more"?

There has never been a social environment in which man has not looked around him and said that what he seeks has not yet come to pass. It is legitimate, especially after the implementation of Marx's theories, to affirm that there shall never be a society in which men will not want more than society offers. There is no social or economic force able to cancel out human alienation and render man totally harmonious. The Soviet Union has proved to the world and, in its own way, the United States has demonstrated that the radical changing of economic and social categories does not radically change man. Soviet artistic endeavors, for example, are human artistic endeavors whose idiom is as understandable in a capitalistic society as they are in a Communist society.

The human spirit transcends those economic forces which exert a considerable influence on life but cannot account for it fully. The literature of the Soviet Union, its prose and poetry, its music and dance, reflect that striving for a spiritual absolute which no human power sets at rest. Sensitive people in the U.S.S.R. and in the United States laugh and weep over the same experiences, cherish the same essential hopes, and recognize in each other a sympathy and a bond which reminds them they are human beings on pilgrimage together rather than different creatures from essentially divergent environments. Though economic systems may be radically distinct, people remain fundamentally similar. In the "new man" of the Soviet Union, Americans see men very much like themselves.

HUMAN DIGNITY AND HUMAN LABOR

Marxism has an appealing community dimension to it. All objects are valueless until man's work gives them a human value and sets them at the service of society. All material realities take on new meaning in human labor so that the commodity produced retains an abiding relationship with those who have transformed its meaning. The identification of man with his work and the thought that man gives value to reality as he makes it into his own image and likeness are original and beautiful concepts. Such a theory presents Christians with a humanistic insight of considerable merit and a religious value which may have its roots in the biblical message.

The Marxist interpretation of how the worker expresses himself in his work is compatible with the creation account in Genesis where man is given dominion; it is harmonious with the eschatological doctrine in Revelation where man is promised a new heaven and a new earth from the work of his hands and the grace of God.

The insufficiency of the person for his own happiness is the virtue and the flaw in Marxism. The community emphasis in interpreting life which Marxism provides is a value. The expendability of the person for the attainment of this objective is inexcusable. Christianity prefers a philosophy of life, however economically implemented in a particular society, which guarantees the inviolability of personal dignity in a community which fosters maximum human development. This preference is not an idle wish. It is capable of concrete expression.

A religion of the absolute future, as Christianity sees itself, insists that no present or future form of society is so absolutely necessary that one generation of men may be sacrificed for the sake of a succeeding generation which, it is supposed, will realize utopia. Christianity does not expect any form of society to be so absolutely satisfying that future man will have more worth or reality than man has today To sacrifice contemporary man for the future or to set limits beforehand on the way future man must live is not to enhance but to retard human development.

Man's future is more absolute than the societies he creates. He transcends not only his present situation but also all the social forms which the future may construct. Christianity is not competent to judge which economic system or social structure is most suitable for man. It does remind us, however, that the person is not negotiable. He is not an item to be bartered even for social progress. The person is not only worth more than the lilies of the field. He is worth more than every social project which seeks his betterment. His is unexpendable because God is somehow present in him; therefore, no contingent value supersedes his value. He remains unfulfilled and goes on striving even in the achievement of those "perfect" orders men devise to bring their fellowmen happiness. He remains alienated in every earthly paradise.

Marx may have been more to the point if he had been more of a materialist. If he had analyzed all those instances *in* history where the dialectic between man and his environment was operative, he would have made a significant economic or social contribution without necessitating the Marxist-Christian rift which occurred. Marx's attempt to impose meaning *on* history led to a different situation.[6] When historical materialism became speculative principle, it tried to say and do too much. Eventually, it claimed to know not only how economics influenced art, history and religion but how it had produced art, history, and religion.

On the other hand, when Marx dealt with one element in the dialectic (namely, human consciousness), he was too much of a materialist and not enough of a dialectician. He defined consciousness so much in terms of materiality that he had little room left to explain man's transcendence over nature. Hence, he limited his anthropology to man's tension with nature. Consequently, Marx's dialectic clarified the antithesis of man to matter more affectively than it illuminated the character of the resulting synthesis. In this, he was less revolutionary and less profound about human transformation than he might have been. He restricted human fulfillment to the satisfaction of material needs and by so doing he diminished the human agent he sought to exalt. This made man more of an object and more of a consumer than Marx may have intended.

Marx's philosophy became excessive when he said that everything beyond material gratification was due to "phantoms in the human brain." He said too much when he insisted that man's development is *determined* by "the material conditions determining . . . production." Short of these extremes, he was unmistakably, indeed movingly, concerned about human development.

This concern Christians share. In fact, Christian social thinking in this century may well prove to have been influenced not only by the Gospel but also by the writings of Karl Marx and the Revolution of 1917. Marxists may be in a better position now than they were before to appreciate the fact that the spiritual aspirations of man to which the Gospel is so effective a witness have accounted for many of the changes which have taken place in the Communist world. Though there are some who turn to religion as an opiate, there

are many who find in it hope and courage, zeal for reform and
strength for renewal.

HUMANISM AND MATERIALISM

Marx is accurate in his assessment of Feuerbach's overidenti-
fication of man with matter. There must be a distinction between man and matter, an essential distinction perhaps, or
else the ensuing dialectic would not lead to a substantially
different event in history but only to an accidental modifica-
tion of the material conditions of life. Marx is disappointing,
however, in his inability to offer a hope or an aspiration
which goes beyond the material. Marx sets in motion a theory
Christianity finds incomplete rather than misdirected. He
links human history so tightly to the world and nature that
he restricts that distinction from physical determinism and
that preeminence of man over matter which his principles
and words declare.

Marx never explains persuasively why men create cultural
values in preference to physical values. Man builds more than
a shelter for himself; he builds castles and temples. He does
not merely clothe himself against the elements; he clothes
himself in such a way that he manifests his rank, his sex, even
his personality. He does not limit himself to the consumption
of food and drink; he uses these as symbols for celebration, as
signs of mourning, as means for friendship.

Man's production is not determined by his material conditions alone. He expresses something else and reaches for
something more in all he makes. His superiority to matter, his
transcendence over animal nature derive from a uniqueness
that is not sufficiently accounted for when one says man is
but developed matter or an antithesis to matter. The more
human man becomes, the more he leaves behind him the
purely physical determinations of his material environment.
And one day he wonders about God and dreams of paradise

and asks himself whether Love made the universe and how men might love one another more.

Man does not accept nature or oppose it. He transforms it in his eagerness to be transformed himself. He turns the world upside down looking for something he seems to have missed, searching for someone to tell him who he is. He impresses his imprint on every inch of the planet and intends to do the same with the universe because he knows that it is man who matters most of all and man alone who gives the world consciousness and forces it to come of age.

Marx was not mistaken in telling us that man is more bound to his material conditions than we may have realized. We take issue, however, with his insistence that man is completely determined by these conditions. Christianity is not naive in its affirmation of the spiritual dimension of human nature. It has demonstrated its impatience with those who make man so independent of matter that they effectively destroy him. Christianity has many times condemned and excluded from its doctrine excessively spiritualistic interpretations of human reality.

Man creates himself in a dialogue with matter, with nature, and with the world. The doctrine of the Incarnation declares that even the Son of God is not a stranger to those material conditions without which human development is impossible.

Marx fails to tell us why man is not only developed in dialogue with his material environment but why he is always dissatisfied with his material environment, even in affluence, and why he feels he must transcend it further. Human dialogue is not achieved as a result of a dialectic between man and matter. It occurs between persons who seek in this dialogue that absolute person some call humanity but whom Christians call Christ.

Man knows instinctively and unmistakably that if he is ever to be saved and fulfilled, the task must be accomplished not by anything emerging from the world of matter but by someone representing the personal order of reality. A person personalizes man more fully than physical force; ultimate salvation, if it occurs, will be given by an absolute person who personalizes man more completely than any or all of the persons he encounters in life.

The essential difference between Marxist and Christian humanism lies in the fact that the former has the entire dialectic for human development occur *within* the world, while the latter admits the need for a dialectic *with* the world but allows for a truly human transcendence beyond the world.

A further insight of Marx which Christians welcome is his insistence on the social and fraternal aspects of man's life. We fear, however, that the restriction of human fraternity and of the social character of man to a collaboration for material improvement alone may deprive men of that mystical brotherhood which makes them partners in a spiritual search. The social aspect of human nature is also revealed in the effort to find an answer for man which is still needed even when man is himself materially satisfied and all his neighbors are given justice.

ALIENATION AND SALVATION

When Marx speaks of alienation, he addresses himself to a problem which has significance, not only for modern philosophy and literature, but also for Christianity. Marx knew man was alienated. He was less accurate in his reduction of alienation to a socio-economic level. Man is alienated in his relationship with his fellowmen and in his capacity for transcendental reality rather than in the imperfections of his economic life. Only a person heals alienation, never a system, not even Christianity. Christianity does not save us. Christ does.

Communist societies have discovered that the source of man's alienation is not his economic environment but his nature and his human activity. Degrading economic and social conditions are not the cause but the effect of human alienation.

Marxism seeks salvation. The search it initiates in this endeavor is neither superficial nor ignoble. Marx promised Western civilization a new unity, a unity it had not experienced since the collapse of Christendom. This is why so many intellectuals and idealists were captivated by the Marxist vision of life.

Men feel insecure in the presence of chaos. They hope always for more unity than they have. If Western men could believe in Christ no longer; if they found Christianity too ethereal and otherworldly for human salvation; if they judged religion repressive or regressive, Marxism enabled them to work for unity and to dream of paradise. Because of Marxism many were able to put their hope in a future salvation.

Marxism is one more indication of how humanly unfulfilling scientism can be. A considerable number who turned to Marx did so because they desired something to believe in, perhaps a cause worth dying for when Christianity seemed no longer worthy of faith or the shedding of blood.[7] Marxism's popularity reveals how many seek something beyond themselves to give their lives for and how ardently man yearns for consecration to a transcendent hope. Man does not want to be skeptical. It is something he resigns himself to rather than something he prefers. Marxism demonstrates the fact that skepticism can only be overcome by a faith in something absolute. Every creed and "ism" men have become passionate about in the last few centuries has offered an absolute interpretation of life. Ambiguous, relative and partial approaches to living, even if accurate, do not inspire soaring faith or lasting hope. History proves this. The less absolute a philosophy or theology is the more it tends to resignation, indifference or ennui; and the less likely it is to provide a secure basis for consecration, dedication and passion.

We must not prejudge the issue we are discussing. Less

absolute approaches lead to less commitment but this is not sufficient reason to conclude that they are, therefore, wrong. The most that can be said is that they occasion a different psychological and personal response and a less secure faith than approaches which are more ultimate and decisive. Later, in a complementary book, we shall ask whether an absolute approach to life is possible, whether it is viable and whether it can command the absolute attention of the believer without tyrannizing and depersonalizing him.

A further distinction of crucial importance requires our recognition of the difference between an absolute approach to life and a total approach to life. Though Christianity offers an absolute answer to life, it must not offer a total answer. Christians cannot perform only explicitly Christian or explicitly religious tasks. Christians must not accept only explicitly Christian or explicitly religious truths. Since the religious level can never be the sole level on which man lives, Christianity should not lead to Christendom.

An absolute system is valid not in its totality but in its ultimacy. Marx tried to dictate and define far more than Christianity does. He created an absolute system. Hence, men could become passionate about the Marxist view of life, but also, unfortunately, he created a total system. Marxism sought to be not only ultimate but so total that no area of life or activity was free from its monolithic categories. Thus, Marxism offered less option, less diversity, less freedom than Christianity even though each seeks to become an absolute answer to life.

SKEPTICISM AND THE FUTURE

In some situations skepticism may seem to be the only choice one has. On occasion, we admire the skeptic for the honesty which led him to the position he has taken. Granted this, we do not say too much or attempt to judge the person when we affirm that doubt about everything fundamental in life is easier and less humanly fulfilling than faith in a tested truth. Genuine faith is more courageous than honest doubt. Christianity, we shall see later, is not a truth which has not been challenged and criticized over the centuries. No other creed, secular or religious men have known has been questioned more and studied more than Christianity.

Complete fairness to Marx requires our saying that, although he constructed a system which had to have total control of society in order to function effectively, he himself seems not to have wanted things to go that far. George Hampsch observes:

Marx abhorred the idea that his words would ever become a stabilized dogma . . . "All I know is I am not a Marxist," declared Marx. . . . What is often forgotten or ignored, however, is that Marx also considered, as Engels points out, that his findings and theories were to serve as guides to the *further* study of history.[8]

If Marxists and Christians consider together a "further" study of history, they will find many similarities in their view of society.[9] We both want to change the world rather than merely interpret it. We both admit that the whole world as an object or commodity is not worth the loss of the human spirit. We both admit that man is mystically identified with and humanly developed by his work. We both seek the redemption of man from his alienation and consider salvation the equivalent of the most intense degree possible of self-realization.

Even when Christians declare their disagreement with Marxism there remains common ground for dialogue. When Christians, for example, profess a belief in God's future judgment on human society, or when they express their faith in God's revelation of himself on the cross and in the Easter event, they are saying in these affirmations that existence is more profound and priceless than men at first suspect. When

Christians state that man is saved by the power of the Other, they make it clear that each man must have a wider understanding of life than his own comfort. This wider understanding includes one's neighbor as much as it includes God. Pope John XXIII observed:

We should not foolishly dream up an artificial opposition—where none really exists—between one's own spiritual perfection and one's active contact with the everyday world, as if a man could not perfect himself as a Christian except by putting aside all temporal activity.[10]

Christians cannot know the concrete conditions in which future man will function. They are able, nonetheless, to predict his nature. Future man will continue to be a questioner, who will seek to transcend his contingent future. His yearning for "more" is so indigenous to him that it will be with him in all his new discoveries. A truly redemptive future must be one realistic enough to admit that man is destined to live with some existential alienation but that his greater hope lies in a future which promises more future without ceasing. Salvation from alienation may be better established in the unspecified awareness that further forms are always open to man than in the limited realization that men have already achieved the future in such and such a discernible manner.

Marxism may unwittingly force men into a mediocre future, one which would not only be predictable but one incapable of progress, once society becomes classless and thus forfeits the dialectic necessary to forward movement in the Marxist system. The friendly competition in a classless society with no class conflict which some Communists believe will keep society dynamic is not consistent with Marxist principles.

Marxism and Christianity do not address themselves to men who feel no need to justify their existence by giving it a sense of service to humanity or a profoundly altruistic meaning. There are undoubtedly such men, but such men never become true Marxists or faithful Christians. Marxism achieves a certain grandeur in its effort to interpret existence and to provide for a self-sacrificing faith. In this, Christians and Marxists are one.

RENEWAL AND SALVATION

Marxism and Christianity are motivated by an advent hope that the "New Man" they await will one day arrive. Marxism describes exactly how he shall appear and seeks to create him from human resources alone. "We shall transform men so thoroughly," Soviet novelist Ilya Ehrenburg prophesied, "that they will hardly know themselves." Christianity believes the "New Man" will one day happen; it is Christ who will become man's future in a mystical brotherhood which has more promise and less prediction to it.

Marx may have weakened his system by expecting man to rest from his labors in a future age when he would not experience himself as a pilgrim on earth. This attempt to settle man is a disservice to him. Man cannot cease his search without undoing himself and condemning himself to unfulfillment.

The absolute future Christianity affirms views everything in terms of a process of arrival. Hence it stimulates historical creativity revealing the transitory character of every historical present.

History may have shown already that Marx's claim to make "out of man and for man the supreme being" offers man less of a future and less salvation than a faith which accounts for the transcendental and mystical tendency in man. This tendency emerges in man's cultural and artistic expressions. It suggests to him the possibility that alienation and aspiration are correlative and that both terminate in divinity, a divinity that will be sufficiently accessible to man only in that absolutely unspecified future he awaits. This future is not only achievement but grace; it is not accomplishment as much as it is gift.

Marx spoke in a manner Christians appreciate when he reminded men that they must be renewed in order to be saved. This salvation was in some respects too extrinsic and in other respects not extrinsic enough.

It was too extrinsic in its preoccupation with the external conditions and environment in which man lives. The need for interior conversion of the heart was thereby neglected.

In other respects, Marxist salvation was too immanentistic. It attempts the salvation of man in a totally human context and, hence, abandons man to the rearrangement of his economic structures as the ultimate hope and final form for salvation.

This excessive concern with economic forces eventually converts Marx's noble humanism into a threat to human dignity. Marx's dismissal of Christianity was so swift and so complete that he excluded not only the deficiencies which characterized nineteenth-century Christianity but also the promise and potential of this same Christianity for human enrichment.

Christians admire, nonetheless, the subject of Marx's philosophy. Marxism is not, as we have stated, a concern with economics but a concern with man as a self-creating, dynamic, historical being. Man is the one who shapes his destiny in a real and not in a purely ideal relationship with the world. Marx considered man's ability to live in fraternal communion with his fellowmen as they adventured together in the transformation of society. Thus, Marxism took as its goal not economic equity but a messianic salvation for all men, a salvation so total that men would no longer need a transcendent redemption. The objective Marx chose was not wrong. It was not even wrong to surmise that man could accomplish this. The mistake lay in thinking that any man could do this if he were not, at the same time, God's Son.

COROLLARY: ATHEISTIC HUMANISM

Marxism with its exalted humanism and its unflagging optimism has raised as much as any system could the question as to why one should bother about Christianity. Albert Camus' writings would later make this question more urgent.[11] If Christianity adds nothing to humanism then Christians must not invite men to become Christian humanists. Yet Christians do not propose atheistic humanism as a viable alternative to Christian humanism. They will settle for atheistic humanism. They may admire much in atheistic humanism, but if they are truly Christian in their approach to life they do not judge such humanism to be of equal value to Christian humanism. Are Christians justified in this assumption? If they have something to offer, what precisely is it they offer?

It may help, first of all, to sketch an outline of the worldview atheistic humanism espouses.[12] The contemporary atheistic humanist views reality essentially in terms of matter. Matter is self-existent, self-active, self-developing, self-enduring, autodynamic. Matter accounts fully for those values we are accustomed to call spiritual or cultural. The atheistic humanist sees no unity to reality other than the existence of pluralities and no destiny to reality other than endurance for as long as possible. Science cannot detect a unity as far back as it can see; nor can it predict a convergence or a unity as far forward as it can conjecture.

This situation causes no despair since reality itself, life itself, is worth living as it is. The fact that we emerge from matter and are destined to extinction does not mean men must cherish life any the less, enjoy it any less vigorously, use it any less selflessly for others. In fact, the idea that there is nothing else for man than what he has here may occasion greater service for one's fellowmen. Men labor not because there is a heaven to justify this, but because there is need all around us. There are men who must be helped even if we lose everything for their sake.

Nature has no plan and no purposeful outcome. It offers us a congenial environment to support human life. In itself, however, it is neither beneficent nor malicious. Reality is neutral, indifferent, nonconstructive.

The atheistic humanist argues that he has a superior ethical system. He gains nothing for his efforts in terms of future beatitude. With Camus, he affirms that in life men do what must be done, looking neither to heaven for help nor to faith for an overall explanation. We save one another as effectively as possible for as long as we can until the plague of death infects us. We try to make one another suffer as little as possible. We comfort, we heal, we simply live.

Ethical awareness demands that we give ourselves to continuous self-development. Morality is bound up with intelligent self-control of nature and with the generous expenditure of our resources for the sake of the total human community. No problem of evil resists our efforts to be good. Resistance derives not from personalized evil but from the severity of nature and the insatiable needs of men. The only damnation which awaits man is human unfulfillment.

Men have demonstrated that noble ethical systems can be constructed without the help of God, the insights of religion, or the sanction of an afterlife. The presumption that man becomes immoral and selfish if he denies God is untrue. In fact, theistic systems retard ethical growth. Christianity, for example, has never managed to make an act of unconditioned faith in man. It offers no plan for action as Comte or Marx have done. Indeed, every major ethical problem of the last century was solved without the need for religion and, tragically, without religious leaders contributing either intelligent voices or concrete plans. Was it religion or man's humanistic spirit which accounted for labor reform, racial justice, nuclear disarmament, population control and concern about automation?

A CHRISTIAN APPRAISAL

It is not my purpose here to answer in detail what Christian humanism offers. This book and its sequel are an effort to answer that question. Fairness demands that we not simplify our task. Christian humanism must not claim that an explicit faith in God is needed for moral living or social reform. The facts prove the contrary, and recent conciliar documents and papal encyclicals recognize this.

We might suggest a few thoughts in passing. A central problem in atheistic-Christian dialogue is the discovery of what reality is. If reality is as measurable and empirically predictable as humanism insists, then Christianity is in error. We should consider more seriously, however, whether the unknown is due solely to the fact that science has not yet analyzed reality completely. Is there not a possibility that mystery will remain even when science has exhausted its resources? Is mystery that which science has not yet mastered, or is it that which adheres to the nature of being and existence?

If life is the central direction toward which matter tends, and if personalism is the goal of this life tendency, Christian humanists wonder whether absolute personalism is not a more likely form the future will take rather than impersonal existinction. Christians ask whether man's search for something imperishably significant in life, a search which continues in all cultures and all periods of history, can be easily dismissed as having been fiction. Is it not reasonable to consider that the goal of contingent personalism, which nature has realized as its highest expression, may be infinite personalism?

William James observed that there are some truths in life

which are not true for us unless we meet them halfway. If going halfway can make an experience true, is it not irrational, or at least less human, not to move unless one is empirically forced to move so that one really does not move at all? This is equivalent to expecting the universe to come to us before we accept it. Has anyone discovered love without meeting it halfway?

Faith is not realized by those who stand where they are until they are pushed. Faith is not less true because one must go halfway, so to speak, to discover its validity. Love is not less real because one must go halfway to perceive its presence. The position of the atheistic humanistic is safer. Whether it is more ultimately humanizing is a debatable question. William James suggested that one should go halfway if the matter were urgent, the stakes were high, and the option were presented by reality itself.

Christians maintain that there is a Person at the end of the process of living. They insist that man must know this. Even if the present horizon seems limitless—the colonization of the planets, the control of this earth, the mastery of genetics—the starting point, namely man, is not infinite. Yet he is as worthy of infinity as his dreams, his race, his horizon.

Man does not achieve an absolute future in living a long time. It is an utterly new type of living man seeks. This renewed existence is not assured in the fulfillment of our many plans unless the person, the starting point, is himself transformed.

Christian humanism is not foolish in its faith that God salvages all the values of the world, not excluding its highest value, human life. Men survive not in their deeds, or in their children, but in their incommunicable singularity. Christians proclaim that all events, death included, are an advent, an expectancy, a patient waiting for transformation and salvation, for more life and absolute personalism. The Incarnation reveals human living as a God-centered experience. The doctrine of divine Fatherhood tells us that reality seeks a Person. The existence of grace is the Church's way of declaring that life resists regression and perversion. Even evolution convinces us that the scale of progress is irreversible in this sense that once a perfection of life is achieved, it is never lost to a lower form of life.

Christianity does not offer humanism ethics or leadership as such, not even morality. Men are ethical and morally effective leaders without Christianity. Christianity offers Christ himself with all that Christ reveals and occasions. Whether this offer should be taken seriously or makes a difference is the subject of this present book and its sequel.

Sigmund Freud

Sigmund Freud was responsible for psychoanalysis. This achievement added a new dimension to man's thinking and experience. Freud thus takes his place with Darwin and Marx in the nineteenth century's list of ingenious men who caused men to think of themselves differently from the way they had considered. The respective theories of psychoanalysis, evolution and social justice which these men devised have had a profound influence on twentieth-century thought and behavior. Each of these contributions has affected man's religious expression and led him to ask anew about the means to happiness and the meaning of salvation.

Freud's parents were Jewish and Vienna was his home from the fourth to the eighty-second year of his life when he was forced to leave. His outlook on life was shaped by the mechanism which characterized nineteenth-century scientism and by the dynamism occasioned by Darwin's discoveries. Freud also learned much from the neurologist Jean Charcot and the Viennese physician Joseph Breuer. He worked in Paris with the former during 1885 on the problem of hysteria. From this research, Freud received hints of a possible relationship between sexual problems and neurosis and even, perhaps, an initial suspicion about the unconscious and its dynamic nature. The latter told Freud of cures from hysteria which could be effected by bringing the patient to recall the origins of his sickness while under hypnosis. Breuer and Freud wrote a study of this work and called their therapy the cathartic method. In reality, this was the beginning of what Freud would later develop and present to the world as psychoanalysis.

Freud went beyond this cathartic method. He substituted free association for hypnosis so that a physician could determine not only the origins of the patient's disorder but also the conscious resistance he offered to the uncovering of repressed experience. The consciousness of the patient also made it possible for Freud to observe the process of transference by which the patient identified with his analyst.

Freud studied for the first time the effects of unconscious forces on consciousness and action. He traced mental conflicts through those defense mechanisms by which instructual tendencies were either excluded from consciousness by repression or modified in consciousness by sublimation. Freud gave the world an original insight into the influence of sexuality and aggressiveness on human behavior which, until his time, had been underestimated.

Freud wrote three books on the nature of religion: *Totem and Taboo* (1913), *The Future of an Illusion* (1927) and *Moses and Monotheism* (1939). The first book presents Freud's ideas concerning the origins of religion and its dependence upon the Oedipus Complex. The second book is Freud's clearest exposition of his understanding of religious experience and of its kinship with neurosis. He concludes in *The Future of an Illusion* that religion is an illusion which has no future. His last book is, perhaps, the weakest and least plausible of all Freud's writings.

Freud was admirable not only in his scientific endeavors

but also in his personal life. His powerful mind and never-failing courage sustained him in his creative and controversial approach to human thinking and human problems.

The last sixteen years of Freud's life were marked by physical and emotional stress. From the first surgery on his jaw for the removal of cancer, Freud's speech was impeded and his pain constant. Yet he worked and wrote to the last. His *Moses and Monotheism* was completed at the end of his life after Nazi authorities deprived him of his books and his home.

Freud was a convinced atheist for almost his entire life. He dismissed religion as an illusion though he gave it so much attention that one wonders whether he considered it more important than he realized. He argued that he would not be deceived, that religion could be explained away, that his own courage needed no illusions to support it, and that he would face reality unafraid even if the universe were barren and ultimately without purpose. Freud's eagerness to dismiss all pretense and deception from his life was vigorous and severely honest. He wanted to confront life exactly as it was.

FREUD'S EMOTIONAL LIFE

There were strange currents which ran through Freud's emotional life. These do not diminish the objective value of his work on religion. They are part of the public record, however, and may shed some light on Freud's inability to be completely objective in his assessment of religion.

It is well known, for example, that Freud was inclined to be superstitious in many respects. He gave undue attention to certain members as 17 or 61 or 62 which supposedly denoted to him the age at which he was to die. Ernest Jones, the definitive authority on the life of Freud, comments that Freud was influenced by "some lingering belief in the significance of . . . numbers."[13]

Freud wondered at times whether there might somehow

be a physical immortality for man here on earth. On one occasion he met a sister of a former patient who had died. The man's sister bore so close a resemblance to her dead brother that Freud reflected: "So, after all, it is true that the dead may return."[14]

Easter Sunday also had a fascination for Freud. Jones mentions two occasions when Easter had taken on unusual significance for him.

The date of . . . his beginning in private practice was Easter Sunday, April 25, 1886, a curious day to choose, since everything in Vienna was closed or suspended on that holy day. In a letter of April 12, 1936, he wrote "Easter Sunday signifies to me the fiftieth anniversary of taking up my medical practice." It has been suggested that Easter had an emotional significance for him. . . .[15]

There is further significance in the fact that Freud would consider Easter Sunday, a movable feast, as his anniversary rather than the fixed date on which he began his career. Freud was, moreover, preoccupied with death.

He had a habit, from his youth, of parting from his friends with the words, "Goodbye, you may never see me again." Freud, we are told, thought of death every day of his life and ascribed this over-concern to "the lasting influence of his death wishes in infancy."[16] Jones writes:

He had been increasingly looking forward to the promised date of his own death in February, 1918, with mingled feelings of dread and longing. Furthermore, we should not forget that the theme of death, the dread of it and the wish for it, had always been a continual preoccupation of Freud's mind as far back as we know anything about it. We can even trace the beginnings of it all to the sinful destruction of his little brother in his earliest infancy.[17]

The reference Jones makes to Freud's brother concerns a wish Freud had that his brother die. When his brother did die, Freud felt guilty about this for the remainder of his life.

He concluded that he deserved to die and both wished for his death and dreaded the event.

Freud's outlook on death, in his life as well as in his work, is reminiscent of Schopenhauer's thinking. In fact, Freud himself spoke of this connection: "We have unwittingly steered our course into the harbour of Schopenhauer's philosophy. For him death is the true result and to that extent the purpose of life, while the sexual instinct is the embodiment of the will to live."[18]

These idiosyncrasies in Freud's behavior discredit neither him nor his work. They do indicate, however, that few are free of illusions and that the rejection of religion and of a transcendental salvation do not always leave men as untroubled as they had expected.

The truth of atheism or religion cannot be judged solely on the basis of the turmoil or severity they bring a person. The issue is larger than this. Atheism, however, does not liberate one from existentially perplexing questions any more than does religion. It will be evident as we proceed that not all of Freud's work is of equal value. His superlative pioneer contributions in psychoanalysis are far more significant than his forays into theology.

Freud was so eager to construct a "metaphychology," as he called it, that he overextended himself. By the end of his life, he had made major pronouncements on psychology, theology, biblical criticism, Egyptology, anthropology and philosophy. Even if Freud's "metapsychology" be valid, no one man could reasonably hope to apply a speculative principle to so many intricate questions in so many complex areas. The resulting unevenness of his work led experts in their respective fields to comment as did W. W. Albright:

As a counterpoise to these serious, though exaggerated, theories we may be pardoned for saying a word about a futile but widely read example of psychological determinism—Freud's *Moses and Monotheism* (1939). The book is simply the latest of a long train of books and papers on history and religion which have been issued by Freud himself and other members of the psychoanalytical school during the past generation. Like them, his new book is totally devoid of serious historical method....[19]

One of the reasons why experts in other fields fail to take Freud's nonpsychoanalytic work seriously in his insistence on holding to a point even in the face of unanimous disagreement from him by those competent to make accurate judgments. From the time when Freud first put forward his hypothesis of the slaying of a primal father, for example, ethnologists have described it as nonsense. Freud knew this and admitted it in *Moses and Monotheism*. He answered, however, that he preferred to hold on to his own version of this possibility.

RELIGION AND NEUROSIS

Freud was intrigued with the similarity between religious activities and compulsive neurosis. He recognized that there were significant differences; the similarities, however seemed so striking that he maintained there was an essential connection. Freud's final judgment was neither hesitant nor qualified. Religion, he wrote, is "a universal obsessional neurosis."[20] He observed that the repetitive acts which characterized compulsive neurosis were present in the prayer and religious activities of believers.

There were three especially noteworthy resemblances in this regard. One observed, for example, the pangs of conscience a neurotic suffered when his ceremonial could not be performed. A religious person experienced the same reaction when he omitted his rites.

Then, too, the complete isolation the neurotic preferred while he was engaged in his ceremonial was akin to the exclusion of all other activities which a religious person insisted upon during the time of his ritual. Both the neurotic and the believer were perturbed if they were disturbed during these times.

Finally, it was difficult not to notice the conscientiousness with which both the neurotic and the religious person carried out the details of their respective ceremonies.

From these observations Freud made his first conclusions about the nature and dynamic of religious activity. Freud saw external behavior and surface symptoms. He had not yet uncovered the root cause of these phenomena. He searched for the sources of these quasi-neurotic compulsions which were apparently so universal that many sought relief from them in religious expression. He felt he had found the reason for the religious phenomenon in his discovery of the illusory character of religious experience and in the presence of a racial unconscious which was linked to the Oedipus complex.

RELIGION AS ILLUSION

Freud's most concerted dismissal of religion was contained in *The Future of an Illusion*. The thesis of the book centers on the definition of religion as an illusion which has no future or, at best, whose future requires the persistence of infantile attitudes among adults.

The first step in the analysis is the examination of the data. It must be admitted that religious ideas "in spite of their incontrovertible lack of authenticity . . . have exercised the very strongest influence on mankind."[21] We must therefore "ask where the inherent strength of these doctrines lies and to what circumstances they owe their efficacy, independent, as it is, of the acknowledgment of reason." They are not verified by an objective consideration of the experience of mature persons nor are they the final result of rational reflection.

Religious ideas "are illusions, fulfillments of the oldest, strongest, and most insistent wishes of mankind; the secret of their strength is the strength of these wishes."[22] Men want to believe in a kindly divine providence which quiets the anxiety they feel in the presence of life's dangers. Such a belief assures the human family of the eventual triumph of justice and preserves it from an overconcern with death by the presence of a future life. Such ideas, however, have neither authenticity nor rational evidence to support them.

Freud did not say that religion was necessarily an error. It was, more precisely, an illusion. "An illusion is not the same as an error; it is indeed not necessarily an error."[23] An illusion was characterized by the fact that it derived from human wishes. It was not the truth or the validity of religious ideas but their illusory nature which gave religion its influence. "If after this survey we turn again to religious doctrines, we may reiterate that they are all illusions; they do not admit of proof, and no one can be compelled to consider them as true or to believe in them."[24]

Freud was determined to rid people of these illusions. He found that "where questions of religion are concerned people are guilty of every possible kind of insincerity and intellectual misdemeanor."[25] Freud was scientific enough in his treatment of religion to narrow and define his scope precisely. "It does not lie within the scope of this enquiry to estimate the value of religious doctrines as truth. It suffices that we have recognized them, psychologically considered, as illusions."[26]

Men create gods and cling to religion because they cannot face reality. "We say to ourselves: it would indeed be very nice if there were a God, who was both creator of the world and benevolent providence; if there were a moral world order and a future life; but at the same time it is very odd that this is all just as we should wish it ourselves."[27] Freud reasoned that religious doctrines kept men from seeing things as they are and, hence, wasted their time and energy. Religion belonged to the past when it performed some useful functions on behalf of human culture. Religion, however, had no future. The future belonged to science.

Religion is an attempt to get control over the sensory world, in which we are placed, by means of the wish-world, which we developed within as a result of biological and psychological necessities. But it cannot achieve its end. Its doctrines carry with them the stamp of the times in which they originated, the ignorant childhood days of the human race. Its consolations deserve no trust. Experience teaches us that the world is not a nursery. The ethical commands, to which religion seeks to lend its weight, require some other foundation instead, since human society cannot do without them, and it is dangerous to link up obedience to them with religious belief.[28]

To Freud, the believer fights a pathetic battle, seeking to defend his religion and preserve his illusions in a struggle he loses "inch by inch." It is a desperate effort to hold out against reality in "a series of pitiable rearguard actions."[29] Religion, of course, manages a few victories. "At such a cost— by the forcible imposition of mental infantalism and including a mass delusion—religion succeeds in saving many people from individual neuroses. But little more. . . ."[30]

RELIGION AS COMPLEX

Freud summarized the thesis he set forth in *Totem and Taboo* in his *Autobiographical Study.* He believed that an all-powerful father in a primal horde of men seized all the women for himself and either drove away or killed his sons as potentially dangerous rivals. "One day, however, the sons came together and united to overwhelm, kill, and devour their father, who had been their enemy but also their ideal."[31]

After this event the sons recognized one another as possible rivals and became conscious of a sense of regret for what they had done. To overcome these threats, they formed a clan and developed the practice of totemism. The clan felt a mystical kinship with some object which served as an emblem of the clan and as a reminder of its ancestry (totem);

it gave expression to this relationship by a series of rites and practices (taboo). The purpose of this totemism was to prevent the repetition of such a deed.

The sons agreed, furthermore, to forego the possession of the women for whom they had killed their father. They were driven to find women elsewhere, and this was the origin of exogamy, or marriage outside one's own group, a practice closely associated with totemism. The totem feast commemorated the horrible crime which was the source of human guilt or "original sin." Freud claimed to have discovered in this theory "the beginning, at once, of social organization, of religion and of ethical restrictions."[32]

In 1919, Freud wrote a preface to Theodor Reik's *Das Ritual*. He stated that he had arrived at "an unexpectedly precise conclusion: namely, that God the Father once walked upon the earth in bodily form and exercised his sovereignty as chieftain of the primal human horde until his sons united to slay him. . . ." All further religions issued from this primal religion. All "are concerned with obliterating the traces of that crime or with expiating it. . . ."[33]

Freud concluded *Totem and Taboo* with words reminiscent of St. John's Gospel: "In the beginning was the deed."[34] This deed was the origin of culture and conscience; it afflicted man with the Oedipus Complex.

I want to state the conclusion that the beginnings of religion, ethics, society, and art meet in the Oedipus Complex. This is in entire accord with the findings of psychoanalysis, namely, that the nucleus of all neuroses as far as our present knowledge of them goes is the Oedipus Complex. It comes as a great surprise to me that these problems of racial psychology can also be solved through a single concrete instance, such as the relation to the father.[5]

Later, Freud reached the same conclusion in *Civilization and Its Discontents*: "We cannot disregard the conclusion that man's sense of guilt has its origin in the Oedipus Complex and was acquired when the father was killed by the association of the brothers."[36]

Freud considered Christianity an unusual development of the Jewish religion. Christianity would also concern itself with the primal crime on which all religion is based, but its description of that crime made it unique. Freud claimed that Paul accepted Jesus as the Messiah after Jesus "whose ethical precepts surpassed even the heights attained by former prophets had in turn been murdered."[37] Christianity, furthermore, translated the primal crime into the doctrine of original sin. "The unmentionable crime was replaced by the fault of the somewhat shadowy concept of original sin."[38] The murder of the Son and the expiation for the first crime which this death achieves makes Christianity a distinctive phenomenon.

A Son of God, innocent himself, had sacrificed himself—and had thereby taken over the guilt of the world. It had to be a Son, since the sin had been the murder of the Father. . . . The Mosaic religion had been a Father religion; Christianity became a Son religion. The old God, the Father, took second place; Christ, the Son, stood in his place, just as in those dark times every son had longed to do. . . . From now on Jewish religion was so to speak, a fossil.[39]

Freud observed that the father complex was a significant factor not only in the beginning but even in the continued presence of religious experience.

Psychoanalysis has made us aware of the intimate connection between the father complex and belief in God, and has taught us that the personal God is psychologically nothing other than a magnified father; it shows us every day how young people can lose their religious faith as soon as the father's authority collapses. We thus recognize the root of religious need as lying in the parental complex.[40]

Freud's analysis of religious experience was original and appealing. His prestige as the originator of psychoanalysis led many to accept completely or at least to be influenced by the application of his scientific insights to the perplexing problem of religion.

Freud's conclusions that religion was a neurosis, an illusion, and a complex derived from his convictions as well as from his observations. Freud had a persistent faith in science, a considerable suspicion of religion, and a certitude that his metapsychology offered men a new approach to religion and to life itself. These premises supposed that the transcendent was non existent and that reason and science could interpret reality. Thus, religion was "nothing other than psychological processes projected into the outer world."[41] The whole complexus of "myths of Paradise, the Fall of Man, of God, of Good and Evil, of Immortality and so on" belonged to metaphysics and could be resolved by "transforming metaphysics into metapsychology." Metapsychology was the application of knowledge gained from individual case histories to the whole of reality.

The debate between Freud and theology does not concern itself with the specifics Freud brought against religion, that is, its neurotic, illusory and complex character. The debate centers around the validity or nonvalidity of the transcendental dimension of life. Freud was convinced that contingent reality was the only reality there is. All else was too vague, too ambiguous, too dependent upon wish fulfillment and guilt feelings to be taken seriously by emotionally mature people. His *Credo* was expressed simply and decisively: "In the long run nothing can withstand reason and experience, and the contradiction religion offers to both is only too palpable."[42]

CRITIQUE

Freud began his discussion of religion with a consideration of its relationship to compulsive neurosis. We do not deny that some religious people are compulsively neurotic. We do question, however, whether religious experience emerges essentially from neurosis and whether those who seriously consider faith do so under neurotic compulsion.

If a percentage of every grouping will be neurotic, a percentage of a grouping as large as that embraced by the term "religious" will also be neurotic. A psychoanalyst would come in contact with a high percentage of neurotic people, religious or otherwise, by the nature of his work. Neurosis, furthermore, tends to manifest itself with regard to important rather than superficial areas of life. Hence, it may well align itself more easily with one's religious convictions than with other experiences which the individual senses to be less critical for life. The fact that religion tends to demand a personal accounting of each individual, that it concerns itself with forces as fundamental as guilt and innocence, the existence of God and the hope for salvation, or the judgment as to whether reality is purposeful, makes religion an area of life where a man's inability to cope with himself may develop into a neurosis with religious symptoms.

Freud's eagerness to dismiss religion as a neurosis led him to simplify his task. In the instances we considered above concerning the relationship between religion and neurosis, it is evident that Freud equates religion with ritual. He limits religious experience to prayer or worship which religious men sometimes turn to but which is not the only form in which religious convictions are expressed. One must examine more than one aspect of religious behavior if he intends to dismiss effectively the entire phenomenon. John Dewey, as we shall see in chapter three, also restricts the definition of religion in his dismissal of it. He narrows religion to doctrine rather than ritual.

Even granted Freud's restricted treatment, his conclusion that religion was a neurosis was too cavalier. Religion, after all, is a normal human experience; neurosis is not. Those who profess faith can see that religious behavior is abnormal when it becomes neurotic. In fact, scrupulosity has been consistently cited by religious men as a malady which requires counsel and therapy rather than admiration or encouragement.

Freud simplifies his task further by choosing as examples the activities of the emotionally distraught, neurotic believer. His evaluation of religious experience does not account for Francis of Assisi, John of the Cross, Francis de Sales, Vincent de Paul. He has no explanation for John XXIII or Dietrich Bonhoeffer.

When Freud claimed that both the neurotic and the religious person suffer "pangs of conscience" when their respective ceremonials are missed, he used the wrong term. The neurotic suffers pathological anxiety, not "pangs of conscience" when his ritual is omitted. Freud also neglected to say that mature religious people make mature religious judgments about when certain rites are to be left undone for the sake of greater values. When a person subordinates everything to the performance of a ritual and suffers anxiety when it is omitted, both religious counselors and medical men know they are dealing with an abnormality.

Freud stated, moreover, that both the religious person and the neurotic are disturbed if their activity is interrupted. Once again, Freud makes his task too easy. The religious person may be annoyed if the interruption is pointless; the neurotic is anxious even if he is interrupted for a serious reason and even though the ceremonial he is performing may be trivial. A mature religious person will not return to his activity if it has been omitted for a good cause; the neurotic feels compelled to do so. The neurotic, furthermore, believes there is something salvific in the very actions he performs. A religious person considers the activity he performs a means to the achievement of something more profound, namely, a deeper love of God, a clearer understanding of himself, or a more selfless service of his neighbor. The neurotic is intense during his ritual; a religious person is recollected but not humorlessly grim. Many Christians are convinced that the central action of Christian worship, the Eucharist, and all the official liturgical celebrations of the Church's life, are enriched by the presence of other persons. The neurotic seeks isolation.

Freud, finally, equated the conscientiousness with which men of faith or neurotics engage in ritual activities. Freud employs the wrong word again. Conscientiousness is a virtue. It means that one is reasonably serious about what he understands to be his obligation or his responsibility. Compulsiveness, on the other hand, is a malady. The neurotic is not conscientious; he is compulsive. If a religious person is compulsive about his activity, he is not conscientious. If he is reasonably serious about a matter he judges to have some importance in his life, he is conscientious.

Freud's analysis of the relationship between religion and neurosis remains very much his personal viewpoint on religion. His analysis of religion, which is unrefined and unscientific, in no way discredits his psychoanalytic method. The evaluation of the validity of that method depends upon the judgment of those competent to assess its worth and, of course, upon its viability as a means of healing emotional disturbance.

WISH FULFILLMENT

Freud's critique of religion included a judgment about its illusory character. He was undeniably accurate in telling us that wish fulfillment can play a part in religious faith. Because of him, we are perhaps more aware of the projection and the rationalization which at times mar the religious behavior of even the most mature men of faith. The fact that wishful thinking occurs in religious experience is not an indication that, therefore, religious experience issues from it. Some wishful thinking in religious behavior no more discredits the validity of religion than some wishful thinking in scientific or psychoanalytic procedure discredit these sciences.

Wishful thinking is a human experience which is present at times in all human activity. We have seen, for example, wishful tendencies in Freud's atheism. This does not mean that his atheism is false or even that it derives from his wishful thinking. It means only that, because a human being is the one who chooses to be an atheist, some wishful thinking accompanies his choices. Whether Freud's atheism is valid or not depends upon factors more significant than his concomitant wishful behavior.

The impulse toward wishful thinking is not restricted to believers. Nor does rigid adherence to psychoanalysis save one from this experience. No one is excused from the presence of wishful thinking, least of all the man who is certain he never thinks wishfully.

Some of Freud's most faithful disciples saw evidence of wishful thinking in *The Future of an Illusion*. Theodor Reik commented in a critical paper the year *The Future of an Illusion* was published:

We shall not withhold our great admiration for this brilliantly delineated picture of the future; but it seems to us less compelling than the foregoing. Moreover, it is admittedly more dependent on subjective factors than the rest. It is not outside the bounds of possibility that this picture of Freud's will become reality; but it is certainly striking that his view of the future in the main seems to conform to our wishes. Whereas the main section of Freud's essay shows the future an illusion, we may say with little exaggeration that this last section presents the illusion of a future.[43]

Freud's dismissal of religion was as susceptible to illusion as the acceptance of religion may be. He never allowed that the believer might face reality as he sees it, not as he wishes it to be. A believer knows he cannot prove the truth of his faith empirically, but he is convinced that more than wishful thinking is at issue in his decision. A believer arrives at faith because he considers faith closer to the truth than doubt or denial. His faith may be, in a way Freud did not permit, a search for meaning and an affirmation of meaning rather than a flight from reality. Even the uneducated believer, if his faith is genuine, comes to religion with this in mind though, of course, he cannot reflexively or conceptually so express himself. Subliminally and intuitively, he comes to religion because he wants to accept reality.

There are those who live a pseudo faith just as there are those who become atheists not from conscientious conviction but from less than noble motives. One cannot judge the substantial validity of religion or atheism by a concentration on the aberrations to which either may lead. There is, furthermore, the likelihood that an uneducated or an educated believer may have made a mature act of faith but not be able to verbalize his experience in a way which is satisfactory to a scientist.

There is more reality testing in religion than Freud admitted or realized. People are not as irrational about their beliefs as Freud surmised. They can reason about their experience of faith, ask questions about it and change their attitudes when they are convinced they are wrong. Freud did not allow for wishful thinking which is certified by reality testing. If there is a reasonable possibility that a wish can be fulfilled, then wishes are useful and become a means for development and growth.

Wishful thinking in religious experience is illusory only if there is no reality testing and only if Freud were correct in assigning to reality the limitations he imposed upon it. If this be true, then religion is an illusion and should be forsaken. Men of faith question, however, the accuracy of Freud's definition of the real. Existential philosophy would also challenge Freud's presuppositions whether one considers the boundary situations of Karl Jaspers or the transcendental character of "Being" in Martin Heidegger.[44] A believer sees no reason why Freud was especially competent to judge what the real is in every area of life. Freud, for example, never refuted or even seriously examined the possibility of God's existence or the meaning behind religious principles. He merely decided beforehand that these questions were unreal and illusory.

Freud engaged in wishful thinking when he made psycho-analysis a veritable religion and when he sought, consequently, to explain everything in psychoanalytic categories. "Thus, one of the world's most determined disillusionists falls into the trap of ruthlessly tearing from his life one of man's great 'illusions,' only to substitute for it another."[45]

Freud accepted the scientific outlook of his age as a complete revelation of truth. Thus, he would not admit the significance of any phenomenon which his version of science could not validate. He could not grant the possibility that a believer might be as emotionally mature as a nonbeliever and that he might be, in addition to this, correct.

THE FATHER FIGURE AND THE TOTEM FEAST

Freud exaggerated the influence of the father figure in man's social and religious life. He argued in *Totem and Taboo*:

However, psychoanalytic investigation of the individual teaches with especial emphasis that god is in every case modelled after the father and that our personal relation to god is dependent upon our relation to our physical father, fluctuating and changing with him, and that god at bottom is nothing but an exalted father.[46]

Freud's observations on the father figure were more applicable to the nineteenth-century Western European family rather than to the human condition as such. He accounts for neither matriarchal societies nor for the contemporary situation in which the authority and influence of the father in the family is less than it was in Freud's day. One wonders, furthermore, whether the concept of God which the mature person has is not dependent upon his general experience of love rather than on any one expression of love or authority. It is more likely that the deprivation or distortion of all love rather than that of the father's love makes of God an impossibility or a threatening deity.

Some accept the biblical message of God as love although they themselves have come from disturbed family situations. Others are frightened by God or hostile to God even though their family environment seems to have been healthy. The influence of parental love on the developing religious life of the child is considerable, and it is undeniable. We are indebted to Freud for having made us more aware of this. We wonder, however, whether that which is crucially important in our lives should be cited as a determining factor.

Freud, furthermore, gave much attention to the totem feast which derived from the primal crime. He saw this feast as an act of expiation for the crime and as a reminder to all who shared in it that the crime must never again be repeated. Sensing a similarity between this feast and the Christian Eucharist, Freud maintained that a communion service is a modern form of the totem feast in which a band of brothers eats and drinks the flesh and blood of the son instead of the father. By so doing, they identify themselves with the son and become holy.

A bottom, however, the Christian communion is a new setting aside of the father, a repetition of the crime that must now be expiated. We see how well justified is Frazer's dictum that "the Christian communion has absorbed within itself a sacrament which is doubtless far older than Christianity."[47]

Freud's thesis is theologically implausible. It depends upon a radical and unjustified reinterpretation of the whole meaning of the Eucharist. No biblical, theological, or even devotional datum supports such a theory. A scientist may not arbitrarily evaluate Christian doctrine any more than a theologian has the right to interpret scientific or psychoanalytic data to his own advantage. Sound scientific and theological procedure demands a rigorous objectivity and total fairness. Both seem absent from Freud's analysis. Most present-day anthropologists, moreover, support Goldenweiser's contention that totemism is difficult to define and that in most groups the totem animal is neither killed nor eaten. The totem feast, furthermore, which figures so largely in Freud's thesis, is extremely rare.[48] Professor A. L. Kroeber questions the entire theory of a primal crime.

The psychoanalytic explanation of culture is intuitive, dogmatic, and wholly unhistorical. It disregards the findings of prehistory and archeology as irrelevant, or at most as dealing only with details of little significance as compared with its own interpretation of the essence of how culture came to be. . . . It is not altogether clear whether the "event" was construed by Freud in its ordinary sense of a single actual happening, or as a "typical" recurrent event. But the explanation comes to nearly the same thing in either case; one mechanism is seized upon as cardinal, all evidence of others is disregarded as inconsquential. The theory is as arbitrary as it is fantastically one-sided.[49]

Freud's words in this area and that of some theologians in other areas evidence an inferiority complex which both scientists and believers sometimes brings to their own concerns. Believers manifest this when they seem to have their faith constantly validated in some way by science; or, when they dismiss completely from their world outlook the challenges and contributions of the sciences. This is not to fault those who rightly expect reasonable assurances before making an act of faith. A need for repeated assurance, however, is a sign of insecurity in the experience of faith or, for that matter, in the experience of any human relationship.

Scientists manifest the same inferiority complex when they

feel compelled to demean or destroy religion. Unless one has a profound distrust of human intelligence and maturity, he can be confident that if religion be false, men will sooner or later abandon it. Likewise, if science overextends itself, people will sooner or later resist the overextension. A patient and candid partnership between science and religion will counteract the fictions and errors from which neither side is immune.

To give Freud his due, his concern with discrediting religion may well have been influenced by his eagerness to rid some people of the emotional disturbances occasioned by their religious training. He also encountered those distorted presentations or religion which no intelligent or mature person can long abide. There were, however, other aspects of the religious phenomenon which Freud cannot be excused for ignoring. A scientist is open to criticism when he entirely dismisses that which he has only partially considered. Freud did not allow the possibility that there may be a truth to religion which survives its misconceptions. He did not realize that his metapsychology may have been "curing" men not only of their problems but of their valid insights into the nature of reality.

FREUDIAN PESSIMISM

We shall never know if Freud's somber pessimism was the cause or the effect of his dismissal of religion. His pessimism, of course, may have had nothing to do with his attitude toward religion, but there is reason to believe there was a relationship. Freud seemed more at home in a universe which proposed no ultimate solution than in one which offered a final meaning. He feared the brighter side of life, sensing perhaps that this might foster illusions. He welcomed darkness as that which requires more courage and partakes of more reality than light. His assessment of fatherhood, sexuality, childhood, and hopeful projection into the future was always correct to a point but eventually brooding, involuted, and deterministic.

Freud was convinced, as he said, that "dark, unfeeling, and unloving powers determine human destiny."[50]

Otto Rank points out that Freud was essentially a man of the nineteenth century whose determinism was as rigid psychologically as Darwin's was biologically and Marx's economically.[51] Freud's pessimism did not derive necessarily from his determinism. Marx was deterministic and yet an optimist. The source of his pessimism may have been due to his voluntaristic outlook on life. Voluntaristic philosophy will be pessimistic (Schopenhauer, Freud) if it emphasizes guilt, or euphorically optimistic (Nietzsche) if it affirms the creative power of the will. Freud had no confidence in the capacity of the human will for creativity or even for prevailing over the problems confronting it.

As therapy, analysis is optimistic, believes as it were in the good in men and some kind of capacity for and possibility of salvation. In theory, it is pessimistic; man has no will and no creative power, is driven by the *id* and repressed by the *super-ego* authorities, is unfree and still guilty.[52]

Freud expressed himself clearly in terms of a pessimistic anthropology:

The bit of truth behind all this—one so eagerly denied—is that men are not gentle, friendly creatures wishing for love, who simply defend themselves if they are attacked, but that a powerful measure of desire for aggression has to be reckoned as part of their instinctual endowment. The result is that their neighbor is to them not only a possible helper or sexual object, but also a temptation to them to gratify their aggressiveness on him, to exploit his capacity for work without recompense, to use him sexually without his consent, to seize his possessions, to humiliate him, to cause him pain, to torture and to kill him. *Homo homini lupus*; who has the courage to dispute it in the face of all the evidence in his own life and in history.[53]

Freud's *Civilization and Its Discontents* is almost a condensed version of the last two books of Schopenhauer's *The*

World as Will and Idea. Freud does not offer a metaphysical explanation concerning the impossibility of human happiness as did Schopenhauer. Freud's observations are more clinical. We are a race so laden with the guilt of a primal murder, so greedy and aggressive in our human relationships, so much at the mercy of sexual and unconscious forces that happiness is an unreasonable expectation.

Freud would not countenance a transcendent salvation, an extrinsic redemption, an ultimately meaningful reality. He was convinced that the search for a final purpose was pathological. Herbert Spencer comments to the contrary that such a concern is normal, instinctive, human. "To the aboriginal man and to every civilized child the problem of the Universe suggests itself. What is it? And whence comes it? are questions that press for a solution, when from time to time, the imagination rises above daily trivialities."[54]

In his own way, Freud viewed his work as offering man a measure of salvation. Psychoanalysis became not only a method but a system built on a philosophical and quasi-religious theory of man. Everything was to be explained in terms of metapsychology, and its canons were sacrosanct. Freud all but defined infallibly the futility of religion, the transcendence of science, and the finality of psychoanalysis as a definitive revelation. Reality was reduced to that which human reason comprehends and the scientific method controls.

The future resulting from this vision was bleak. Men were determined to helplessness and anxiety in the face of overwhelming odds against them. Freud claimed that he did not make the odds but that it was his mission to make men aware of their plight. He dismissed as an illusion the idea that ultimate hope inspired men with courage and self-sacrifice and joyful creativity. As we saw above in the quotation from *Civilization and Its Discontents,* Freud recognized human frailty but he seemed more angry at it than compassionate toward it.

Freud thought he had found the fundamental truth which

sets men free. Men would be saved in a shattering and total awareness of what we were like and how barren reality is. Freud sought to save us by his method, not for happiness, of course, but to save us nonetheless from the alienation of our neuroses, illusions, complexes and unconscious anxieties. This stark self-knowledge would inspire us to re-create ourselves into new men who would live in maturity if not in content-ment. Such salvation was the only salvation possible.

In spite of Freud's mishandling of the religious question, his genius and his work fortunately survive. We believe he would have been closer to the truth had he limited his scope and adhered more rigidly to his statement that "reality will always remain 'unknowable.' "[55]

The unknowableness of reality and the reasonable as-sumption that reality is ultimately favorable to man leads men of faith to consider a salvation more total and more joyous than that offered by Freud.

2

The Religious Phenomenon

The religious aspirations of men urge them beyond theories of transcendence to worship. Religious experience is less concerned with conceptual certitude than it is with awe and reverence. In this, philosophy and religion differ.

Men affirm religion as they reach out in hope for salvation toward transcendence. Faith does not limit salvation to this world nor reduce it to rational categories. As men sense the need to be saved by something not available to human resources, they create religions. Religion, then, is a universal sign of our universal need. It is, furthermore, a universal act of hope in the eventuality of salvation. Since we engage religious men on a more complex level than reason, religion expresses itself in reason but more often in symbol and ritual.

The religious phenomenon is further attestation of the scope and magnitude of the human need for transcendent salvation. This phenomenon is so polyvalent and transconceptual that it is difficult to simplify or comprehend its reality. Man's desire for scientific certitude is easier to explain than his sensitivity to the sacred or the mystical. Even the history of religion cannot account adequately for the motives and hopes which make men religious. Man, it seems, is not only a religious being who reveals his religious nature in the course of history; he is also a human being who, therefore, fails to manifest in a concrete and comprehensible manner all he is and all he seeks to become. Man as such, certainly religious man in particular, performs actions and utters words which he knows do not show him as he is. Each man is more than he can express in a communitarian or historical manner. A history of religion is, by its definition, limited to the societal forms religion takes, and it is restricted, consequently, to that in religious experience which can be recorded.

In religion man perceives not only the sacred but the sacred as saving. An experience which inspires terror and terminates in terror is not a religious experience. Religion, Eastern or Western, reveals order in spite of chaos and discovers reasons for hope and means by which human existence is justified or else it is not religion.

Religion is involved with a perception of the sacred. When man stands in the midst of his fellowmen, he may sense his importance. When he confronts the cosmos, he may become aware of his dominion or superiority. This is especially true today. Before the sacred, however, man is confronted with his "unimportance," as it were. He turns toward the sacred, even in primitive societies, as we shall see, because he is anxious for more being.

Religion is often a human way of discovering something more substantial than the "trivialities" of everyday existence; religion is man's most enduring symbol; and the content of this symbol is an affirmation of beauty and meaning in spite of the distortions and absurdities of life. In every age of history, religion becomes a means by which the unity of reality is declared. The religious man learns thereby to regard reality as a purposeful harmony and himself as an intelligible creature despite the contradictory, and at times destructive, tendencies he suffers in his own personality. Religion is, therefore, "irrelevant" to everyday life because it brings to the surface realities not realized in daily existence but realities which are as much a part of us as our everydays.

Regardless of what the "nonreligious" person thinks of religious experience, it is for the man who lives in its influence a grace and a source of further life and beauty. The "nonreligious" man can maintain cogently that he can live in happiness and die in peace without religion. This is true. Religion, does not intend a more effective management of the life we have. Obviously, "nonreligious" man does not lose control of himself nor even of his capacity for goodness. Religious man is not concerned, however, only with an understanding or mastery of the life we are given. He has become aware of another dimension of life. This causes him to wonder if the life "nonreligious" man affirms, a life totally committed to the profane, is really life. The question is not whether profane life can be handled intelligently and morally without religious experience. It can be. The question is whether a radically profane life is diminished life, a life which has not yet discovered its grandeur or its destiny, a life which, therefore, has missed something life ought not to miss.

The stubborn survival of religion in history is an indication that it offers men a life experience not available to them elsewhere. Granted the validity of this discussion, we might describe religion as an existence based upon some absolute meaning of life; this meaning must inspire reverence and evoke in the human spirit a hope for salvation; this meaning, finally, must be attuned to a transcendent definition of reality even if transcendence is not recognized as such. Religion differs from philosophy because it seeks, in addition to absolute meaning, devotion, salvation and relationship with that which is more than human. More simply defined, religion is a search in devotion for salvation which derives, essentially if not completely, from a transcendent principle or person.

Religion, furthermore, must pervade one's whole life. This does not mean that one constantly performs explicitly re-

ligious actions. It does not even require that explicitly religious
actions be performed more often than explicitly profane ones.
In fact, the intensity of explicitly religious actions demands
that they be performed less frequently than explicitly profane
actions. Religion pervades one's life when it inspires men to
a freely given devotion to an absolute sphere of life. This requires that he live his life, not minute by minute, nor only in
terms of his practical and necessary tasks but in virtue of an
absolute value, transcending, enriching, unifying and solemn-
izing daily living. This consecration to an absolute sphere is
accompanied by a yearning to be saved for more life and to be
preserved from the terror of nonbeing, nonlife, chaos, or
absurdity.

A man is completely "nonreligious" only when his life lacks
devotion to absoluteness. Thus, religious experience is wider
than the historical form of religion, as Christianity is more universal than the institutional structure of the Church.

The description of religion we have given is suitable to all
religions and even to the "nonreligious" religious spirit. These
religions attest to the need and desire for salvation which is
the object of our present study. We shall consider briefly the
world's major religions so that we might determine whether
the salvation themes we discovered in modern philosophy are
operative in the more expansive area of religious awareness.

Primitive Religions

Primitive man was more sophisticated in his religious expression than appears at first sight. One wonders, for example,
whether modern man's view of himself as a chance creature
lost in a remote corner of a meaningless universe is the better
part of wisdom. The inability of many modern men to discover human intelligibility in reality or purposeful destiny for
the human family may be an indication that we are not as
superior to primitive men as we often suppose.

Primitive man was unwilling to consider the objects or persons he encountered in life to be real unless he could relate these with something transcendent. We grant, of course, that the relationship was, on occasion, confused and distorted. Of greater significance, however, is the fact that primitive man thought such a relationship was possible and sought to establish it. When the supposed relationship was achieved, primitive man was convinced that objects or persons had been saved from their profanity. They had been sacralized, redeemed, given meaning, inserted into the process of reality.

Primitive man formulated religious practices because he could not abide the terror of meaninglessness. Religion negated nonbeing for him and reminded him "that suffering is never final; that death is always followed by resurrection; that every defeat is annulled and transcended by the final victory."[56] Religion gave his life devotion, his activity solemnity, his suffering purpose, his success durability.

Primitive man understood, in some preconceptual fashion, that human beings cannot live in chaos. He became religious because he was eager for more being and more reality than he was given. Because he was certain this was available to him, he never became pessimistic.

It must be admitted, of course, that the symbols and words used for God are today more accurate. We have realized greater precision and, as a consequence, conceptualize God far more adequately than primitive man did. Whether we experience God any more deeply is questionable, however.

Primitive man believed, for example, that nature revealed and mediated the sacred. His world was sacramental, at times foolishly so, but sacramental nonetheless. Thus we discover in primitive man a remarkable religious awareness. Common to primitive religions is a sense of filial confidence in a Great God and an undiminished hope for a future life with this Great God. Primitive religions also converge in the affirmation that there was a time when the Great God conversed with men.

Indeed, this God can be reached as a saving God if sacrifices are offered. Sacrifice is universal among primitive men.

It is noteworthy that primitive religion does not become a religion of human perfection achieved by human resources, but, rather, it tends to be a "supernatural" religion. No human can save man; only God is capable of this.

Primitive man is a creature sensitive to the religious and the sacred. He often perceives God in spatial terms, much as medieval man will perceive God in terms of order and modern man in terms of the future. The Great God is most high, dwells in the sky, knows all things and can do whatever he wishes. This Great God will save man.

Only the Great God is a saving God. The lesser gods could not effect this. Thus, "in an extremely critical situation, in which the very existence of the community is at stake, the divinities who in normal times ensure and exalt life are abandoned in favor of the supreme god . . . all these . . . gods were unable to *save* them, that is, to ensure their existence in really critical moments."[57]

Hinduism

Hinduism is the oldest of man's major religions. Hinduism and Judeo-Christianity are the only major religions which are not derivative from a former major religion. Hence, these two religions may tell us more than any other religion about the fundamental and instinctive religious yearnings of the human heart. Buddhism borrowed from Hinduism, and Islamism was influenced by Judeo-Christianity. Hinduism and Judeo-Christianity developed, however, independently from each other.

Our concern in this section is not an analysis of each religion nor even an effort at comparative religious expression. The intent is to discover whether man creates his major religions because he seeks through them some form of tran-

scendent salvation. It is worth noting that if Hinduism and
Judeo-Christianity from which all other major religions derive
exhibit obvious salvation themselves we have discovered a
universal hope for salvation in the human spirit.

Hinduism evolved from *Vedism*, was a polytheistic religion structured around a salvation principle: a good life
would lead to life after death in the company of the gods.
Before Vedism became Hinduism, it went through a form
called *Brahmanism*. Here the aspiration for salvation is intensified. Brahmanism encourages asceticism and affirms *samsara*
(transmigration) and *karma* (acts which have a beneficient
influence on the process of the individual's reincarnation).

The desire for salvation in Hinduism was not systematically
expressed until the Upanishad or sacred writings were com-
posed. The *Upanishad* teaches that contemplation and ascetical practice can liberate man from the necessity of being
reborn and eventually allow man's finite spirit to return to a
pantheistic union with the Absolute.

The *Upanishad* invites the reader to a salvation influenced
by karma. These good actions liberate one from the transmigration (samsara) which continues until definitive freedom is
given. *Moksha* is the final grace which abolishes the need to
be reborn constantly. *Moksha* is ultimate happiness, total salvation. It brings suffering to an end and ushers one into sublimity.

The goal of life is union with the God, Brahman-Atman.
Peace and salvation are conferred on the human spirit when
one abides in a state of moksha with Brahman. At this moment transfiguration occurs. The contradictions and ambiguities, the dualities and defective options of living are
reduced to unity. So radical is this unity that all difference between the individual and Brahman are abolished.

Hinduism contains a pervasive mystical element. It admits
the possibility that one may achieve moksha even in this life.

If one is given this great grace, he will not be able to speak of it. To speak is to affirm opposites. Moksha, however, is a unity beyond all opposites. One cannot, therefore, describe it in human language. The awareness of moksha must occur in contemplation and silence.

The *Upanishad* witnesses to a soaring aspiration toward salvation. In another of Hinduism's sacred books, the *Bhagavad-Gita,* or joyous songs, this possibility for salvation takes on an incarnational form. The *Bhagavad-Gita* is a dialogue between *Arjuna,* a celestial figure, and *Krishna* who is god in human form. The *Bhagavad-Gita* explains that Krishna is at the heart of all things. Everything is a manifestation or revelation of Krishna. Krishna, who apparently came into the world as man, has given men an example of *bhakti.* This is a selfless love; it is the only love able to destroy egoism.

The *Bhagavad-Gita* is the most spiritual and the most popular of the Hindu sacred books. The incarnational form of salvation presented in this book well account for its influence. Indeed, the *Bhagavad-Gita* has been called the Gospel of Hinduism.

The Brahman or supreme god of Hinduism appears in Hindu mythology in a trinity of functions. Brahman appears as Brahma who creates each new universe, as Vishnu who sustains, and as Shiva who destroys. Vishnu is a god of love who is worshipped in his nine incarnations, the chief of which is Krishna. Vishnu took on physical flesh in each of these incarnations so that evil might be overcome and salvation assured.

The description we have given of Hinduism is concerned with its classic expression. Today Hinduism is less a religion than a collection of religions. It is so tolerant of divergent thought that it includes both atheism and monotheism in its various acceptable manifestations. Of interest for our purpose, however, is the model or traditional structure of the religion.

All other tendencies or developments find their norm in this "official" Hinduism. In much the same way as Western man may express his desire for salvation in secular rather than sacred categories, Eastern man may be occupied about salvation in erratic forms of Hinduism. It would take another study to examine each of these forms. It is clear, in the meantime, that Hinduism testifies to the antiquity and depth of man's hope for transcendent salvation. In a fashion typical of the religious phenomenon, this concern with transcendent salvation is optimistic. It has none of the despairing pessimism characteristic of Schopenhauer's philosophy of transcendent salvation.

Christianity will have difficulty with the Hindu insistence that the world is *maya* or illusion. Hinduism does not accept the world as seriously as a Christian prefers; nor does it regard history as decisive. Despite these differences, Hinduism speaks of salvation, as does Christianity. It believes in the power of prayer to affect this salvation, even prayer for the dead who may be thereby relieved of the need to be reborn.

The Hindu description of God includes a revelation from God in the sacred books and a salvation opportunity because of God. Ascetical practices and contemplation are stressed because aspirations toward salvation are vivid. This salvation terminates in a union with a God who ultimately saves man by incorporating man into his unity. This God, as we have seen, appears even incarnationally so that man may know he is not forsaken in his efforts to find salvation.

Considerations such as these led the Second Vatican Council to declare:

Thus in Hinduism men contemplate the divine mystery and express it through an inexhaustible abundance of myth and through searching philosophical inquiry. They seek freedom from the anguish of our human condition either through ascetical practices or profound meditation or a flight to God with love and trust.[58]

Buddhism

Gautama Siddhartha, the Buddha or Enlightened One, was born a Hindu. He reacted, however, against both Brahmanism and Hinduism. Buddhism is concerned with salvation but it stresses man's ability to achieve this without reliance on a transcendent source. In theological terms one might say Buddhism tends toward Pelagianism.

The practical aspect of Buddhism's search for salvation are emphasized by its substitution of psychological attitudes and concrete deeds for the ritual and myth which are prevalent in Hinduism. To continue the use of theological language, one notices in Buddhism an effort to eliminate interest in the world and attachment to the body. In this, it is akin to Albigensianism. Finally, Buddhism's insistence that little or no help comes from the gods approximates Deism.

The psychological interest of Buddhism is manifest in its reinterpretation of Hindu *karma*. *Karma*, for the Buddhist, is achieved in the way one looks at the world rather than in specific actions. One must have, above all, good will and compassion. Buddhism is not as concerned with the cosmological speculation which intrigues the Hindu. Practical living and emotional withdrawal from the world are of paramount importance. Austere practices, therefore, are not essential; invocation of God is unnecessary.

Buddhism hopes for salvation from the unfortunate necessity of rebirth.

Freedom from this suffering is attained when the individual destroys all craving for this world or the body by an admixture of meditation and abstention from pleasure. The result of this process is *Nirvana*, or a state of total silence, complete detachment, passionless serenity.

The central urgency of withdrawal from the world has led to an emphasis on monastic life. The Buddhist monk is expected to be a model of detachment. His possessions are kept to a minimum; he meditates on the qualities of Buddha while counting the prayer beads he carries. He is encouraged to exemplify in even the smallest detail the Buddhist precept which obliges one to a refusal to take life. Thus, in spite of his limited possessions, he carries a filter to strain insects from drinking water so that he might not inflict suffering on living things. His diet is, preferably, vegetarian for the same reason. The Buddhist monk affirms poverty, inoffensiveness and celibacy as he pursues a state of Zen or enlightenment which is often the fruit of years of meditation.

The salvation themes in Buddhism, with transcendental considerations, emerge more clearly in Mahayana Buddhism than they do in the Hinayana form. Hinayana Buddhism is a sect in comparison with the massive numbers who follow Mahayana Buddhism. This Mahayana form teaches that the historical Buddha was but a partial incarnation of the Celestial Buddha. In addition to this historical Buddha, countless Bodhisattva aid the salvation of men by various terrestrial incarnations. These Bodhisattva are closely allied with the Divine Rbsolute and refuse to enter Nirvana until they have helped men to salvation. In a further Buddhist tradition, both the historical Buddha and the Bodhisattva are unable to save men until *Amida,* a divine emanation of the Celestial Buddha, comes to forgive sins.

Both Buddhism and Hinduism evidence a salvation tendency. In at least some forms of Buddhism, incarnations and emanations from the Celestial Buddha attest to this in a transcendental manner. In all forms of Buddhism, men strive to be saved from suffering and rebirth by detachment and meditation.

It can be said with adequate justification that Hinduism and Buddhism reflect basic human needs, instincts and longings. Critical to these is a yearning for salvation, a yearning sometimes ill-directed toward a salvation which is obscurely defined. There remains in Hinduism, nonetheless, an elaborate structure of myths and ascetical practices, of incarnations and hopes for union with God which seek salvation. Buddhism, moreover, counsels contemplation and compassion, detachment and enlightened thinking as a means to that salvation which lifts man from the imprisonment of this world and his body to freedom.

The Second Vatican Council took note of Buddhism in this manner:

Again, Buddhism, in its various forms, realizes the radical insufficiency of this changeable world; it teaches a way by which men, in a devout and confident spirit, may be able either to acquire the state of perfect liberation, or attain, by their own efforts or through higher help, supreme illumination.[59]

Islamism

Islam is the religion of "submission" to God's Will. Allah, the one and only God, has spoken his Word (the Koran) to his servants; he has given a law to Islam; and he promises salvation to those who are faithful to his Will and his law. Islamism is a religion of prayer and almsgiving, of fasting and pilgrimage, of holydays and of unambiguous proclamation: "There is no God but Allah; Mohammed is the messenger of Allah." Islam is God's kingdom on earth; God meets those who identify with this kingdom with his promises and his salvation.

Islam requires a more specific faith than Hinduism or Buddhism. The creed is simple but it is clear. When a Moslem dies, the profession of faith is whispered into his ear: "Who is your God? Allah. What is your religion? Islam. Who is your prophet? Mohammed." Allah is a saving God, but he is also a judging God who condemns those who do not believe in him.

Islam counsels brotherhool although brotherhood is defined in terms more ethnical than those Christianity considers. In Mohammed's last speech, he advised: "Know that every Moslem is a brother to every other Moslem and know that you are now one brotherhood."

Islam places strong emphasis on the supreme dominion of God, his omnipotent will, his awesome majesty. In this, its salvation concern is less man-centered than that of Buddhism and less mystical than that of Hinduism. Officially, the religion is uncomfortable with the notion of friendship with God since it deems such friendship too exalted for man. It prefers a master-servant relationship between God and man. There is, however, a mystical tradition which developed after the first few centuries of Islam's existence. It continues into the present and accounts for the presence of religious communities where the contemplative life is stressed and where a personal relationship with God is sought.

It seems that no major religion is content to consider God as aloof from us. With remarkable frequency, an incarnational expression of salvation appears in world religion. For the Moslem, this incarnationalism is not symbolized in a specific figure who is divine in some way, as is the case in Hinduism and Buddhism. The transcendent Allah does, however, send man his prophet (Mohammed) and he does reveal himself in a clear manner (the Koran). Allah is reached by prayer and identifies himself, in a sense, with the Kingdom of Islam.

In two of its documents the Second Vatican Council commented on Islam. The earlier of these documents is brief: "The plan of salvation also includes those who acknowledge the Creator. In the first place among these are the Moslems who, professing to hold the faith of Abraham, along with us adore the one and merciful God, who on the last day will judge mankind."[60]

The Council returned on another occasion to a more detailed consideration of Islam:

Upon the Moslems, too, the Church looks with esteem. They adore one God, living and enduring, merciful and all-powerful, Maker of heaven and earth and Speaker to men. They strive to submit wholeheartedly even to his inscrutable decrees, just as did Abraham, with whom the Islamic faith is pleased to associate itself. Though they do not acknowledge Jesus as God, they revere him as a prophet. They also honor Mary, his virgin mother; at times they call on her, too, with devotion. In addition they await the day of judgement when God will give each man his due after raising him up. Consequently, they prize the moral life, and give worship to God especially through prayer, almsgiving, and fasting.[61]

CONCLUSION

It is not necessary that all men profess a religion although it is remarkable how many do. The numbers who turn to religion, the durability of the world's major religions and the centrality of salvation themes in them indicate the universality and force of man's hope for redemption. We have seen how modern man seeks salvation in his philosophy; this concern is even more explicit in his religious expression. Obviously, salvation is a crucial element in the definition of man, the formation of his history, the construction of his philosophy, and the existence of his religions.

Mircea Eliade reminds us that man never does away with religion:

. . . profane existence is never found in the pure state. To whatever degree he may have desacralized the world, the man who has made his choice in favor of a profane life never succeeds in completely doing away with religious behavior . . . even the most desacralized existence still preserves traces of a religious valorization of the world.[62]

Only recently has man conceived of himself as the sole agent and unique subject of history. This may be one reason why he senses his alienation. It is difficult for man to feel he belongs to a world which has neither plan nor purpose, neither healing grace nor eventual salvation. Man's discontent with this situation leads him to create salvation philosophies such as Marxism, or to preserve irrational relationships with the powers beyond him by superstition or astrology. This is further proof that the purely rational man whom Western civilization admires does not exist and has never existed.

A philosophy is most captivating when its reasoning allows for mysticism. Marxism does this as do some forms of Existentialism. A religion, furthermore, which is structured on logic alone, discounting ritual or mystery, symbol or faith is inadequate to the total man and insufficient to meet the human need for complete salvation.

Modern man who, as we have said, is not as alone in the universe as he thinks, or as rational as he supposes is also not as nonreligious as he presumes:

> ... nonreligion is equivalent to a new "fall" of man ... after the first "fall," his ancestor, the primordial man, retained intelligence enough to enable him to rediscover the traces of God that are visible in the world. After the first "fall", the religious sense descended to the level of the "divided consciousness"; now, after the second, it has fallen even further, into the depths of the unconscious; it has been "forgotten."[63]

With the advent of Judeo-Christianity, something utterly new happened to religious man. Judeo-Christianity spoke to religious man for the first time of faith, strictly so-called, and it discovered history as a way in which God reveals himself.

> This God of the Jewish people is no longer an Oriental divinity, creator of archetypal gestures, but a personality who ceaselessly intervenes in history, who reveals his will through events (invasions, sieges, battles and so on). Historical facts thus become "situations" of man in respect to God, and as such they acquire a religious value that nothing had previously been able to confer on

them. It may, then, be said with truth that the Hebrews were the first to discover the meaning of history as the epiphany of God, and this conception, as we should expect, was taken up and amplified by Christianity.[64]

Our ultimate intention is to demonstrate not only the magnitude of the theme of salvation, as we do in this book, but in a further book to relate Christ to this universal need. Before we do this, however, it may help us as Americans to know whether we are motivated by a desire for salvation and, if this be so, how we are motivated by it. The next two chapters will consider the American scene in which the ever-recurring drama of man's search for salvation is enacted although in a distinctively American manner.

Peter Berger made an observation which serves well as the conclusion for this chapter.

All Christology is concerned with salvation. To speak of Christ is to speak of man's redemption. . . . A quest for redemption is by no means the prerogative of the biblical tradition. One has only to recall the importance of the idea of moksha in the religious formulations of ancient India. And, despite the vast differences in the conceptions of just what man is to be redeemed from and how this might be accomplished (as, say, between a biblical conception of man's sin and the Hindu view of man's predicament), there is a common, empirically given human reality that underlies all quests for redemption. . . . The discovery of Christ implies the discovery of the redeeming presence of God within the anguish of human experience. Now God is perceived not only in terrible confrontation with the world of man, but present within it as suffering love. This presence makes possible the ultimate vindication of creation . . . it vindicates the hope that human suffering has redeeming significance.[65]

3

The American Experiment

George Santayana once wrote that "to be an American is of itself almost a moral condition, an education, and a career."[66] It is not our purpose to explain Santayana's statement but to explore in our own way the phenomenon which led him to speak as he did. The reader may wonder why a description of the American experiment is fitting in a study which has Christ as its ultimate object and the search for salvation as its proximate intent. I think it is suitable for two reasons.

The search for salvation has taken a unique and distinctive form in these United States. Americans are not inclined to the pessimism of Schopenhauer or Freud. They have shown little interest in the type of religious society Comte devised or the monolithic economic determinism Marx declared. They have demonstrated a sympathy for Mill's utilitarianism, but they did not find a congenial philosophy until John Dewey derived a philosophy from the American experience.

Americans are an experimental people. They are inveterate tinkerers whose experience has taught them that if they really wanted to they could change anything. Things men had only wondered and theorized about became concrete realities in the American experiment. Whatever may have been attempted before interested the American, but it did not thrill him as much as the possibility that he might try what no one had tried before. "It is in his blood," Santayana wrote, "to be socially a radical, though perhaps not intellectually. What has existed in the past, especially the remote past, seems to him not only not authoritative, but irrelevant, inferior, and outworn. . . . But his enthusiasm for the future is profound. . . . It is the necessary faith of the pioneer."[67]

The confidence of the American with regard to the future is justified, it seems, by his past record and present accomplishments.

[Americans] could not consistently accept determinism. . . . They could believe in progress; their own history was the most convincing proof of the validity of that concept. America had been a gamble that had paid off, an experiment that had succeeded; it had enlisted the average man, had required him to play his part in a common enterprise, and had rewarded his courage and audacity with boundless generosity . . . [Americans] had assumed the worth of democracy, of equality, of freedom, assessed the practical consequences of these assumptions, and committed themselves to their realization. When they had pledged their lives, their fortunes, and their sacred honor to the triumph of the doctrines of the Declaration, they had acted pragmatically. Every American knew that the world in which he lived was, in part, of his own making, that he had bent Nature to his will . . . to break with the past, reject traditional habits, try new methods, put beliefs to a vote, make a future to order, excited not only sympathy but a feeling of familiarity.[68]

In addition to the American penchant to approach reality in a new way, there is a second reason why this discussion is germane to our topic: American theology ought not to be a European theology translated to the new world. It must be a distinctively Christian theology, of course, but one which is at least conscious of the depth and magnitude of the American experiment. Such a theology will not always approve of that experiment. This is understandable. To ignore the experiment, however, is unpardonable.

An acceptance of the American experiment does not require that we exaggerate its importance. There does not have to be, indeed, cannot be a characteristically American approach to every aspect of Christian doctrine. The American experiment influences theology in a more subtle and less universal manner.

The methodology we employ in this two-volume study of Christology in an American perspective, a methodology we first used in *The Estranged God*, may be one example of an American approach. The eagerness to explore options, to consider alternative opinions seriously, to find optimistic implications in even the most severe Christian doctrines, to theologize, not only from Christian tradition but from the philosophical or literary forces which influence the contemporary scene, may lead Americans to create a theology different in tone, perhaps in substance, from that developed by other cultures.

The two reasons we have given justify, we believe, our present interest in the American experiment. Since there is a danger that an American examining his own culture or a theologian assessing his own society might become subjective or arbitrary, we shall rely almost exclusively on non-American commentators for the validation of our observations. We shall, furthermore, limit the commentators we consider to those who are recognized for the cogency and incisiveness of their comments so that the positive interpretation we intend to give the American experiment may not appear naive.

Since the question we are about to consider is complex, it may simplify our presentation if we divide this chapter into four parts: a general commentary on the classic features in the American cultural profile; John Dewey and pragmatism; contemporary concerns in American culture; literary expressions of the American temper.

A General Commentary on the Classic
Features in the American Cultural Profile

This discussion will be restricted to those characteristics in
the American cultural profile which will influence the religious
or nonreligious attitudes Americans may adopt. We are not
concerned here with the political, economic or artistic insights
of American culture. We are eager to know, however, what
Americans expect from Christianity, how Christianity should
be presented to them, and, finally, in the concluding chapter
of the book which will follow this one, whether a distinctively
American spirituality is possible.

AMERICANS DO NOT EASILY ACCEPT
TRANSCENDENCE OR MYSTERY

This characteristic is not recently true of us. It has not been
the result of twentieth-century technology; it was observable
in our culture long before we became the mighty industrial-
scientific complex we are today. Alexis de Tocqueville saw
this feature of our national personality when he visited this
country in 1831. He later recorded his impressions:

As [Americans] perceive that they succeed in resolving without
assistance, all the little difficulties which their practical life presents, they readily conclude that everything in the world may be
explained and that nothing in it transcends the limits of their
understanding. Thus they fall to denying what they cannot comprehend, which leaves them but little faith for whatever is extraordinary, and an almost insurmountable distaste for whatever
is supernatural.[69]

This led de Tocqueville to comment on the philosophical
attitude of Americans.

I think that in no country in the civilized world is less attention
paid to philosophy than in the United States. . . . To evade the

bondage of system and habit . . . to accept tradition only as a means of information . . . to seek the reason of things for one's self, and in one's self alone . . . such are the principal characteristics of what I shall call the philosophical method of the Americans.[70]

The concern with this world of which de Tocqueville was speaking was in the first half of the nineteenth century so much a part of the American outlook that Henry Steele Commager could comment in the second half of the twentieth century:

. . . from the beginning most Americans, except Negro slaves, found this world a paradise rather than a purgatory. Whatever they may have said, or sung, they preferred this life to the next, and when they imagined heaven, they thought of it as operating under an American constitution.[71]

De Tocqueville reasoned that the democratic principle on which the new country was founded accounted for a lack of interest in the transcendent.

Equality begets in man the desire of judging everything for himself; it gives him, in all things, a taste for the tangible and the real, a contempt for tradition and for forms . . . [Americans] mistrust systems; they adhere closely to facts. . . . As they do not easily defer to the mere name of any fellowman, they are never inclined to rest upon any man's authority; but, on the contrary, they are unremitting in their efforts to find out the weaker points of their neighbor's doctrine.[72]

Even the transcendentalism which a few Americans became interested in during the nineteenth century was not exactly what Europeans would have recognized as a typical transcendental approach. American transcendentalism was practical and uncomplicated when compared to the German metaphysics which influenced the movement. The American stamp on transcendentalism was visible in its optimism, its faith in the spiritual resources of man, its emphasis on individual inspiration, its conviction that intuitive truth could be validated by effective action.

Transcendentalism, even in its American form, never appealed to the country at large. William James' abandonment of transcendentalism and John Dewey's lack of interest in Hegelian idealism which had at first attracted him led both philosophers to devise the pragmatism which was typically American and which caught the American imagination. De Tocqueville's observation that there was little philosophical interest among Americans is valid although the situation changed somewhat in the twentieth century. Pragmatism, which some judge not to be a philosophy, but at best a method and at worst a mistake, was about as close as Americans were likely to come to an interest in philosophical questions.

AMERICANS ARE A PEOPLE ON THE MOVE, ANXIOUS FOR CHANGE AND, HENCE, A PEOPLE COMMITTED TO THE PERFECTIBILITY OF MAN

Well over a century ago, de Tocqueville said it accurately in one sentence: "Every one is in motion."[73]

In proportion as castes disappear and the classes of society approximate . . . the image of an ideal but always fugitive perfection presents itself to the human mind. Continual changes are then every instant occurring under the observation of every man . . . he learns but too well that no people and no individual, how enlightened soever they may be, can lay claim to infallibility . . . he infers that man is endowed with an indefinite faculty of improvement.

De Tocqueville gives an example of this attitude:

I accost an American sailor, and inquire why the ships of his country are built so as to last but a short time; he answers without hesitation, that the art of navigation is every day making such rapid progress, that the finest vessel would become almost useless if it lasted beyond a few years. In these words, which fell accidentally, and on a particular subject, from an uninstructed man, I recognize the general and systematic idea upon which a great people direct all their concerns.[74]

What de Tocqueville called "the restless ambition which equality begets,"[75] another Frenchman found still typical of us. Jacques Maritain comments:

Americans seem to live in their own land as pilgrims. . . . They are always on the move. . . . They are not settled, installed. . . . A skyscraper in New York does not lay claim to brave the centuries any more than does a tent in the desert. . . . And now Americans are demolishing houses and constructing new buildings all over New York. . . . this American mood seems to me to be close to Christian detachment, to the Christian sense of the impermanence of earthly things.[76]

This same characteristic leads Harvey Cox to call mobility a feature of the secular city. The American city is typified by the cloverleaf, the airport control tower, escalators, elevators and subways. American literature, Cox observes, is filled with heroes on the move. "Americans have always been a mobile people. They had to be, even to come here . . . mobile people are generally tolerant of new ideas and possibilities."[77]

The restlessness of the American scene conditioned the culture to concern itself with the eventual perfectibility of man. Since many Americans were convinced this was possible, they tended to be optimistic. "For three hundred years Calvinism had taught the depravity of man without any perceptible effect on the cheerfulness, kindliness, or optimism of Americans. . . ."[78]

In the mid-twentieth century, Americans "were by no means so sure of the benevolence of God and of Nature or the perfectibility of man as they had been a century earlier," although "nothing had as yet persuaded them to acquiesce in a philosophy of despair."[79]

Santayana made note of the goodwill and hope for perfection in the American.

. . . America has been the land of universal goodwill, confidence in life, inexperience of poisons. Until yesterday it believed itself immune from the hereditary plagues of mankind . . . [the American cannot detect] vanity or wickedness in the ultimate aims of a man, including himself. He thinks life splendid and blameless without stopping to consider how far folly and malice may be inherent in it. . . . American orthodoxy . . . has a keener sense for destiny than for policy. It is confident of a happy and triumphant future.[80]

No American could believe that he was damned, and Jefferson spoke for most of them when he acknowledged an overruling Providence which by all its dispensations proves that it delights in the happiness of man here and his greater happiness hereafter.[81]

AMERICANS ARE DEEPLY INFLUENCED
BY THE PRESSURE OF PUBLIC OPINION

This pressure was so prevalent that it was detectable in the early nineteenth century, even in the area of religious concerns. De Tocqueville observes:

In ages of equality, kings may often command obedience, but the majority always commands belief: to the majority, therefore, deference is to be paid in whatsoever is not contrary to faith. . . . All the American clergy know and respect the intellectual supremacy exercised by the majority; they never sustain any but necessary conflicts with it. . . . Public opinion is therefore never hostile to them; it rather supports and protects them . . . religion herself holds sway [in the United States] much less as a doctrine of revelation than as a commonly received opinion.[82]

At first sight, this susceptibility to the pressure of public opinion seems odd in a culture which is also noted for its self-reliance.

There is little doubt that a spirit of self-reliance is assertive in our culture. Santayana once observed: "[Americans] are men with principles and fond of stating them. Moreover, they have an intense self-reliance; to exercise private judgment is not only a habit with them but a conscious duty."[83]

It was, perhaps, the early constitutionalization of the country, the immediate implementation of the democratic principle, the fear of authority when it is exercised by the few which led Americans to affirm their self-reliance, but to do so in a context of interdependence. Eventually this made possible the pressures of the peer group which we shall speak of later. Americans had to work together from the beginning. "Society as a whole was . . . interdependent, and with interdependence went some impatience with independence."[84]

If cooperation was imperative, individualism and self-reliance were equally extolled. The American character tended to be voluntaristic rather than rationalistic. There is an impatience with authority unless Americans feel they have a part to play in its exercise. On the whole, Americans are more impressed with the teachings of experience than the dictates of logic.

The harmony of this apparent contradiction between self-reliance and group pressure was perhaps best explained by Santayana:

The general instinct is to run and help, to assume direction, to pull through somehow by mutual adaptation, and by seizing on the readiest practical measures and working compromises. Each man joins in and gives a helping hand, without a preconceived plan or a prior motive. Even the leader, when he is a natural leader and not a professional, has nothing up his sleeve to force on the rest. . . . All meet in a general spirit of consultation; eager to persuade but ready to be persuaded, with a cheery confidence in their average ability. . . . . It is implicitly agreed, in every case, that disputed questions shall be put to a vote, and that the minority will loyally acquiesce in the decision of the majority and build henceforth upon it, without a thought of ever resisting it.[85]

Americans seek the support of the majority. This support is considered more important in our culture than in other cultures. There is, Maritain maintains, a great dislike for being too individual.

I am thinking in particular of that kind of outshining others which can sometimes be observed in academic circles. Many an American professor seems to be anxious not to be more brilliant or more original than the average member of the teaching community. After all, is not genius always harmful to mutual tolerance and a good state of affairs in the community, and is not mediocrity of good standing preferable to any occasion for jealousy, strife, and rivalry?[86]

Once again, Santayana's analysis is perceptive:

. . . the bubbles also must swim with the stream. Even what is best in American life is compulsory—the idealism, the zeal, the beautiful happy unison of its great moments. You must wave, you must cheer, you must push with the irresistible crowd; otherwise you will feel like a traitor, a soulless outcast, a deserted ship high and dry on the shore. In America there is but one way of being saved, though it is not particular to any of the official religions, which must themselves silently conform to the national orthodoxy, or else become impotent and merely ornamental. This national faith and morality are vague in idea, but inexorable in spirit; they are the gospel of work and the belief in progress. By them, in a country where all men are free, every man finds that what matters most has been settled for him beforehand.

Nevertheless, American life *is* free as a whole, because it is mobile, because every atom that swims in it has a momentum of its own which is felt and respected throughout the mass, like the weight of an atom in the solar system, even if the deflection it may cause is infinitesimal. In temper America is docile and not at all tyrannical; it has not predetermined its career, and its merciless momentum is a passive resultant.[87]

AMERICANS ARE NOT A
MATERIALISTIC PEOPLE

Alexis de Tocqueville gives us a starting point for this consideration.

> The love of well-being is there [in the United States] displayed as a tenacious, exclusive, universal passion; but its range is confined. To build enormous palaces, to conquer or to mimic nature, to ransack the world in order to gratify the passions of a man is not thought of; but to add a few rods of land to your field, to plant an orchard, to enlarge a dwelling, to be always making life more comfortable and convenient, to avoid trouble, and to satisfy the smallest wants without effort and almost without cost.[88]

Not only is the search for material possessions moderate but it is a search limited by moral restraints.

> . . . it is difficult to depart from the common rule by one's vices as by one's virtues . . . good morals contribute to public tranquillity and are favorable to industry . . . men wish to be well off as they can in this world, without foregoing their chance of another . . . a kind of virtuous materialism may ultimately be established . . .[89]

De Tocqueville's observation helps explain why Americans sometimes feel guilty about the wealth they desire. The wealthy class in the United States differs considerably, for example, from the wealthy class in Latin America. In speaking of America's wealthy class, Santayana noted: "The rich have helped the public more than they have fleeced it, and they have been emulated more than hated or served by the enterprising poor."[90] As Americans, we are aware of harsher aspects of this picture than Santayana takes into consideration. We shall have the opportunity to discuss these later. Nonetheless,

Santayana's comment retains its validity. The wealthy class in the United States tended to spend their money less ostentatiously than the same class in other cultures; they felt guilty about wealth on occasion and used it to benefit the public at large to an unprecedented extent. One can, of course, question the motivation, recall the greed of big business in the beginning of this century, cite tax considerations as a reason why the wealthy share. All this is true and yet there remains something more to say. One must account for the distinctive behavior of the wealthy in this country, a distinctiveness which is previous to the other factors we have just enumerated.

Maritain energetically refutes what he calls "the old tag" of American materialism. He records the first impressions he had of this country: "They were freedom-loving and mankind-loving people, people clinging to the importance of ethical standards, anxious to save the world, the most humane and the least materialist among modern people which had reached the industrial stage."[91]

The conviction that moral standards are important remained unchanged from the nineteenth into the twentieth century. Moral practices may have changed; the authority of institutions sustaining moral standards may have been diminished; the sanctions which once enforced the standards are less severe; but Americans continue to emphasize ethical behavior and deem it of greater significance than reason or logic. The moral conduct of a political leader, for example, even in his private life, is sometimes judged of more consequence than his competence for his office and his honesty in the public arena.

Margaret Mead in her study, New Lives for Old, quotes the reactions of the Manus of New Guinea. A million Americans passed through the island of this primitive people during the Second World War. They evaluated the American character in the following manner:

The Americans treated us like individuals, like brothers . . . Americans believe in having work done by machines so that men can live to old age instead of dying worn out while they are still young . . . the Americans believed that every human being's life and health was of inestimable value, something for which no amount of property, time, and effort was too much to sacrifice. . . . From the Americans we learned that human beings are irreplaceable and unexpendable, while all material things are replaceable and so expendable. . . . From the Americans we learned that it is *only* human beings that are important.[92]

This American passion for humanitarianism became both a restraining influence on materialism and a form of national religion. Religion was often considered the most effective way of expressing this humanitarianism. The humanitarian American tended, therefore, to view religion less in terms of its theology, metaphysics or authority and more in terms of its capacity to reinforce American optimism for the future of man and trust in the untapped resources of the life we live in this world. This gospel of humanitarianism sent Americans on an extensive missionary venture on its behalf through the preaching of the democratic system, the expenditure of funds for foreign aid, and the commission of groups similar to the Peace Corps.

THOUGH NOT MATERIALISTIC, AMERICANS ARE INSTINCTIVELY RESPONSIVE TO SECULARITY

De Tocqueville noticed this in the early days of this country's formation.

The American ministers of the Gospel do not attempt to draw or to fix all the thoughts of man upon the life to come; they are willing to surrender a portion of his heart to the cares of the present . . . whilst they never cease to point to the other world as part of the great object of the hopes and fears of the believer, they do not forbid him honestly to court prosperity in this.[93]

De Tocqueville marveled at how quickly and enthusiastically Americans gave themselves to the construction of their secular city.

... a stranger is constantly amazed at the immense public works executed by a nation which contains, so to speak, no rich men. The Americans arrived but as yesterday on the territory which they inhabit, and they have already changed the whole order of nature for their own advantage. They have joined the Hudson to the Mississippi, and made the Atlantic Ocean communicate with the Gulf of Mexico, across a continent of more than five hundred leagues which separates the two seas. The longest railroads which have been constructed, up to the present time, are in America.[94]

Maritain distinguishes between secularity which is open to spiritual values and materialism which is closed to them. The fact that the American spirit forced the industrial regime in this country beyond pure capitalism to a more humane economic system is one indication of this distinction. Frequently, the secular American seems materialistic to Europeans because Europeans often identify spirituality with a contempt for or, at least, a neutrality toward material improvement.

It may be difficult for some Europeans to discover asceticism in American life. The asceticism is present, I suggest, but it takes a different form in this culture. One denies himself not so much in a voluntary renunciation of what he might have enjoyed as in unremitting work. A resistance to selfish desire is not measured by Americans in terms of tangible objects which are sacrificed but in terms of energy expended on behalf of goals. A man who works hard is respected and admired and is seldom considered a hedonist.

This asceticism does not always have a religious outlet. It

sometimes leads to self-seeking just as a voluntary renunciation of pleasure may become a subtle form of self-seeking. This asceticism is present, nonetheless, and tempers materialistic concerns with some restraint. It makes life in these United States hectic, and it is unrelenting in its demands that time must be given to constant purposeful activity. Because the work drive in this country can often be measured only in terms of possessions acquired or secular success, Americans frequently wonder where their hectic pace is leading them. Materialism is not enough; yet self-denying work seems to terminate only there. Americans may, therefore, be eager for a contemporary approach to asceticism, one which is meaningful, demanding, and more humanly fulfilling than their work or possessions. We shall discuss this later in the concluding chapter of the book which will follow upon this one.

CONCLUSION

The observations we have made in this section give us some indication of how Americans may approach religion. There is clearly something new and distinctive about the American spirit. A nation disinclined to transcendence, suspicious of fixed principle and stable life patterns, responsive to public opinion and committed to secularity ought to be irreligious. Yet there remains in America a dissatisfaction with the material and a yearning for spiritual values. Americans surprisingly are unmistakably and irreversibly religious. A few words on how this is possible are now in order.

There was little doubt in de Tocqueville's mind that "the Americans are a very religious people."[95] Santayana marveled at the same phenomenon: "[Americans] are traditionally exercised about religion, and adrift on the subject more than any other people on earth. . . ."[96]

Many of the effects of this commitment can be identified in the religious residue which is part of the American self-image. An ingrained moral purpose, a ceaseless search for salvation, a passion for righteousness and for justice, a dissatisfaction with material achievements, an interest in the spiritual (which sometimes becomes so erratic that hundreds of denominations vie with one another) must be considered in any effective definition of the American spirit.

Strangely enough, this concern with religion was so instinctive that nineteenth and even twentieth-century science caused violent but no fatal conflicts with religion. "The most scientific-minded people in the Western world were, on the whole, those whose faith was least impaired by science."[97] This persistent loyalty to religious principles was not always commendable. It often degenerated into a fundamentalism which required a resistance to facts for its continued existence. Of more interest for our purposes is the durability rather than the form of this religious interest.

As science revealed the mysterious character of the universe, many Americans clung more devoutly to their familiar God, resented the invasion of religion by science, and, at times, in an unfortunate disparity, considered their faith as so different from the empirical world that it could not be affected by developments in the secular realm.

Will Herberg, in his classic study of religious sociology in America, makes an observation which would seem contradictory if one did not know the American spirit. "America seems to be at once the most religious and the most secular of all nations."[98]

This simultaneous faith in religion and secularity caused Americans little difficulty, at least on the surface. Later, in our fourth chapter, we shall discuss the problems occasioned by this attitude as F. Scott Fitzgerald analyzed them. For the moment, it is sufficient to comment that Americans approached religion determined that their ever-present goodwill, their native idealism, their confident trust in the future and in the national experiment would not be destroyed by their religious faith. They resisted religion, perhaps only by passive nonacceptance, whenever it seemed to undermine those secular virtues and that secular vision which a cultural consensus had endorsed.

Santayana makes a careful distinction between speculative idealism which he considers dangerous and pragmatic American idealism which he admires.

. . . a man who does not idealize his experience, but idealizes a priori is incapable of true prophecy; when he dreams he raves and the more he criticizes the less he helps. American idealism, on the contrary, is nothing if not helpful, nothing if not pertinent to practicable transformations; and when the American frets, it is because whatever is useless and impertinent, be it idealism or inertia, irritates him; for it frustrates the good results which he sees might so easily have been obtained. The American is wonderfully alive . . . his vitality . . . makes him appear agitated on the surface . . . yet his vitality is not superficial; it is inwardly prompted, and . . . sensitive . . . He is inquisitive, and ready with an answer to any question that he may put to himself of his own accord; but if you try to pour instruction into him, on matters that do not touch his own spontaneous life, he shows the most extraordinary powers of resistance; so that he often is remarkably expert in some directions and surprisingly obtuse in others. . . . In a word, he is young.[99]

This goodwill and idealism encouraged Americans to trust in the future, not the distant future, for which Americans may be too impatient, but at least in the immediate future.

. . . the American is imaginative; for where life is intense, imagination is intense also. Were he not imaginative he would not live so much in the future. But his imagination is practical and the future it forecasts is immediate; it works with the clearest and least ambiguous terms known to his experience, in terms of number, measure, contrivance, economy, and speed. He is an idealist working on matter. Understanding as he does the material potentialities of things, he is successful in invention, conservative in reform, and quick in emergencies. All his life he jumps into the train after it has started and jumps out before it has stopped; and he never once gets left behind, or breaks a leg. . . . Idealism in the American accordingly goes hand in hand with present contentment and with foresight of what the future very likely will actually bring . . . he believes he is already on the right track and moving toward an excellent destiny. . . . In the United States . . . the scale and speed of life have made everything strangely un-English. There is cheeriness instead of doggedness, confidence instead of circumspection; there is a desire to quizz and dazzle rather than a fear of being mistaken or of being shocked; there is a pervasive cordiality, exaggeration, and farcical humour; and in the presence of the Englishman, when by chance he turns up or is thought of, there is an invincible impatience and irritation that his point of view should be so fixed, his mind so literal. . . .[100]

AMERICAN RELIGIOSITY

These forces and qualities are present in all genuinely American expressions of religious experience. Continuing American interest in religion would surprise those who, fifty years ago, thought that science and reason had fatally discredited religion. If ever a country seemed less in need of religion, it was this country. Here secularity was so massive and affluence so abundant that religion, it was felt, could not survive once it lost its intellectual credibility. This had apparently happened and soon, some predicted, religion would disappear.

Although, at the moment, there is a certain disenchantment with institutional religion, religious experience is deemed valuable, especially by young people. The many Americans who attend church "are not fools or hypocrites" as Herberg observes. "They are honest, intelligent people who take their religion quite seriously."[101] Herberg repeats what others before him noticed: "Americans believe in religion in a way that perhaps no other people do."[102] The American approach to religion emphasizes deed rather than creed. This is to be expected in a culture which is pragmatic and which shows little interest in philosophy. Americans often have faith in faith rather than in God. They become religious about religion rather than about God. "Religious Americans speak of God and Christ, but what they seem to regard as really redemptive is primarily religion, the 'positive' attitudes of believing."[103]

Americans want concrete results from all they do. Religion is no exception. It is sometimes a means of getting the most out of life. Religion is expected to bring about peace of mind, happiness and secular success. Granted our survey of classic features in the American profile, it does not surprise us to discover that American religion is humanistic. Without a vital transcendent concern, it easily becomes a religion in which man is served rather than God. God is often expected to serve man's designs. American "religion, however sincere and well-meant, is ultimately vitiated by a strong and pervasive idolatrous element."[104]

These observations reflect a search for spiritual values which is frequently confused but by no means absent in the American people taken as a whole. "Particularly among the more sensitive young men and women" in America today "there is a groping for a spiritual base."[105]

Maritain, for his part, sees a "thirst for spiritual life which is deep in the American soul. . . . In a number of people it is more or less unconscious, more or less repressed by the conditions of existence and the tyranny of unceasing activity. For all that, it is real and alive. . . ."[106]

Americans may not respond instinctively to transcendence but they remain inarticulately sensitive to it. "American literature, in its most objectively careful scrutinies, has been preoccupied with the beyond and the nameless . . . from *Moby Dick* and *The Scarlet Letter* to *Look Homeward, Angel* and *Requiem for a Nun*."[107]

We shall consider American literature seriously in terms of

its transcendence and interest in salvation in the following chapter.

The religious problem in America is not a problem concerned with whether religion will survive. It will. The problem is not the presence of religion in American life but the impact it can make on American society and whether it will develop in a manner which will respond to the profound spiritual needs of the American people. "As long ago as 1914, Walter Lippmann could say that the Church . . . was answering questions that were not being asked and refusing to face those that were."[108]

Americans love life deeply. They want religion to encourage this love for life and give it some direction. For, in spite of this love, they quickly lose heart. ". . . Americans are not patient with life. They are not patient with their own life, as a rule. And they get disturbed and discouraged very soon, if the work they have undertaken is slow to succeed."[109]

In spite of surface bravado, there is in America a fear and an inner insecurity, which is typical of young people and young cultures. Americans are anxious for stable and dogmatic principles in life provided they are real and not artificial, supportive rather than repressive, pragmatic instead of clever.

John Dewey and Pragmatism

John Dewey's philosophy emerged from the spirit of the American experiment. Whatever American philosophy there was before Dewey was pragmatic.

Benjamin Franklin urged Americans to be self-reliant and to occupy themselves with pragmatic objectives rather than transcendental concerns. His axioms were so fitting that they often became American colloquialisms.

God helps them that help themselves.
Get what you can and what you get hold.

Keep thy shop and thy shop will keep thee.
Love your neighbor; yet don't pull down your hedge.

The American disinclination toward transcendence found clear expression in the writings of Thomas Jefferson. "To talk of immaterial existence is to talk of nothings. To say that the human soul, angels, God, are immaterial is to say they are nothings. . . . I cannot reason otherwise. . . ."[110]

American resistance to transcendental categories takes the form of indifference rather than vigorous opposition. Pragmatic projects are so numerous and urgent that speculation seems pointless. Jefferson observed: "I am satisfied, and sufficiently occupied with the things which are, without tormenting or troubling myself about those, which may indeed be, but of which I have no evidence."[111]

As Americans became immersed in the pragmatic, their religious instincts found expression in humanitarianism rather than in theological or metaphysical efforts. "What is serving God?", Benjamin Franklin once asked. " 'Tis doing good to man."

Jefferson was impatient with anything other than man as an object of religious interest. Dogmatic affirmations or definitions of the transcendental were impossible and pointless.

Jesus has told us only that God is good and perfect, but has not defined him. I am, therefore, of his theology, believing that we have neither words nor ideas adequate to that definition. And if we could all, after his example, leave the subject as indefinable, we should all be of one sect, doers of good and eschewers of evil.[112]

Jefferson reflected in his writings that ambivalent American attitude toward religion which finds religion acceptable if it does not emphasize a distinctive approach to life and yet somehow reprehensible if it does. "If by religion we are to understand sectarian dogmas, in which no two of them agree, then your exclamation on them is just" that this would be the best of all possible worlds, if there were no religion in it.[113]

In spite of this, the Declaration of Independence reflects the spirit of a religious people. The Declaration, Jefferson explains, "was intended to be an expression of the American mind and to give to that expression the proper tone and spirit called for by the occasion."[114]

These were some of the influences on John Dewey's thought. He was to become the most systematic and most representative exponent of American pragmatism. From Hegel, he borrowed the concept of the dialectic and defined intelligence as a dialectic between experience and nature. Meaningful activity emerged from the dialectic between the natural conditions men discovered and human intervention in them so that broad social consequences might follow.

Dewey developed the Darwinian thesis that our biological structure was the result of our need to cope with our environment. Dewey utilized this principle to develop a theory on the origin of human intelligence. He argued that men were governed by instincts in the beginning and learned to think only when they saw that a thoughtful reaction to one's environment led to more significant human control of it than did mere instinctual response. Thus, a pragmatic and utilitarian interest in the environment forced us to discover thinking.

This utilitarianism was neither crass nor selfish. The objective was to bring about broad social benefits. Dewey became interested in the effort John Stuart Mill had made to use philosophy as an instrument for social reform. He especially liked Mill's ability to achieve an ethical system and a plan for social reconstruction from his philosophical insights.

Even Marx, with whom Dewey differed, impressed him. Marx's thesis that the social situation accounts for our ideas and that the social consequences of our thinking determine truth and morality was expressed by Dewey in another form, but it was essentially attuned to Marx's observation. Dewey criticized Marx in *Freedom and Culture* because of his concept of class warfare and his outdated scientific approach. The affirmation of one, rigid law which necessitated and explained all human activity was a result of nineteenth-century scientism rather than an enlightened twentieth-century insight. Contemporary science recognizes pluralism and probability, Dewey argued. Yet Marxism requires a monolithic interpretation of reality through an acceptance of inflexible certitudes. Thus, Marxism did not use a valid scientific methodology. It became instead a theology, relying on its own a priori's rather than on reality for its validation. Nonetheless, Dewey could not be unsympathetic to Marx's explanation of human consciousness in terms of social existence, nor to Marx's belief that human intervention in the social order was a moral duty.

On the American scene, William James was an obvious influence on Dewey's philosophy. He was responsive to James' insistence that "there can be no difference which doesn't make a difference—no difference in abstract truth which does not express itself in a difference of concrete fact."[115] "The ultimate test for us of what a truth means is indeed the conduct it dictates or inspires."[116]

Pragmatism, as James envisioned it, does not stand alone but finds agreement with related philosophical approaches to life. "[Pragmatism] agrees with Nominalism, for instance, in always appealing to particulars; with Utilitarianism in emphasizing practical aspects; with Positivism in its disdain for verbal solutions, useless questions, and metaphysical abstractions."[117]

James observed that the real is that which produces experimental, concrete, measurable effects. "[Man] turns toward concreteness and adequacy, towards facts, towards action, and towards power . . . as against dogma, artificiality, and the pretense of finality in truth."

Dewey reasoned that philosophy should benefit society. It

could not do this unless it was based on the experience of living as interpreted by scientific investigation. The proof that one's method and conclusions were valid depended upon the social utility which resulted. Dewey felt that Americans had to get away from the Greek influence on philosophy.

The Greeks, especially Plato, had something to teach us in their methodology of continuous inquiry and in their passion for a moral reconstruction of their environment. Eventually, however, the Greeks developed a preference for knowing over doing, for contemplation over action. Thus, they lost the opportunity of making their philosophy humanly effective.

Philosophy needed reconstruction. This would require our abandoning any hope for final truth. Nothing was fixed; everything changed. It was urgent, therefore, that philosophers consider the changing nature of reality rather than speculate on the intrinsic nature of man. Men learned about life when they allowed experience to instruct them and when they made the most of the present situation in which they found themselves.

In *Human Nature and Conduct*, Dewey claimed that ethical systems were unreal when they were based on theological and metaphysical considerations. Such systems became negative because they were not based on the positive forces in human nature but on not doing certain things, on avoiding evil, and observing prohibitions. Morality would prove to be socially effective and humanly enriching only if it grew out of experience and observation.

This dualism between morality and reality, between thinking and action, between philosophy and life could be overcome if a dialectical approach were taken. In *Reconstruction in Philosophy*, Dewey attacked traditional philosophy on two counts. It claimed to be more scientific than science by pretending to be a means to final truth. Furthermore, it necessitated dualism by its insistence that the metaphysical be kept distinct from the practical affairs of the everyday world.

Dewey, finally, exerted a considerable influence on American education. His educational theory was one with his philosophical outlook. In *The School and Society*, the most widely read of all Dewey's books, he argued that a child learns from life itself. Hence, education must be less teacher-centered and less preoccupied with handing down fixed and final principles for living. It must become more student-oriented and more interested in creating a social life and community environment in the classroom, from which the child would receive experience and knowledge. Education is not a preparation for later life but a process of gaining from the present the opportunities for growth it offers. The problem with past educational procedure was its emphasis on knowledge for the sake of knowledge rather than on the practical utility of knowledge for life itself. The child would benefit if the school were not geared to the listening student but to the dynamic, active, involved, experiencing student.

Dewey's system was ideally suited, on the philosophical and the educational level, for a society which was creative, democratic, pragmatic, a society which relied on cooperative activity for its survival and growth.

DEWEY'S CONCEPT OF TRUTH

Dewey argued that classicists sought for truth on a supposed higher level of knowledge, a level above experience. He seems to have Hegel and the post-Kantian idealists in mind. Such an approach overemphasized reason as the source of meaning and morality.

Thought, however, does not originate in reason. It originates in a need for action. In other words, thought is functional; it is mind in use, "intelligently conducted doing." Intelligence is simply a mode of human behavior which is not operative unless there is need to solve a problem. Thus, the chief determinant of all human thinking is the social environment. And all human thinking takes its value from its ability to reconstruct society in an intelligent, effective, human manner. Ideas, therefore, have value only if they are socially useful. If this occurs, the ideas are true.

Thinking was never meant for knowledge, according to Dewey. It was meant to be an instrument by which the environment was controlled. Evolution supports this contention. The higher the form of life, the more it reconstructs its environment. Life on a lower level is inert, passive. It waits for something to happen to it before it reacts. As life becomes more complex it becomes more active in seizing its environment and transforming it. Knowledge is what occurs in this dialectic and struggle between one form of life and the environment it rearranges. Hence, knowledge is always involved in the experience by which one perceives himself and the task to be done. No knowledge is separate from experience or self-sufficient. The experience which emerges from the individual's confrontation with his environment is the raw material from which knowledge proceeds, the test of its truth, and the measure of its value. Since experience issues from the encounter with a specified environment, no one can say beforehand what the experience will be or formulate previous principles to solve a problem which has not yet occurred. All experience is empirical and the intelligent person becomes the one who uses his empirical experience in a socially constructive fashion. Science is of considerable value in helping one to understand his environment and to determine the task to be undertaken.

Dewey saw his experimental method as one which was the very antithesis of changelessness. The static absolutistic concerns of traditional philosophy had to cede to this new, dynamic interpretation of thought, morality and society. Philosophy was never meant to be fixed or rigid. It was meant to change with the needs of the times. When the times required some intelligent explanation of what was occurring and what had to be done, then philosophy became useful. The significance of philosophy lies in its social purpose and in its ability to apply human thinking to practical affairs. The thinking agent not only originates in society; he becomes a means by which society can be forced to reconstruct itself. The experimental approach requires free intelligence so that one can face the real problems which each age brings to the fore. No one can know beforehand what institutions or traditions will be placed in jeopardy by the reaction of human thinking to new problems in a spirit of free inquiry. "Every thinker puts some portion of an apparently stable world in peril and no one can wholly predict what will emerge in its place."[118]

Philosophy can no longer afford to avoid the scientific method. This method, which has proved its indisputable effectiveness for physical and biological questions, must be applied to human affairs as well. The substance of this method is its emphasis on inquiry and discovery in contrast to a-priori dogmas and certitudes. The scientific method discovers truth in process and accomplishment. The resulting truth is not predetermined and need not be final. What is true today may be false tomorrow.

The method is reliable because it is self-correcting. It learns from its successes and failures. A philosophy which ignores the scientific method is doomed to social irrelevance and dissipates its energy in arbitrary questions and useless solutions. Such a philosophy is more interested in the validity of its own system rather than in the truth of the situation.

Traditional philosophy defines the person as an individual who is already something fixed and unchanging. Dewey argued that his experimental philosophy saw the person as an individual who evolved in his achievements. He was not to be defined in terms of his "nature" but in terms of his initiative, his resourcefulness, his ability to make ever-new choices in belief and conduct. He was, therefore, in a continual dialectical relationship with his empirical environment. He could test the value of his truth and morality by the social consequences of his faith and behavior. The aim of living, Dewey wrote in *Reconstruction in Philosophy*, is "not perfection as a final goal but the ever-enduring process of perfecting, maturing, refining."

This ongoing process creates truth and makes morality. Growth is the only moral good; its goal is the fullest experience possible in a socially useful context. The good is that which diminishes the existing wrong. It is not possible to be good unless something must be done. One is then good or evil in terms of the social utility involved in the solution of his task.

THE SPIRIT OF MODERN LIFE

John Dewey believed that there were a number of characteristics which typified the modern age, marking it off from traditional and classical eras. The modern age was so distinctive that it required its own philosophy. It could not live by the philosophy of former ages. Dewey was convinced that we must philosophize from our experience. The experience modern man perceived was so different from the experience of previous times that only a reconstruction in philosophy could adequately interpret what was happening.

The modern age had witnessed a shift in attention from an affirmation of the universal and eternal to an interest in the specific, the changing, the concrete. The supermaterialism and otherworldliness of the Middle Ages had been replaced by a concern for this world and for science.

This shift in attention brought with it a resistance to the authority of all static institutions, especially those which offered men an interpretation of the experience of living before men had experienced living. Secular institutions would be resisted but institutions which were not only traditional but supernaturally oriented would be rejected outright. Authority would be challenged whenever it imperiled free inquiry. It was not precedent or authority but experience which would be accepted as the ultimate norm of truth and morality.

As men become involved in this world and a free inquiry approach to it, they come to emphasize the future rather than the past. The future is to be realized not by repeating the patterns of the past but by continual, indefinite, ceaseless progress. The past has little to teach us because present experience and hope for future progress could not be measured by previous events. Progress implies a departure from the past and utilizes present experience as the starting point for something new and the means by which the new would be conceived of, executed and adopted.

A further characteristic of the modern age is the specific manner in which progress is understood. Progress would depend upon an experimental analysis of the environment and its adaptation to social purposes. A philosophical method which derived from the notion of progress would help men discover truth, live ethically, and promote the happiness of their fellow men. Such a philosophy would affirm unequivocally that change was neither undesirable nor a sign of imperfection. Indeed, change was the only opportunity for improvement which man had.

Older philosophies had retarded progress by their faith in the value of contemplation, pure knowledge and ideals. The new philosophy was practical and promised progress. Its practicality, however, did not derive from self-seeking utilitarianism. It was practical because it was true, in tune with reality and dependent upon the experience of the age. The new philosophy allowed man to express his idealism and humanitarian aspirations by immersing him in the social and moral problems of his times. Unless modern man eliminated concrete evils, he would not be ethical. Unless he developed a more effective present and dreamed of a better future, he could not claim he was in contact with truth.

The faith by which modern men would live would be a common faith with concrete moral goals and clear insights into the nature of truth. Although the new philosophy would not emphasize the past, it would not despise it. A record of the experience of the past could help men move intelligently into the future provided that the past was used creatively and selectively. Under no circumstances, must the past be obligatory. The new philosophy thus harmonized valid past experience with explorative intelligence in the present for the safe of a future which would not be predictable in the form it would take. The sole certitude the future offered was the promise of progress. "Philosophy recovers itself when it ceases to be a device for dealing with the problems of philosophers and becomes a method, cultivated by philosophers, for dealing with the problems of men."[119]

On another occasion, Dewey expressed himself clearly on the most pressing problem of the present: "The problem of restoring integration and cooperation between man's beliefs about the world in which he lives and his beliefs about the values and purposes that should direct his conduct is the deepest problem of modern life."[120]

A COMMON FAITH

In 1934, John Dewey published A Common Faith as his statement on the religious meaning of his philosophy and on the reasons why he found religions oppressive.

Dewey was convinced that a careful distinction had to be made between being religious and belonging to a religion. It was inaccurate for religions to assume that they were the only legitimate categories through which religious convictions could be expressed. Many men were religious without having to concern themselves with the artificial and restrictive burdens religions imposed.

When one understands Dewey's philosophy, he realizes why Dewey rejected religion. Religion defined itself in a way which made the past important, authority essential, and institutionalization indispensable. Was it possible, Dewey asked, to be religious without being bound to the past, indebted to authority or loyal to an institution? Dewey claimed this was possible, desirable and attainable so long as one was religious without religion.

The first objective Dewey had in mind was a dismissal of the past concerns which kept religions from being religious, made them unreal in their beliefs, and ineffective for social reform.

[Logic] demands that in imagination we wipe the slate clean and start afresh by asking what would be the idea of the unseen, of the manner of its control over us and the ways in which reverence and obedience would be manifested, if whatever is basically religious in experience had the opportunity to express itself free from all historic encumbrances.[121]

Starting anew requires not only freedom from the past but freedom from authority as well.

. . . when we begin to select, to choose, and say that some present ways of thinking about the unseen powers are better than others; that the reverence shown by a free and self-respecting human being is better than servile obedience rendered to an arbitrary power by frightened men . . . we have reached a point that invites us to proceed farther.[122]

Another burden the religious spirit must throw off is institutionalism:

. . . the moment we have a religion whether that of the Sioux Indians or of Judaism or of Christianity, that moment the ideal factors in experience that may be called religious take on a load that is not inherent in them, a load of current beliefs and of institutional practices that are irrelevant to them.[123]

Dewey feels that many are religious and unaware of this. The artificiality of religion compels them to reject all religions. But they have been conditioned to think that the rejection of religion is the same as the denial of the religious spirit. "I believe that many persons are so repelled from what exists as a religion by its intellectual and moral implications, that they are not even aware of attitudes in themselves that if they came to fruition would be genuinely religious."[124]

Dewey's philosophical system placed a great value on experience and the meaning of the present. He sees in a proper relationship to one's environment the beginnings of what he calls a religious outlook. "Let us then for the moment drop the term religious and ask what are the attitudes that lend deep and enduring support to the process of living. I have, for example, used the words 'adjustment' and 'orientation'."[125]

Dewey defines the religious spirit in terms of a principle of unification which gives wholeness and cohesiveness to one's conception of reality. Although he defines faith and God as well as "religious," in his own way, he retains the terminology. He was convinced that there was a common faith as distinct from former faiths as his philosophy may have been different from previous philosophies. The differences, however, were not so great that Dewey could not call his belief a faith or his system of thought a philosophy.

Dewey describes faith and the religious spirit in the following manner:

The artist, scientist, citizen, parent, as far as they are actuated by the spirit of their callings, are controlled by the unseen. For all endeavor for the better is moved by faith in what is possible, not by adherence to the actual ... it is pertinent to note that the unification of the self throughout the ceaseless flux of what it does, suffers, and achieves, cannot be attained in terms of itself .... and so its own unification depends upon the idea of the integration of the shifting scenes of the world into that imaginative totality we call the Universe. . . . Faith in the continued disclosing of truth through directed cooperative human endeavor is more religious in quality than is any faith in a completed revelation.[126]

Dewey's favorite themes emerge in this effort to define realities as elusive as faith and religious meaning. The future, the need for integration with and interpretation of reality, the concern with change and trust in cooperative human action are key features in Dewey's concept of a common faith. The scientific method, furthermore, serves as a paradigm and a method for meaningful faith.

. . . the natural interactions between man and his environment will breed more intelligence and generate more knowledge provided the scientific methods that define intelligence in operation are pushed further into the mysteries of the world, being themselves promoted and improved in the operation.[127]

Dewey's thoroughness leads him to attempt a definition of God.

Suppose for the moment that the word "God" means the ideal ends that at a given time and place one acknowledges as having authority over his volition and emotion, the values to which one is supremely devoted, as far as these ends, through imagination, take on unity.[128]

Dewey's common faith, as well as his philosophy, are American in their inspiration. One sees in this common faith some of the classic features in the American profile: the uneasiness with transcendence, the eagerness for change, the concomitant rejection of materialism and affirmation of secularity, the pervasiveness of optimism, the concern with practical results from faith, the faith in faith and the service of man rather than God.

CRITIQUE

A critique of John Dewey's work which makes even a pretense of being fair must express admiration for the clarity and originality of his contribution. Few Americans will be unmoved as they read Dewey. Dewey was true to his philosophical principles: he derived his thought from the American experience, and he brought his thinking to bear on the reconstruction of the society which inspired his insights. Dewey's dialectic led him to assimilate his experience and react to it. He was pragmatic at every turn and socially concerned in his every book.

No one should fault him for his optimism, for his hope in the future, for his statement that some philosophical systems exist solely for their own sake. Even in his religious thought, Dewey was not wholly beside the point. Anyone familiar with the American religious scene is aware of the illusions, the unnecessary dogmatism, the flight from reality and the artificial pretensions of some religious groups.

Dewey searched for a religious interpretation which would not exclude those who could not, in conscience, accept a religion and would not abide a church which made growth all but impossible. He wanted, in effect, a theology for the American scene. If he made us more aware of this need, we are in his debt even though we shall not subscribe uncritically to his approach.

George Santayana, on the other hand, was not alone in his denunciation of pragmatism. The irrationality of this system, Santayana wrote, "gave me a rude shock. I could not stomach that way of speaking about truth; and the continual substitution of human psychology . . . for the universe . . . seemed to me a confused remnant of idealism and not serious."

Critics point out that pragmatism is anti-intellectual, arbitrary, destructive of disciplined thinking, and susceptible to eccentricities, illusions, and emotions rather than sound and sober reasoning. It was whimsical and fortuitous; suited to social reform and functional projects but unsuited to the great ideas men think as they poetically, philosophically and religiously gain insights into the mystery of the human condition. Critics argue that the new philosophy has no capacity for sublimity. It sees man as a problem-solving animal rather than as a being whose spirit soared to heights beyond the reaches of social concerns and pragmatic tasks. It is a common philosophy, one which neither enriches nor challenges man in the depths of his human existence. It is a philosophy for technocrats, accurate at times but never inspiring.

Pragmatism, Santayana argued, led to "hazardous views about truth, such as that an idea is true so long as it is believed to be true; or that it is true if it is good and useful; or that it is not true until it is verified."[129]

There are deficiencies in Dewey's system when viewed in a Christian perspective. He does not provide for those human ideas and ideals which have meaning and no function, ideas and ideals men have never completely explained nor totally dismissed. The principle of unification which Dewey sought in life could not be found in the context of his system. When one defines a principle of unification in exclusively secular and rational categories, he concludes with answers similar to those of Comte or Mill, of Marx or Freud.

Dewey stated accurately that there is a socially conditioned dimension to our thinking. He was incomplete, however, in assuming that our thinking is socially determined and that it had no further purpose than social utility. We share with Dewey his rejection of a static contemplation of truth as the norm for philosophical inquiry. We do not share with him his insistence that life and reality change so often and so radically that every truth is relative, functional and transitory. There is place in philosophy for a conception of truth which occupies the middle ground between the utterly static and ceaselessly changing. Human life is perhaps the most striking example of this synthesis.

Every human life is undefinable until one has lived it completely. It is open to change, unpredictability, growth, regression, nobility or baseness. Yet in the process by which a human life is constantly changed there remains a givenness, a constancy, an identity with self which assures us that it is the same person who has changed. There is a continuity to each human life and to reality which allows identification at every point in the process as well as openness to the unforeseeable at every step. The adventure of human personhood and the mystery of reality derive from the concomitant capacities for endless growth and constant stability. We are not the cavemen, and yet our fundamental hopes and fears are not at odds with those they experienced.

Dewey argued that all values are relative and that the facts we face in life determine the values we affirm. He reasoned that all values are created by men in their effort to adjust to their environment.

There is more to account for in human experience than Dewey's pragmatism or instrumentalism allow. Dewey's system excludes an antecedent personal reality before man or a cosmic design which is teleologically personal and meaningful. He could account in no way for the "beyond" of which Jaspers spoke, or the call of Being which intrigued Heidegger, or the radial energy and aspiring consciousness Chardin described. Though there may be few final truths for our social concerns, there may well be final truths for the meaning of life. A final truth need not be static; it need only be ultimate. For Christians, it is also purposeful. The history of Christian thought is proof that the acceptance of a final truth, an absolute value or a transcendent reality do not foreclose inquiry or change.

RELIGIOUS THOUGHT

Dewey's developed his common faith because he maintained that there was no bridge between the religious spirit and religion. He is eloquent in his denunciation of the shortcomings of religion. He seems unaware of the fact that men without religion have not lived a perfect existence. Had that been the case, no honest and idealistic person would affirm religion to have a meaning. In spite of Dewey's disclaimer, many sense that the religious spirit is enriched in religion and is diminished and compromised without religion. Obviously, one does not find utopia in religion any more than the "unfettered" religious spirit does. Religion frequently becomes the means by which a man tests the validity of his religious spirit, much as Dewey argued that the environment must become the means by which the validity of our ideas and goals are tested.

At times, Dewey wearily rehearses the glories of science and its effectiveness in discrediting religion. Without realizing it, he cites how science discounted the empirical view of the world which accompanied some Christian doctrines. This is not the same as disproving the value or truth which lay behind the empirical conditions in which a doctrine is expressed. There may be a truth to original sin, for example, whether monogenism or polygenism is factual. Christ may be present in the Eucharist whether or not Aristotelian or Thomistic metaphysics is accurate.

Dewey's panegyric to the scientific method seems dated:

. . . new methods of inquiry and reflection have become for the educated man today the final arbiter of all questions of fact, existence, and intellectual assent. Nothing less than a revolution in the 'seat of intellectual authority' has taken place. . . . In this revolution, every defeat is a stimulus to renewed inquiry; every victory won is the open door to more discoveries. . . . The mind of man is being habituated to a new method and ideal. There is but one sure road of access to truth—the road of patient, cooperative inquiry operating by means of observation, experiment, record, and controlled reflection.[130]

Dewey's designation of "but one sure road of access to truth" seems narrow. His common faith, admittedly, allows for mystical experience. There is no reason why, as Dewey persuasively argued, religious feeling or mystical aspirations need be confined to those who align themselves with a concrete religion. Religions do not necessitate, guarantee or monopolize religious awareness. They do, however, attempt to say what this awareness means, whether it is delusion, how it is to be interpreted, why it occurs and to what it is directed. A religion is valid not in terms of the quality of each member's religious spirit but in terms of its ability to relate this spirit to a meaning which is open to the transcendent without being insensitive to the concrete world we inhabit.

The root of Dewey's rejection of religion lay in his conviction that the natural and the supernatural were incompatible. There may have been good reason why he came to believe this. The concrete religions he encountered may well have forced him to this conclusion. The question, however, is not whether some religions are based on a disruption between the natural and the supernatural, or whether Dewey had no alternative except to conclude as he did. We must be concerned with the nature of the case.

Neither the New Testament, nor the doctrine of the Incarnation, nor the Christian ethic of love of neighbor suggest an antithesis between the natural and the supernatural. Faith in God either strengthens one's faith in man, or it is misguided. The affirmation that Jesus of Nazareth was the Son of God made flesh calls for an almost scandalous belief in the value of human living and an unheard-of interrelationship between the natural and the supernatural. A supernaturalism which neglects the concrete world in which we live is ignorant

of the meaning of creation, untrue to the synthesis of the
Gospel and simultaneously destructive of man's human dignity
and religious vocation.

Dewey's common faith was an act of faith in the ability of
the human family to be the origin and guarantor of all religious values.

> The reality of ideal ends and values in their authority over us is
> an undoubted fact. The validity of justice, affection, and that in-
> tellectual correspondence of our ideas with realities that we call
> truth, is so assured in its hold upon humanity that it is unneces-
> sary for the religious attitude to encumber itself with the apparatus
> of dogma and doctrine. Any other conception of the religious
> attitude, when it is adequately analyzed, means that those who
> hold it care more for force than for ideal values—since all that an
> Existence can add is force to establish, to punish, and to reward.[131]

Dewey defines religion only in terms of its limitations: over-
concern with the past, overbearing in authority, overstruc-
tured in its institutional forms. He describes transcendent
Existence as a source of punishment, force and reward. Never
once does he concede a single value to any religion. Never
once does he consider that a man may put his faith in God,
not because he is fearful or greedy for rewards, but because
faith in God gives him more hope in others and in life.
Gabriel Marcel has remarked that every twentieth-century
mass movement which denied God and transcendent values
came to despise rather than to cherish human life.

Dewey was undeniably perceptive when he wrote that
"ideals change as they are applied in existent conditions."[132]
We must ask, however, whether *all* ideals change. Some ideals
transcend all cultures and all eras and emerge as human ideals
rather than as the ideals of a particular moment in history.
These ideals assume new forms, admittedly, but fundamentally the freedom and life, the happiness and love man has always sought he seeks today, although he uses another lan-

guage and different customs to articulate the needs of his
heart. Modern man can still discover himself as he reads
Genesis or Homer or Shakespeare.

Dewey's case for a common faith is a contribution to religious thinking insofar as he aids the purification of religion.
Dewey, however, insists that religion must be abolished. It is
doubtful that his common faith has a deeper hold on reality
or offers men a more humanizing influence than Christian
faith. Dewey wrote of the many values which his common
faith would provide. Like Freud, he wanted no illusions in
religious behavior. As an American, he would abide no dogmatism. As a process thinker, he favored unlimited possibilities for growth and unrestricted human experience in a socially useful context. Contemporary Christianity agrees with
every one of those objectives.

Life, however, is so complex that it is not manageable in
terms of the scientific method or pragmatism. Ambiguities
are not the same as illusions. There is sufficient structure and
continuity to human thought to permit the formulation of
abiding doctrinal principles without engaging in dogmatism.
Whether one defines the American spirit, Christian experience or human life, he can emunciate certain propositions
which are not restrictive but merely a means of self-identifi-
cation and self-realization in change.

These propositions need not be fixed or final in their construction, but they should link the past and the future. The
discovery of self-identifying, unitive principles does not lead
to dogmatism but to wisdom and perception. Growth is most
meaningful when one has some awareness of what he is growing in relationship to, and what he is growing toward.

Dewey's eagerness for unlimited growth and unrestricted
experience is an elusive ideal unless it is defined in a certain
context. No one is opposed to growth and meaningful experience, but one cannot say much of them unless these
ideals are articulated in a specific manner. Growth is never

unlimited nor experience unrestricted except in our imagination. Limitation and restriction are contributive to development if they are delineated with development in mind. Civilization and society always require limitation and restriction, but they contribute to development nonetheless.

CONCLUSION

Was John Dewey a philosopher who articulated a doctrine of salvation? He said as much in his own words:

It is even now possible to examine complex social phenomena sufficiently to put the finger on things that are wrong. It is possible to trace to some extent these evils to their causes, and to causes that are something very different from abstract moral forces. . . . The outcome will not be a gospel of salvation, but it will be in line with that pursued, for example, in matters of disease and health. The method, if used, would not only accomplish something toward social health, but it would accomplish a greater thing; it would forward the development of social intelligence so that it could act with greater hardihood and on a larger scale. . . . The importation of general moral causes . . . the sinfulness of man, the corruption of the heart, his self-love . . . to explain present *social* phenomena is . . . reinforced by . . . traditional religions and . . . stifles the growth of . . . social intelligence . . .[133]

Dewey may have had good reason to see in some forms of religion a force resisting social intelligence. We are not concerned with the justification of his observation or even with the accuracy of his judgments in these instances. We are concerned with the nature of the case. If Dewey argues for a clearer distinction between the sacred and the secular so that the former does not intrude on the latter, and so that the latter is reconcilable with the former, we agree with him.

It is necessary to recall that the validity of the question religion poses does not depend upon its relationship with secular reform except secondarily and obliquely. Religion poses a question concerning the meaning of a reality beyond our secular tasks. Dewey, in limiting human hopes to natural existence, restricts them. We endorse Dewey's passion for social reconstruction. We accept his indictment against religion's indifference at times to social reform. We wish, however, to say something about men which transcends, without diminishing, all his pragmatic projects and his service of his contemporaries. This requires our confessing a faith not only in the human enterprise and social reconstruction but also in the antecedence, transcendence, and teleology of the human phenomenon in a mystery we call God. We know we cannot be modern men effectively without the science, intelligence and education in which Dewey placed all his hopes for man. But we believe it is possible to labor on behalf of these values with the same passion and devotion of John Dewey and yet to speak a further word about man, a word we proclaim, not because we sense restriction in it but creative possibilities, a word we confess, not because we love men less, but because we care too much not to ask ultimate questions about human life and death.

We are one with Dewey in his wish to save man. Dewey envisioned this salvation as taking place exclusively in a social context which disturbs and develops us. We see human salvation more fully expressed in Someone who entered our social context to disturb and develop us. Christ came, we believe, with goals and insights, with values and possibilities we would not have considered seriously without his revelation. He came to save us in a socially useful context but to save us for something even more meaningful than this.

We have made clear our exceptions to and objections with John Dewey. We affirm with equal vigor the contributions he made. These contributions are not any less impressive because we disagreed with aspects of his thought. Although not en-

dorsing everything Dewey says in this final quotation, we read
in his words values America and Christianity can ignore only
at their own peril.

I cannot understand how any realization of the democratic ideal
as a vital moral and spiritual ideal in human affairs is possible without surrender of the conception of the basic division to which
supernatural Christianity is committed. Whether or not we are,
save in some metaphorical sense, all brothers, we are at least all
in the same boat traversing the same turbulent ocean. The potential religious significance of this fact is infinite. . . . The things
in civilization we most prize are not ourselves. They exist by grace
of the doings and sufferings of the continuous human community
in which we are a link. Ours is the responsibility of conserving,
transmitting, rectifying and expanding the heritage of values we
have received that those who come after us may receive it more
solid and secure, more widely accessible and more generously
shared than we have received it. Here are all the elements for a
religious faith that shall not be confined to sect, class or race. Such
a faith has always been implicitly the common faith of mankind.
It remains to make it explicit and militant.[134]

Contemporary Concerns
in American Culture

Our study is not a sociological study. Hence, the most we can
do is make a number of observations which seem cogent and
which we should be aware of as we preach the Gospel or explain theology on the American scene.

When we discussed the classic features of the American
profile, we noted that Americans are deeply influenced by the
pressure of public opinion. This, no doubt, derived from the
democratic principle on which the country was built and the
spirit of interdependence which organized this society. At this
point in our history, however, public opinion and forced interdependence have made the contemporary American lonely

because he seldom makes contact with others or with himself. This is a thesis which David Riesman articulates in *The Lonely Crowd*. Without entering into a technical evaluation of this work and without discussing those sections of his study which sociologists dispute, we can subscribe to a number of his insights.

Riesman argues that codes of conformity may be endangering the flexibility of the American character. This seems to be valid even when one considers those who protest against this conformity. Many young people rebel in a rigid, conformist pattern, replete with similar dress, clichés and faddish causes. This is not to demean what they seek to accomplish but merely to point out how patterns of conformity emerge even in the effort to be nonconformist. These codes of conformity may be a logical development of some of the features of the classic American profile.

Riesman's study is important for those who articulate a Christian value system for Americans. He makes it clear that the other-directed personality is prevalent in our society. One characteristic of other-directedness is an eagerness for approval and acceptance. The other-directed person has a more than normal need to sense he belongs; he looks constantly to others for his values and even for the meaning of life.

Once again, Riesman's description does not contradict what one might almost have predicted, granted the American profile we discussed earlier. The implications of this societal behavior for religion and morality are considerable. Such a behavioral attitude favors historical relativism, a relativism John Dewey's philosophy articulates. Erich Fromm, in another manner, parallels Riesman's thesis that contemporary America idealizes approval and acceptance.

It is difficult for other-directed people to accept a doctrinal, authoritative, nonrelativistic religion. For the most part, an other-directed culture looks to society for the answers to life and feels oppressed by an authority which is nonsocial in origin and which demands at times resistance to the popular trend in belief and conduct.

"Everybody's doing it" is an Americanism. Catholics, in this country, will have special difficulty accepting clerical celibacy, prohibition of divorce or disapproval of artifical birth control because these decisions are not supported by a popular consensus and do not derive their wisdom from such a consensus. Thus, Catholics may tend to feel embarrassed or hesitant by what seems to them the interansigence and "unreality" of Catholic belief and moral norms. The consequent tension between what the individual prefers, what society approves and what religion requires will be felt more acutely in this country than elsewhere. Inner-directed people are less anxious in the face of this conflict.

An other-directed culture lends great authority to the peer group. The peer group in an other-directed environment judges in terms of taste and is characterized by the rapid adoption and rejection of fads. It is preoccupied with what is "in" or "out"; it labels people villains and heroes with less subtlety and more decisiveness than inner-directed cultures do.

A hazard of other-directedness is insecurity, a fear that one can easily be "out" if he is not careful, a fear that, though he is a hero today, he may be a villain tomorrow, a fear that he may not be accepted or liked (a fear which causes the tragedy of Willy Loman in *The Death of a Salesman*, as we shall see later).

The inner-directed person also suffers from nonacceptance. This is a human rather than a cultural reaction. But nonacceptance is more catastrophic for the other-directed person; he is less well equipped to handle peer group rejection and feels the punishment of this exclusion more severely. Since peer group acceptance is so fragile, the other-directed person often worries about his worth. Maritain was, therefore, accurate when he said, as we quoted earlier, that Americans easily become discouraged with life and with themselves.

An outer-directed culture leads many to test the value of their opinions not by whether they are true or false but by whether they result in peer group acceptance or rejection. The other-directed person can spend much of his life conforming to the superficial tastes of people rather than in the development of substantive beliefs and moral norms. He is susceptible to a hectic style of life and a frantic search for values.

In an outer-directed culture, the person can lose his individuality since there is little time and less encouragement for reflection, privacy, thought, solitude. The other-directed person is seldom alone and yet constantly lonely. In other-direct edness, the currency into which values are converted is not money but appraisal by the peer group. Americans acquire wealth less for its own sake than for the sake of proving they are worthwhile.

The competitive energies an inner-directed person applies to success in achievement, the other-directed person channels into winning approval. Success for the other-directed is not measured in terms of overcoming the environment or mastering a difficult task. People, rather than goals, make demands on him and judge his worth. Winning becomes important because everybody likes a winner. Failure is an anxious fear. How will one face others when he has failed? What will they say? No one, in any culture, takes failure easily, but outer-directed people have more at stake in their failure. One thinks again of Willy Loman.

INNER-DIRECTED CULTURE

If society is tradition-directed or inner-directed, the person works for his self-improvement. He may even prefer to be different, original, at times unpopular. Although he gains a measure of freedom from the tyranny of peer group pressure, the inner-directed person is not without his own problems.

He is anxious lest he let go of himself, fearful that a lack of discipline may undo him. He believes he can easily drift, and he indicts others for their sloth because it relieves his own fears and convinces him that he is industrious.

The inner-directed person is likely to lecture others and give advice. The other-directed person tries to discover what the other wants to hear. If the inner-directed person does not achieve his goals in life, he feels inadequate. The outer-directed person is disappointed if he does not meet his goals, but he is more interested in being liked. The inner-directed person abhors flippancy and thinks that if people are not working, they are wasting time. When he does not have work to do, he does not know what to do with himself. The inner-directed man is confused by leisure, except after a hard day's work. Since he is less people-oriented, he approves of artistic enterprises, but he does not understand a man motivated by artistic interests. We shall see later how this is exemplified in Sinclair Lewis' *Main Street*.

In terms of commitment, inner-directeds differ from outer-directeds. An inner-directed person is less anxious when he must commit his life to a goal or cause. In outer-directed culture, there is more uncertainty, and hence the person fears long-term commitments. He is unsure of himself and his values. Things change quickly; people change quickly. He wonders what he will do if those things he believed in are believable no longer, or if those people whose approval supported him need him no more. The outer-directed person is especially concerned with the social utility of his vocation and with the acceptance by his contemporaries of the social usefulness of what he is doing. *Doing* something is preferable to *being* something.

The growth in counseling services and books dealing with "happiness" or "success," and the interest in group dynamics or psychological maturity testify to the outer-directed emphasis on group adjustment. The inner-directed person uses group dynamics if it helps get the job done. He does not take psychology as seriously as the outer-directed person.

The outer-directed person is anxious to find someone who loves him. He needs this as a reassurance of his value. The inner-directed person knows he has a value even if he is not loved.

The outer-directed person finds that acceptance by the peer group is never as convincing as he thought it would be. He is at the mercy of change, never sure who he is or what he is for.

The high premium we place on sincerity in those we meet is another aspect of an outer-directed society's longing for acceptance and approval. Today in the United States the most effective people in terms of influence on the population are not those who wield maximum power but those who draw most attention to their sincerity and personality. Indeed, truthfulness has become more appealing than truth. An outer-directed society is more eager to know exactly what someone thinks, even if he be mistaken or have no answers. Whether that which the truthful person says is true is important but secondary.

It is clear from what we have discussed that the outer-directed person has a problem with the internalization and interiority of his values. Since his values are so strongly influenced by his peer group, he finds it easier to adopt many values relativistically rather than to affirm a few values absolutely. He has less fear of the crowd than of lifelong principles. He is eager to dialogue because he sees truth as a reality subject to process and abiding in people.

The inner-directed person is less interested in talk, in "chatter." His concept of dialogue differs from that of outer-directeds. He will share his opinion and hear the other side, but he frequently leaves dialogue more conscious of what the opposition feels but not very much changed by it. He responds more easily to "reality" and power, to unavoidable facts than he does to a dialogical situation. He does not need

to be liked as much as the outer-directed person. He has discovered principles by which to live; he considers these principles too sacred for "negotiation."

One of the most distinctive features of outer-directed culture is its need to communicate. Americans will talk to anyone and expect a response from everyone. Inner-directed people tend to hear the "other side" not because they hope to
learn something significant for themselves but to know what
the opposition thinks, either because they are curious, or because they see this information as a means of overcoming
those who disagree with them. The outer-directed person feels
ill at ease when opposing sides are not speaking to each other.
When he does present his position, he looks about him for
support. If there is none, he is lonely and uncertain. As he
gains numerical strength, he becomes more convinced of his
position. If he represents a majority viewpoint, he rests assured
that he is infallible. He believes that if a vote is taken and he
wins, the minority has not only been overcome but must be
in error as well.

The outer-directed person is anxious to have his position
presented in a way which will influence people. Articulation
and persuasion, flexibility and a certain agnosticism typify his
presentation. The inner-directed person cares less for the
words used, prefers a sharp and precise distinction to ambiguity and betrays no doubt of the rightness of his cause or
the accuracy of his insights.

GENERATION CONFLICTS
AND WESTERN FOLKLORE

The outer-directed person seeks adjustment rather than power.
Adjustment with the peer group guides him in his choices. He
knows that the contemporary American can do almost anything he chooses, and he looks to the peer group to see how
people are choosing. The choices before him are numerically

so immense, and his uncertainty about himself is so painfully obvious that he relies on the peer group to narrow those choices and support him in the choice he makes.

The outer-directed person resists the limitation of his choices by authority. He trusts authority less than he trusts the majority. Authority is often unpopular; the majority never is. Authority, he suspects, limits choice arbitrarily; the majority will try anything and choose what is best.

This problem is especially acute in the United States because our interest in the future and our belief in the indefinite perfectibility of man leads us to overemphasize the insights of the youngest generation. The youngest generation is never in authority. Hence, a generation conflict develops. The youngest generation thinks it must blaze its own path with little assistance from tradition and no help from authority. The older generation fears that its failure to adjust to the youngest generation may be a sign they are old in a young country, attuned to the past in a futuristic society, alligned with forces or repression in a culture which prizes freedom.

Inner-directed or tradition-directed cultures do not take the youngest generation seriously. Youth is something the young always manage to get over. It is noteworthy that in the United States the golden years are one's youth; in France, the golden years are one's middle age; in Spain, the golden years are one's final decades of life.

The ideal would be a fusion of the virtues of outer-directedness and inner-directedness. If this is possible, religion may be able to effect this. Whether it shall is not predictable. But it seems to have within it the potential, provided it maintains its inner convictions and simultaneously acquires a sensitivity to outer-directedness.

The autonomous person in an outer-directed culture is unfortunately a loner, yet he is needed. He measures his culture by a standard inward to himself or by a standard not taken from his social setting. History, philosophy or the Gospel influence him more than the present or, at least, qualify his acceptance of the present. He does not see tradition as restrictive, metaphysics as unreal or evangelical values as a threat to human development. An inner-directed person is able to resist the unfavorable forces which exist outside him and to affirm who he is despite the efforts of others to make him into what they want him to be.

American folklore, especially the Western, continues to admire this type of person. The hero stands against overwhelming odds. Though many contemporary Americans will not imitate the Western hero, they wish they were as sure of themselves as he seems to be. Somehow the type of life the Western hero represents seems freer than the type of life they lead even though the Western hero had fewer opportunities and choices than his twentieth-century counterpart. At least, however, he was his own man.

The American Western follows a stylized pattern which is at odds with the outer-directed preoccupations of the present. The Western hero comes from nowhere and goes forth at the end of his mission to an unknown but obviously meaningful future. He comes on the scene to save someone or some situation. He is a savior who finds himself alone and always on the side of goodness. There is no ambiguity about him. Evil has no hold on him. He is victorious because he knows who he is and because his inner strength and personal skill prevail. There is little support from those in positions of authority or power. In fact, those in positions of authority or power are ineffective. The sheriff is seldom adequate to the task; the law is well-meaning but weak. Those who represent the Eastern establishment or philosophical values cannot cope with their problems. The banker, the lawyer, the wealthy in town may be followers, but they are not leaders. They are confused, powerless or evil. Only someone who is completely innocent and totally inner-directed, a pragmatist, a man of action rather than a man of talk can be of assistance.

The Western hero does not need the support of the community in what he must do. His inner resources are sufficient. His moral code, incidentally, is puritanical. The Western hero is not interested in sex. He sees his horse as his only friend. Women are attracted to him, but he is impervious to their charm or affection. The Western hero is never passionately in love with a woman. He is passionate about his cause or justice. The hero either refuses to drink liquor or, if he does, it is with obvious disinterest. He works hard, but he is not concerned with money. Nor is he given to gambling. If he does play cards, it is not because he sees a value in this but because he wishes to beat evil at its own game. He never speaks much, and he is never afraid. A loquacious or trembling Western hero is unthinkable.

The combination of inner strength and moral innocence assure the Western hero of victory. He is not only uncorrupted by evil forces, but he is unharmed by them. The most he sustains is a flesh wound.

The American admiration for such inner-direction and assimilation of many outer-directed values holds out some promise that a new character type may emerge in the future, one not so much a loner as the Western hero nor so much bound to the peer group as the contemporary American.

BOREDOM

De Tocqueville once warned that Americans would one day overemphasize social virtues and overexpose the individual to prevailing opinion and the tyranny of the majority.

The contemporary American suffers from boredom. Indeed, boredom has become the way we suffer. Americans try too vigorously to make a "big deal" of everything. Even unimportant events in the lives of American children are fussed over, photographed, and treasured. Vacations must be more than vacations. They must be something one can talk about glowingly afterward. The vacation must be a "big deal." Ironically, since everything is emphasized, nothing is truly important.

The successes of their children, the successes of their vacations and parties are utilized by Americans to prove to themselves and their peer group how significant their life is. More than one's work, one's ability to get along with his fellow workers and to enter his children and vacations into competition with others prove to the American that he counts and must be noticed. Americans work so hard at proving their significance before the peer group that all the individual moments of living become meaningful while life itself becomes empty and boring.

As long as the American is at the mercy of the peer group, he does not discover the cause of his boredom. Everything is going well and yet nothing is going well. He does not know what else he needs and yet he feels indigent. He knows more about himself than any of his predecessors did. He is aware of his physical strengths and weaknesses, his psychological profile, his vocational aptitudes and yet he is more a stranger to himself than previous generations were. He has mobility but no stability.

This may be a hopeful sign. The outer-directed person who verges on autonomy and inner-direction is unhappy about the values his culture has given him. Because Americans are reaching toward a consciousness of every dimension of human life in a way they seldom have before, Christianity has an unparalleled opportunity to help. If America's search for values terminates in excessive dependence on a new culture or a new peer group rather than in transcultural values, the search will have been in vain.

The search for spiritual enrichment requires not only a fusion of inner-directedness with outer-directedness and the discovery of something transcendental but also a communication between the generations. Spiritual depth is a total ex-

perience. Just as no culture has all the answers, no genera-
tion is self-sufficient in its reaching out for wisdom and truth.
In measuring the ground between fifty years of age and twenty,
Adlai Stevenson once put it this way to his students at
Princeton:

What a man knows at 50 that he did not know at 20 boils down
to something like this: the knowledge that he has acquired with
age is not the knowledge of formulas, or forms of words, but of
people, places, actions—a knowledge not gained by words but by
touch, sight, sound, victories, failures, sleeplessness, devotion, love
—the human experiences and emotions of this earth; and perhaps, too, a little faith and a little reverence for the things you
cannot see.

Literary Expressions
of the American Temper

This final section will have as its objective the consideration
of three short literary works which exemplify some of the
themes we have explored in our study of the American experiment. The first of these is *Main Street*, a novel written by
Sinclair Lewis.

In a previous work, *The Job* (1917), Lewis was sharply
critical of the enslavement of the individual in a business-
centered society. In *Main Street* he explores a number of
themes which reflect the American temper. He speaks of the
conformity and the pressure of public opinion exerted in
small-town America. Public opinion dictates the morality
(narrow, puritanical, suspicious) and the cultural values of
the community. These values are either nonexistent or hectic. The Thanatopsis Club in Gopher Prairie decides to explain all the English poets in one meeting, all essayists and
writers of fiction in a second meeting and Scandinavian, Rus-
sian, and Polish literature in a third.

Main Street (1920) is the story of Carol Kennicott and her unsuccessful efforts to save Gopher Prairie from its mediocrity and provincialism. In Carol Kennicott, Lewis embodies many American qualities. Carol is an idealist with a sincere desire for a career of service to others. Despite her powers of observation and her constant analysis of her environment, she is extremely naive.

She is dismayed when she discovers that her efforts to improve the world are met with indifference and even hostility. This hostility is due, in part, to the spiritually improverished and culturally deprived condition of the people she seeks to help. Their hostility, however, is attributable, not only to their inadequacy, but to Carol's insensitivity in trying to accomplish her task too quickly. She is so eager to help that she ignores laws of human psychology. Therefore, she embarrasses people by her swiftness. The rapidity with which she goes about her work indicts the people she might have changed more effectively had she tried to understand their values and had led them gradually to a new outlook.

Carol comes from the outside as a savior, a sign of contradiction, someone with a mission. Unfortunately, she never identifies with those whose ignorance she wishes to dispel. In the first chapter of the novel, Carol is a sincere but confused college senior who wishes to help people reach fulfillment, but she is uncertain of her own goals. She senses vaguely in herself those instincts which form part of the classic and contemporary American profile. She is not comfortable with materialism and experiences an indefinable dissatisfaction. Her dissatisfaction is linked with a spiritual quest and a cultural crisis rather than with a lack of physical conveniences. She gropes constantly for something she cannot attain, straining restlessly to proceed beyond the nearest horizon and around the next turning of the road.

Carol is caught in a crosscurrent of cultural complexities.

She is aware that past values are not viable in the new age coming to American society, an age in need of more sophistication than small-town life or national insularity provide. This experience would be less painful if the present were not so ill-defined. Carol, however, moves forward conscious that the past is not sufficient but unable to understand what must be done to heal this insufficiency.

Sinclair Lewis continues in *Main Street* the theme of the alienated person which he explored in *Babbitt* and *Arrow-smith*. The issue Carol faces in the context of small-town America is akin to that faced by Babbitt in the business world and by Arrowsmith among his medical colleagues. The issue is revolt or acquiescence. Such an issue is a live problem in contemporary America.

The barrier Carol confronts does not emerge from her environment as much as it comes from herself. She is a person who has not found herself and whose sense of identity is, therefore, weak. She is an idealist, it is true, but idealism can become a way in which we cope with others without having been reconciled either to them or to ourselves. Carol's mistake is not the mistake of idealism which, all things being equal, is a virtue. Her mistake comes from the naivete which leads her to suppose that the world will not resist idealism, or that idealism need not have enemies to endure.

All the fault is not Carol's, of course. Her environment is a deficient environment, one which prefers the renunciation of liberty for the sake of conformity or the surrender of inner values for the sake of the crowd. In a sense, Lewis' small-town America is as outer-directed and as impatient of individuality as the later America of David Riesman's *The Lonely Crowd*.

The American character is expressed more completely in Carol than in Gopher Prairie. The failure of the village is a universal failure, one which includes more than the American scene. The root failure is the failure of people to transcend

with love the inhibitions and taboo's which a restrictive culture creates. Carol's failure, however, is more distinctively an
American failure.

Carol is more able to articulate her desire to help than she
is to articulate the finality or purpose of her assistance. She
prefers to think she is an idealist, but she is not as unselfish
as she supposes. Her idealism is also her way of wanting to
dominate and assert her own influence. This is borne out by
her impatience and by the frequency with which she goes
against the grain of the human condition when she might as
easily have gone with it.

The society Carol seeks to transform is in urgent need of
transformation. She seems more conscious of this than she is
conscious of the equally urgent need to help people bear with
the pain which transformation requires. Thus, one is forced to
conclude that Carol is more passionate about reform than she
is about people.

THORNTON WILDER'S OUR TOWN

We mentioned earlier that there is a basic humanism at the
heart of American culture. This humanism is, in part, the result of a cultural problem with transcendence or mystery. It
led Margaret Mead to cite the observations of the Manus of
New Guinea. It influenced Americans to view religion as the
service of man rather than of God and to emphasize deed
rather than creed.

This humanism was given its most striking expression in
Thornton Wilder's *Our Town*. Human life is portrayed in
this play as the central force in the universe. The wonder and
awe of life are so sublime that reliving even one day can be
too painful to endure. Emily explains as she returns from
the dead to live her twelfth birthday again: "I can't bear it.
. . . I can't look at everything hard enough. . . . I can't. I

can't go on. It goes so fast. We don't have time to look at one another."[135]

The play seeks to give an awareness of the tragic waste of life. This waste is evident in the folly of war:

"Want to tell you something about that boy Joe Crowell there. Joe was awful bright—graduated from high school here, head of his class. So he got a scholarship to Massachusetts Tech. Graduated head of his class there, too. It was all wrote up in the Boston paper at the time. Goin' to be a great engineer, Joe was. But the war broke out and he died in France—All that education for nothing."[136]

The waste of life is also evident in the folly of the way we live. We have little awareness of the importance of our everydays. Emily asks a key question in the play: "Do any human beings ever realize life while they live it—every, every minute?" The stage manager answers: "No . . . the saints and poets, maybe—they do some."[137]

Wilder calls attention to the significance of life by reminding contemporary man that he is one with men of all times. The setting is unmistakably American. Those who appear in the play include a paperboy, the milkman, a soda jerk, a high school baseball hero, the church organist, the country doctor. Yet Wilder reminds his audience that "Grover's Corners lies on the old Pleistocene granite of the Appalachian range. I may say it's some of the oldest land in the world. We're very proud of that."[138] He goes on to relate the history of man in that area of the world.

At a later point in the play we are reminded that "Babylon once had two million people in it. . . . Yet every night all those families sat down to supper, and the father came home from his work, and the smoke went up the chimney—same as here."[139]

Wilder's message is especially appropriate for Americans

who tend to secularize life rather than to discover its contemplative dimensions or who easily dismiss the wisdom of lived experience or tradition. It is clear that Wilder senses the sacredness of life. *Our Town* is written so that we might recall "the way we were: in our growing up, and in our marrying, and in our living and in our dying." For life to redeem these promises, one must be sensitive to it and in love with it. "You've got to love life to have life."[140] Sensitivity to life includes sensitivity to its deeper meaning. "Each individual's assertion to an absolute reality can only be inner, very inner."[141] This deeper meaning is linked inextricably with an awareness that life is not trivial, that it is, in fact, immortal.

"We all know that *something* is eternal. And it ain't houses and it ain't names, and it ain't earth, and it ain't even the stars . . . everybody knows in their bones that *something* is eternal, and that something has to do with human beings. All the greatest people ever lived have been telling us that for five thousand years and yet you'd be surprised how people are always losing hold of it. There's something way down deep that's eternal about every human being. . . . They're waitin'. They're waitin' for something that they feel is comin'. Something important, and great. Aren't they waitin' for the eternal part in them to come out clear?"[142]

ARTHUR MILLER'S
DEATH OF A SALESMAN

Death of a Salesman witnesses to the universality of the fall. It brings the tragic flaw in human nature to the surface in an "average" man. As it does this *Death of a Salesman* raises some intriguing questions. Is Willy Loman responsible for his demise? Could he have been different? Or is he determined to doom by a commercial and competitive system which is irresistible? Is he an unwilling or a consenting victim?

The tragedy of Willy Loman is set in an American context.

Willy is anxious to define values by which he might live, sensing that the values his environment offers are superficial, experiencing how quickly they change and yet, in a typically American fashion, resisting the traditional or stable.

Willy confesses this inner insecurity: "Dad left when I was such a baby, and I never had a chance to talk to him, and I still feel—kind of temporary about myself."[143] The same weakness is transmitted to Willy's son, Happy, who tries to explain his failure as a person to his brother: "See, Biff, everybody around me is so false that I'm constantly lowering my ideals. . . ."[144]

Confusion about values leads Willy to seek his identity in success rather than within himself. For the sake of this success, he abandons himself. Even while he is succeeding, he is unhappy as is evident in his need to keep a mistress in Boston as a relief for his loneliness. When success is no longer present, he is desperate and eventually suicidal.

Willy's affirmation of success as a total value system necessitates his choice of success as a more significant value than life. Thus, his failure in his job makes his suicide inevitable. Even the circumstances surrounding his death underscore this distortion. Willy dies so that his family may acquire insurance money from his death and thus see that his life, after all, was a success. The society in which Willy finds himself and the value system he develops convinces him that even life is a commodity.

Willy's idea of success is based on his need "to beat the system," to win all the top prizes, but, most of all, to reach the supreme achievement of popularity. In this he represents the classic American character. Linda, his wife, appreciates Willy as a person and decries the situation which is making him think he is worthless. "Why must everybody conquer the world?"[145] she asks. But she is not strong enough to prevail.

Willy becomes a pathetic figure as he pursues the elusive

dream of popularity so that he may realize the yet more ambiguous goal of "success." "The man who makes an appearance in the business world . . . is the man who gets ahead. Be
liked and you will never want."[146]

In an especially revealing moment, Willy tells Linda that
he has some awareness of the demon which torments him:
"You know, the trouble is, Linda, people don't seem to take
to me. . . . I know it when I walk in. They seem to laugh at
me. . . . I'm not noticed."[147]

Torn between his desire for recognition and his demand for
achievement, Willy turns to his employer and erstwhile friend,
Howard, for help. It is a painfully sensitive moment for him
since he must plead. In his pleading he must confront his
maddening and heartbreaking failure, his realization that his
life has misfired, his inability to know why this happened or
how he can recover.

Although Willy is responsible for his fall, the responsibility is not all his. He turns to the system, to society, to the
structure for help. Redemption is still possible, but it depends
upon an objective world more capable of healing than the one
Willy finds. The success syndrome which has disturbed
Willy's inner harmony has also broken the bonds of human
relationships which were meant to save us but now systematically torment us. Howard hardly hears Willy. While Willy
bares his heart, Howard is more interested in a new tape recorder he has purchased. The lesson is obvious. Things matter
more than people. The tape recorder works perfectly. It is not
a problem. Willy, however, does not function unerringly. He
is, furthermore, an onus. In a commodity-conscious, machine-
oriented culture, one must run smoothly or be disregarded.
Before he dies, Willy expresses his plight: "Funny, y' know?
After all the highways and the trains, and the appointments,
and the years, you end up worth more dead than alive."[148]

In a flashback he recalls a conversation with his Uncle Ben, the embodiment of the American success story.

BEN: What are you building? Lay your hand on it. Where is it?

WILLY: That's true, Linda, there's nothing . . . it's not what you do, Ben. It's who you know and the smile on your face! It's contacts, Ben, contacts! . . . that's the wonder, the wonder of this country, that a man can end with diamonds here on the basis of being liked! . . . Ben, am I right? Don't you think I'm right?[149]

The tragedy of Willy Loman is the tragedy of the fall translated to a new world which was supposed to be an earthly paradise and a place for freedom. Miller reminds us in *Death of a Salesman* that a culture which idolizes popularity and success is a culture in which the sting of failure and the dull ache of frustration destroy us. In such a culture, Biff can say of himself and his father: "Pop! I'm a dime a dozen, and so are you.!"[150]

The tragedy of *Death of a Salesman* is heightened by the fact that Willy was not a dime a dozen but was made to feel in his lifetime that he was. He had little sense of the dignity of his humanity which Wilder wrote about so well in *Our Town*. He saw no way to begin a transformation of his environment as Carol Kennicott did in *Main Street*. He was a victim throughout, sometimes consenting, sometimes unwilling, but a victim nonetheless.

Willy thought he accomplished nothing. He is, indeed, the alienated man of our times, the man on whose head a price has been set, the man who was told he was worth so much, and who never realized he was priceless.

Biff is only partially right when he says of his father at the burial: "He had the wrong dreams. All—all wrong. . . . He never knew who he was."[151]

Biff was only partially right because he considered the wrongness of Willy's dreams rather than the fact that Willy dreamed. Willy wanted to do what was right, to save himself, to heal his family and to find the values which would enable him to accomplish these things. He was a man who was made conscious of the fall of man but not of his redemptive value. Since he could find no dreams worthy of his aspirations, he devised lesser dreams. When he was made desperate by his dreams, he died for them rather than live with no dreams. Willy wanted something more from life than the life he had to live could offer. He summed himself up most accurately in an offhand remark he made midway in the play: "Gotta break your neck to see a star in this yard."[152]

SUMMARY OF SALVATION
THEMES AND THE MODERN AGE

There is a persistent quest in the history and nature of man. It is a quest which defines itself neither transcendentally nor immanently but as an admixture of both. Any effort to limit salvation to that which occurs exclusively in and beyond death (Arthur Schopenhauer) is proximately unfulfilling and ultimately unattainable. If salvation were meant to happen elsewhere, the Incarnation would have been an obstacle rather than a revelation of the way man must take to discover himself.

The tendency of the modern age has not been a tendency to exclude salvation from our concerns but to intensify it. Never before have we tried so concertedly to find a savior. Never before have so many lives been sacrificed, so much labor expended, so many false hopes inflamed in the hope that this or that plan, this or that prophet might save us.

If we sense we are more unsaved than we have ever been, it is not because we chose to be unredeemed or because we care little about our absence of redemption. Our mistake has been the mistake of laying down the wrong conditions before we would accept salvation. Our basic condition has been the insistence that salvation must happen exclusively here before we would believe it or participate in it.

Moralists like Mill, planners like Comte, economic philosophers like Marx, fatalistic metapsychologists like Freud, socially conscious pragmatists like Dewey devised theologies of salvation. Often they borrowed from the Christian message; sometimes, they sought to undo it. One by one, however, they and their theories were abandoned, leaving behind not so much the ingenious systems they developed but a permanent record of man's yearning for salvation.

Even American culture has become an effort to find a viable salvation with little or no reference to the transcendent. Its classic features and its contemporary style attest to the success and failure of a culture which once thought man would happen here, on this continent, in a new way. There was hope that human renewal would come less from grace and from our dependence on God than from the power of our dreams, the massiveness of our efforts, the newness of our environment.

Americans have learned decisively in this century that man is a limited creature whose hunger for the limitless neither human freedom, political justice nor affluence can satisfy. For this reason, among others, idealism cannot escape disillusionment if it limits itself to cultural enrichment (Carol Kennicott); for this reason, humanism continually raises the spectre of the eternal (*Our Town*); for this reason, human success must be a success which is fundamentally measureless; such a success is the only success which saves us from the fate of Willy Loman, the fate of wasting life on "the wrong dreams," the dreams which are "all, all wrong."

4

Salvation Themes in American Literature

Whenever men become sensitive about life, they turn not only to one another but also to the literature or art, the philosophy or theology which sensitive men create. It often happens that in our turning to one another we cannot express what we are experiencing or what this means in terms of who we are or where we are tending. It is then that literature, especially, becomes a joyful experience and an instructive insight.

There is a danger that a theologian might preempt literature and use it polemically for his own purposes. When he does this he performs a distinct disservice to literature whose artistic message he circumvents and to theology, since he theologizes from his own preconceptions rather than from objective data.

In every case the theologian must seek to avoid this hazard. He ought, however, to utilize literature when he is speaking to his own culture. Literature provides him with a language his culture recognizes as its own. It guarantees, furthermore, that the theologian will address his message to the real concerns of people, to those concerns which need a religious interpretation, to the concerns we become most aware of in those sensitive and profound moments all men know.

Literature is often a witness to the fact that grace and God have been met in this cultural situation. Literature is the way a particular culture expresses this occurrence. Obviously, a work of art is not formulated in theological categories; but, if it is a work of art, it attests to that reality which theology also declares.

The mistake which either theologian or literary critic can make in evaluating a piece of writing is to expect it to be explicitly theological or exclusively artistic. A theologian who sees theology only where it evidently and categorically expresses itself as such is a fundamentalist. A literary critic who cannot perceive the religious dimensions of literature because they are obliquely handled is also a fundamentalist. He judges that a literary effort must be interpreted uniquely in terms of its verbal clarity and not in terms of its intuitive and inarticulate expression of what is deepest in the human heart. The fundamentalistic theologian denies theology creativity and universality. The fundamentalistic literary critic cannot justify a subtle reading of text. In so doing he denies literature its transcendental and religious scope.

Whether American culture has given literary expression to a need for salvation and a discovery of grace is the question we now wish to consider. We shall give the reasons and the literary references which lead us to draw the religious conclusions we do. In this way we hope to minimize, if not totally eliminate, arbitrariness in our analysis.

F. Scott Fitzgerald

Although much of F. Scott Fitzgerald's writing is a search for a paradise lost, *The Great Gatsby* is a particularly striking expression of this theme.

The nostalgia for a Garden of Eden, the hope for a new world, the belief that innocence is recoverable are themes American literature often explores. Such aspirations attest to

a spiritual yearning in American culture, the virtuous materialism which de Tocqueville observed. Beneath the world
of illusion Americans devise, a world brilliantly described by
F. Scott Fitzgerald and, later, by Tennessee Williams, there
is an intense yearning for the real coupled with a refusal to
accept the real unless it is gracious and saving, beneficent and
healing. Illusions may be the product of immaturity, but they
are hope's sometimes misguided way of saying that reality
is not ultimately harsh.

If secularity or economic affluence are destined to be the
American style of life, this "materialism" must be transformed
into an idealistic materialism, or else it will be incapable of
bearing the cultural and spiritual burdens we intend to impose
upon it. Because this has not yet occurred, Jay Gatsby is dis-
contented by the spiritual waste which accompanies our material wealth. More is needed. Thus, Nick Carroway, the narrator of *The Great Gatsby*, reminds Americans that they need
discipline more than comfort, a "world . . . at a sort of moral
attention forever."[153]

The Great Gatsby is a story narrated by Nick Carroway concerning the exploits of Jay Gatsby, his love for Daisy Buchanan and his fascination with the world created by her and
her husband, Thomas. From his first appearance in the novel
to his eventual murder, Gatsby is less aware than the reader or
Carroway that what Gatsby wants cannot be discovered in the
selfish concerns of Daisy or in the surface materialism of Tom.

The tragedy of Jay Gatsby is rooted in his unawareness of
his spiritual needs. This unawareness is the consequence of
those aspects of American culture which make success and
possessions so essential that Americans neglect their instinctive idealism. This idealism becomes a motive force for discontent precisely because it cannot find adequate expression.
Fitzgerald artfully creates Gatsby as a symbol of the universal
human need for spiritual meaning. More concretely, however,
Gatsby is a dramatization of that fundamental dichotomy in

American culture which makes us discontent with material success and discontent without it.

Carroway sees, as Gatsby does not, the spiritual desolation of the Buchanan world and the inevitable tragedy awaiting those who seek to find spiritual substance in it. The Buchanan world is so grossly material that every spiritual value is a disadvantage. Gatsby seeks to become part of this world in terms of love, moral pride and commitment. His failure to realize his dream is presented by Fitzgerald as an American tragedy, a tragedy which touches not only Gatsby but all Americans who take the same road.

The second and third decades of the twentieth century in the United States were acutely aware of the spiritual poverty and value crisis beneath the surface and extravagant wealth. Gatsby is swept up into the gaiety of "the whisperings and the champagne and the stars."[154] When these do not offer faith, he becomes unable to function and is disjointed by the consequent conflicting confusions.

SYMBOLISM AND WASTELAND

There is a complex series of symbols and rituals in *The Great Gatsby* which together with its imagery of a spiritual wasteland made it a favorite of T. S. Eliot, Thomas Hardy and J. D. Salinger. What Carroway describes as Gatsby's "heightened sensitivity to the promises of life,"[155] is symbolized by the mystic rite which accompanies Gatsby's first appearance in the novel. Alone in the dark, facing the water, he stretches his hand toward a distant green light in a gesture of supplication and yearning, similar to that of a worshipper before a shrine. ". . . he stretched out his arms toward the dark water in a curious way, and . . . I could have sworn he was trembling. . . . I glanced seaward—and distinguished nothing except a single green light."[156]

The green light suggests hope by its color and the future

by its distance. Gatsby is denied both because of the vantage point from which he reaches for them.

This vantage point is a landscape of desolation over which Dr. T. J. Eckleburg presides. Eckleburg is a bleak symbol, a large face painted on a billboard, overlooking an uninhabited territory with unseeing, unresponsive, indifferent eyes. Eckleburg looks down on everything, Godlike, but does so in a commercialized manner, that is, from an advertisement. The billboard is a fitting symbol of what Carroway calls a culture's acceptance of "a vast, vulgar, and meretricious beauty."

In this wasteland Gatsby is destroyed. He is destroyed because of his virtues. His romanticism was too immature to allow him to commit himself simultaneously, as American culture demands, to raw power and romance. His dream demanded the transformation of materialism into enchantment, a stubborn faith in the indefinite perfectibility of man achieved in the hope that the material world could do more than the material world can actually do. This attempt to make the spiritual material and the material spiritual leads Gatsby to lose both. He is unsatisfied with what he has and fearful of being without it. Thus, his purity and innocence, his childlike trust and sense of wonder are transferred into trivial concerns and false values. He refuses, however, to surrender his idealism. The result is a bizarre type of religion in which the acquisition of wealth is ritualized. Even his shirts become sacred realities which, in a famous scene, he touches reverently as one would the beads of a rosary or a religious object.

Buchanan is not destroyed in the wasteland because he matches his ideals to "reality" and success, rejecting everything which is not useful, forsaking the spiritual and affirming, in its place, the "nature of things", the pragmatic. Gatsby, unable to do this, replaces reality with the Ideal, trying to "fulfill his Platonic conception of himself." This resistance to a "real" world of moral expediency and material dreams leads Gatsby to create illusions as it will later lead Laura and Blanche to do the same in *The Glass Menagerie* and in *A Streetcar Named Desire*, respectively. Indeed, this conflict between illusion and reality is a characteristic theme in American literature.

SPIRITUAL WASTE
AND PARADISE LOST

The tragedy of *The Great Gatsby* is the tragedy which follows upon the waste of spiritual resources. Jay Gatsby could have been, as his father says after his death, "a great man" had the world in which he lived not confused dreams with reality or material possessions and public acclaim with happiness. Gatsby, the typical American, was capable of a quest, the quest of the green light. He was willing to sacrifice himself for a dream, but he was trapped by a faith which sought to do the impossible with the material world.

F. Scott Fitzgerald explained in *This Side of Paradise* that he was writing for a generation that had "grown up to find all gods dead, all wars fought, all faiths in man shaken." *The Great Gatsby* was one effort at analysis and observation. *Tender is the Night* was a second attempt. The psychological structure of both novels is similar. In this case, Dick Diver is the idealist and Tom Barban is the man completely without ideals.

Diver encounters and fails to solve the same dilemma which confronted Gatsby. He pursues wealth because he knows it to be a crucial element in the cultural definition of worth, and yet he distrusts the cultural pressure which compels a man to equate wealth with personal value. He is torn between the outer-directed need to belong and the inner-directed force to be himself. "When people have so much for outsides, didn't it indicate a lack of inner intensity?"[157] Since he is unwilling to surrender "real" success for the sake of an elusive ideal and equally unwilling to sacrifice the ideal to what seems to be a vulgar reality, he remains uncommitted, confused, divided in his identity.

Fitzgerald develops in *Tender is the Night* the theme of paradise lost which accounts for the ambivalence in American culture. Diver's ideal world is a world of service to his fellowmen; Gatsby's ideal world was a world of beauty discovered and possessed. Diver cannot believe in his own worth unless he is helping someone and is hailed by others for having done so. He is an embodiment of the deed rather than creed approach of Americans, an exemplification of Dewey's premise that doing pragmatic tasks is equivalent to *being*.

Diver eventually realizes that he is loved for the services he performs rather than for himself. His service becomes his assurance that he is worthwhile as a person. And it is not enough. Gatsby, likewise, needed some material assurance that he had encountered his ideal of beauty. Beauty had to be something one had or was about to have as a possession rather than something which possessed the beholder. For Gatsby, beauty had to become something others could see and acclaim one for achieving rather than that which a man serves, realizes internally and silently reverences. Beauty had to be an object rather than a reality larger than wealth and more elusive than those trivial things men own.

HISTORY AND
THE DREAM OF GLORY

Americans may have developed their culture in this ambiguous manner because of the historical conditions which occasioned their cultural identity. They knew themselves to be the inheritors of a new world with all the promise and idealistic energy which such a connotation implies. They also knew that they had discovered an earthly paradise of unimaginable power and wealth with all the mundane and material opportunities which such largesse provides. They tried to become simultaneously men who were renewed and men who were resplendent in affluence. The effort misfired not because renewal and wealth are incompatible, but because wealth cannot become the means to renewal. What proved unworkable was the equation of wealth with worth, the material with the spiritual, glitter with substance.

In *The Great Gatsby* and *Tender is the Night* a dream of glory is dreamed. It is a dream that the divine and the material might be realized in an earthly context. The new world became man's last chance to displace religious concerns with human reason and pure secularity. This is why so many religious references occur in Fitzgerald's writings.

Gatsby defines his devotion in terms of shirts and green lights. Nicole, in *Tender is the Night*, "put on the first ankle-length day dress that she had owned for many years and crossed herself reverently with Chanel Sixteen." Diver, at the end of the novel, "blesses" the Riviera beach "with a papal cross."

The impossible hope of combining the sacred and the profane by a total reduction of one to the other is described in these two novels. Gatsby and Diver sense the foolishness of the success craze although they are trapped by it. They perceive in their disillusionment the rottenness beneath the surface of splendor in their lives; they become gradually aware of the futility of rushing from achievement to achievement only to discover that they have gone nowhere.

In *The Great Gatsby*, especially, the "heightened sensitivity to the promises of life" leads to nothing; the enjoyment of life is artificially produced, desperately clung to, superficially sustained. Confidence in self is sought not in love or real values or genuine human relationships but in excitement and objects. Consequently, there is winning but no victory; motion but neither meaning nor purpose; romance but no persevering love nor permanent commitment. Jay Gatsby for all his dreams of glory lives in a wasteland.

The tragedy of Gatsby derives from the fact that he was a good man who, like Willy Loman, "had the wrong dreams. All, all wrong. . . . He never knew who he was." His world, like Loman's, was one in which a person is saved only if he is acclaimed, happy, enchanted. In such a world, salvation is possible as long as the external appearance of one's life remains intact.

The goodness of Gatsby is intensified by his devotion to an ideal. He was devoted even though he was devoted wrongly. He did things less for himself than for his dream. He was, at heart, innocent and yet destroyed by a world whose values he believed in, as did Loman, and whose evil he never saw. Nick Carroway saw what Jay Gatsby was unable to see. He saw beneath the surface charm of Tom and Daisy a world of sterility, corruption and death; he saw beneath Gatsby's surface a spiritual strength, confused and misspent, but present nonetheless. Gatsby's career was a search for the promise life seems to offer; "he had committed himself to the following of a grail."[158]

Tennessee Williams later dramatized even further the antithesis between flesh and spirit in American culture which Fitzgerald portrays in the novels we have discussed. Laura in *The Glass Menagerie*, Blanche in *A Streetcar Named Desire*, Brick in *Cat on a Hot Tin Roof* and Alma in *Summer and Smoke* opt for the spirit and are damaged or destroyed by the world of flesh. Stanley in *A Streetcar Named Desire* and John in *Summer and Smoke* build a world of material values alone and, in the former case at least, succeed in the same way as Buchanan succeeds in *The Great Gatsby* or Barban in *Tender is the Night*. The conflict Fitzgerald describes is a recurring theme in American literature.

When Jay Gatsby first kisses Daisy, he realizes that the idealistic enchantment of their relationship must vanish and that the spirit cannot endure once physical contact is made.

> He knew that when he kissed this girl, and forever wed his unutterable visions to her perishable breath, his mind would never romp again like the mind of God. . . . Then he kissed her. At lips' touch she blossomed for him like a flower and the incarnation was complete.[159]

Reality is quite the reverse. The "incarnation" is not "complete." The "real" is either the gross, represented by Buchanan, or the gossamer, symbolized by Gatsby; it is either self-seeking impulse or unfocused romanticism. The world is a world in which neither God nor man is affirmed sufficiently, a world preoccupied with success so that the spiritual is not sensed in its severity nor the material enjoyed in its legitimate sensuousness. The American dream becomes a curious blending of Calvinistic and non-Calvinistic elements. Calvinistically, there is an emphasis on unrelenting labor and saving success. This is accompanied, inconsistently, with a conviction that man is, by nature, good and innocent. Gatsby is optimistic. He believes in an earthly Paradise and an ideal world more than he believes in sin or damnation, an avenging God or a dark eternity.

FUNDAMENTAL WEAKNESSES
IN AMERICAN CULTURE

Fitzgerald pinpoints two fundamental weaknesses in American culture. He shows us that America tends to offer secular objects to satisfy the religious instincts of the human heart. Ernest Hemingway will later develop this insight further. Gatsby's religious search was totally secularized. "He was a son of God . . . and he must be about His Father's business, the service of a vast, vulgar, and meretricious beauty."

American culture, moreover, attempts to transcend the concrete, the finite, the material without accepting the fact that the flesh makes its demands, demands which are sanctifying so long as one senses other demands in the human person, demands not satisfied when one has conquered the world, mastered its wealth, and made the environment comfortable. There may be a certain evasion of historical responsibility in the American desire to escape time by a compulsive youth cult or to escape space by the construction of an earthly paradise.

A hope for salvation is expressed in the effort by which time is suspended, space transformed, evil denied, imperfection evaded. Nick Carroway rubs out an obscene word scrawled on the white steps of Gatsby's mansion, as Holden Caulfield in *The Catcher in the Rye* erases vulgarities from school walls. The world must be perfect so that salvation, the survival of goodness and innocence, may be assured.

The two fundamental weaknesses in American culture converge in an incarnational problem: secular objects substitute for rather than tend toward religious values; the real and the ideal are set against each other so that an affirmation of one necessitates a denial of the other. There is an absence of harmony between the material and the spiritual, the concrete and the transcendent, the pragmatic and the contemplative. One element in the equation is expected to strike a balance without the other; one polarity is affirmed without allowing a healthy tension to exist between two poles which are different from each other but not at odds with each other.

The questions Fitzgerald raises in his fiction are religious questions: the meaning of death, God, good and evil, individual responsibility, salvation. There is a search in his writing for a world in which one forever sees "the city from the Queensboro Bridge." There the city is "seen . . . in its first wild promise of . . . mystery and . . . beauty."[160]

Unfortunately, the magic cannot last. Carroway visits Gatsby's house after the murder: "I could still hear the music and the laughter. . . . One night I did hear a material car there, and saw its lights stop at the front step. . . . Probably it was some final guest who had been at the ends of the earth and didn't know that the party was over."[161]

The closing words of *The Great Gatsby* combine the impressions of the first explorers of the new world with the aspiration of Jay Gatsby. In both cases, there was a firm faith that life was filled with promise, the future secure, salvation inevitable. The early explorers saw in America:

> . . . the last and greatest of all human dreams; for a transitory enchanted moment man must have held his breath in the presence of this continent . . . face to face for the last time in history with something commensurate to his capacity for wonder. . . . Gatsby believed in . . . the . . . future. It eluded us then, but that's no matter—tomorrow we will run faster, stretch out our arms further. . . .[162]

Ernest Hemingway

De Tocqueville observed that there is a split in the American personality between thought and experience, between theory and practice, between dream and reality. F. Scott Fitzgerald wrote of the dream world of the American. He tried to tell us why we dream and where our dreams went wrong. His intention is not to stop the dreaming but to redirect it.

Ernest Hemingway, conversely, is concerned with the reality world of the American. He prefers the pragmatic, the concrete, the uncomplicated world of action and clarity. Dreams are too ambiguous, uncertain, deceptive.

For Hemingway, it is possible that life may consist of only surface realities and sense experiences. Fitzgerald referred to our dead gods and our shattered beliefs. He knew we had failed and asked in his work why this had happened. Hemingway sensed the same failure and endorsed Gertrude Stein's description of his contemporaries as a lost generation. He was not interested in exploring the *why* of the failure but in making certain it would never happen again. Hemingway's affirmation of surface realities rather than visions or creeds was his way of saying that we cannot be deceived if we commit ourselves to tangible, manageable, infallible certitudes.

Hemingway's acceptance of the world in its naked reality was not as simplistic as it sounds at first hearing. There are religious and ritualistic dimensions to the Hemingway universe which can easily be overlooked. The religious dimensions are expressed in Hemingway's sensitivity to the holiness of the world. His writing is a celebration of life, a tribute to the nobility of creation and a reminder of our accountability to the glory which surrounds us.

Hemingway is convinced that honor is possible even when the struggle we face is brutal. Honor is realized when men are in communion with the mystery at the heart of nature's grandeur; when they are consecrated to ritualistic form or "grace under pressure"; when they cleanse themselves and the tasks they must perform by discipline and courage.

This religious instinct is the motive force behind the rituals, legends, sacraments and symbols Hemingway employs in his writing. There is something transcendent in reality which makes us reverent and demands our homage. We hallow the tests life gives us when we meet them with fortitude, in terror, perhaps, but never in craven fear or frenzied panic.

Ritual is Hemingway's requirement to impose meaning on the *nada* or nothingness which overcomes us in death, or sooner if we live as cowards. If men are not careful, they will be undone by this annihilating force.

Our nada who art in nada, nada be thy name, thy kingdom nada thy will be nada in nada as it is in nada. Give us this nada our nada and nada us our nada as we nada our nadas and nada us not into nada but deliver us from nada: pues nada. Hail nothing, full of nothing, nothing is with thee.[163]

Ritual is a redemption or salvation from total defeat. The loneliness and failure all men meet are redeemed by dignity, grace and steadfastness. This ritual is religious in its essence. It is pure. It is performed, not for a pragmatic purpose but to express a meaning too deep for words and best approximated in symbol. This ritual saves one from collapse and renders a measure of respect to the mysterious Presence in reality which allows nobility.

The bullfighter, for example, must kill cleanly, in exquisite form, with no malice or fear. That he kills and wins the contest does not matter. It is how he kills and whether he prevails which is significant. These ritualistic actions by which we must live are rites of exorcism purifying reality and offering creation the clean oblation of human effort and manly victory.

HEMINGWAY AND THE TRANSCENDENT

Hemingway seeks to describe life as a manageable reality, a phenomenon which yields momentarily to discipline, permits itself to be interpreted simply, and accepts the man who meets it in grace, with no pretense and unfailing strength. The President of the Swedish Academy described Hemingway's intention and success in bringing it to completion when the author was awarded the 1954 Nobel Prize for literature. His writing concentrates on the:

... heroic pathos which forms the basic element in his awareness of life ... a natural admiration of every individual who fights the good fight in a world of reality overshadowed by violence and death ... the bearing of one who is put to the test and who steels himself to meet the cold cruelty of existence without by so doing repudiating the great and generous moments. . . . He is one of the great writers of our time, one of those who, honestly and undauntedly, reproduces the genuine features of the hard countenance of the age.

Yet, surprisingly, Hemingway is not insensitive to the intimation of a transcendent reality in creation. There is a progressive acceptance in his novels of a Power beyond us. The Power is, however, impersonal, unable to help and indifferent. This Power is that Something in nature which accepts our offering of disciplined courage, of hallowed honor and gracious fortitude.

Even the vehemence with which Hemingway declares there is *nada* emerges from a heart in need of meaning, perhaps of God. The "nothingness" which overcomes Frederick and Catherine in *A Farewell to Arms* is less harsh with Santiago in *The Old Man and the Sea.* Santiago is also overcome, but he does not go down as decisively before the forces of *nada.* It is he, Hemingway's most refined presentation of the human voyager, who reminds us that "man is not made for defeat. . . . A man can be destroyed but not defeated."[164]

Santiago adds to his ritual a love not only for a woman, as Frederick does, but a love for all creation, perhaps for a Power beyond it. He transforms reality in ritualized love and achieves in the process a redemption which survives destruction even though the redemption is brief and tragic. Thus, he is not defeated.

Hemingway's stoicism deprives life of humanizing joy. He is a voluntarist and suffers from the pessimism which is typical of voluntarists from Schopenhauer to Freud. In place of happiness, there is discipline; in place of spiritual and intellectual experiences, there is action. Action, in fact, becomes an escape from those aspects of human experience which make their presence felt but cannot be accounted for in activity. In Hemingway, the will alone saves man. It does not overcome *nada*. This is impossible. It merely holds *nada* at bay and defies it.

We commented earlier that the apparent simplicity in Hemingway's work is complicated by a sophisticated approach to ritualism. The stoicism in Hemingway is, likewise, refined by a tentative affirmation of the divine in human living. The sacredness of human life is revealed when men are true to their humanity.

This sacredness is not completely humanistic since it involves a responsibility not only to one's self but also to the created order which is seen as transcendent and sacred. The struggle of man is, for Hemingway, a struggle to confront his own mortality and spiritualize it. In "Today is Friday," Hemingway pays tribute to the fact that Jesus accomplished this on the cross. Five times in that short story, the first soldier expresses admiration for the crucified Christ: "He was pretty good in there today."

The spiritual dimensions of human victory are most graphically portrayed in *The Old Man and the Sea*. Santiago, the old man, has little physical strength for the ritualized struggle with the great fish. He does have spiritual resources, and he relies on these for the final conflict of his life. The Christological references in the novel are multiple and worthy of later note. Santiago reveals to us the spiritual strength of the human heart as does Christ. The human heart is capable of such greatness that this revelation does not preclude the possibility of even a divine opportunity for man.

THE ALONENESS OF MAN

Hemingway, unfortunately, limits his concern with salvation to individualism. His characters are constantly tested but never in a social context or a corporate effort. In this, Hemingway differs from John Dewey. Frederick Henry in *A Farewell to Arms*, Robert Jordan in *For Whom the Bell Tolls* and Santiago in *The Old Man and the Sea* are alone when they face the moment of truth, as alone as the matador must be in the ring, as alone as Jesus was on the cross.

This aloneness is so stark that each man must formulate his own creed, his own morality and his own response to the harshness of reality. Love and religion help little.

Catherine dies at that moment when Frederick in *A Farewell to Arms,* most needed her to make "a separate peace" during a time of war. Robert Jordan must send his beloved Maria away as he summons courage for his final struggle and impending death. Santiago prays, but he knows his prayers will not affect the outcome of his struggle. His prayers are as unavailing as are those of Frederick who discovers Catherine has died soon after he had prayed ardently that she might live.

Man is alone, even though *The Old Man and the Sea* shows Hemingway more sensitive to solidarity than he was in any other novel. There is no salvation except an individual salvation; there is no saving grace except the grace of a ritual, individually performed and courageously sustained despite one's forsakenness.

F. Scott Fitzgerald was more concerned with cultural salvation or salvation in community. Ultimately, Hemingway maintains that salvation is for the few, for the elite. In this, his Pelagianism manages to become also a Gnosticism. Man saves himself by his will alone. Only a minority, the enlightened, are able to be saved. The others, the majority of mankind, are often unaware of their desperate situation and frequently ignorant of the greatness of the noble and redeemed in their midst.

Hemingway was troubled by the ignorance of the many. While Catherine is dying and Frederick is undergoing a personal ordeal, he overhears the nurses in the hospital comment on how fortunate they are to be seeing their first Caesarian. "It's a Caesarian," one said. "They're going to do a Caesarian." The other one laughed. "We're just in time. Aren't we lucky?"[165]

Later, Frederick takes lunch and supper in a nearby cafe, awaiting the outcome of Catherine's operation but fearing the worst. Those around him talk busily and laugh loudly, unaware that there is a man among them whose world is coming to an end.

The closing scene in *The Old Man and the Sea* depicts curious tourists who stare but who have no idea of what the skeleton of the fish, the empty boat and Santiago's struggle mean. They know little of ritual, suffering, gallantry.

"What's that?" she asked a waiter and pointed to the backbone of the great fish that was now just garbage waiting to go out with the tide....
"Shark." ...
"I didn't know sharks had such handsome, beautifully formed tails."[166]

If Hemingway felt the need to create a stern code and to limit his commitments to those truths certified by sense experience, it is because his generation, a lost generation, asked: "What else can we do?" We can do this much, Hemingway maintained. We can hope for the salvation life makes possible. We can do more. We can wrest this salvation, in grace under pressure, from a cold, empty universe and, thus, seize a momentary, ritualized meaning from *nada*. No peace is possible; no final saving grace will be given us. We have no God, but we are men to the very end. We are, therefore, capable of courage even in our forsakenness and crucifixion. This may not be everything, but it is something.

THE SUN ALSO RISES AND
A FAREWELL TO ARMS

There is general agreement that the two novels we are about to consider, and the two we shall study after them

(*For Whom the Bell Tolls* and *The Old Man and the Sea*) are the best of Hemingway's novels. *The Sun Also Rises* is involved with the problem of time, the impermanence of man and the cyclic futility which leads him nowhere. *A Farewell to Arms* is the story of a man lost in a world where God does not exist and where each must create his own rules for life. It is concerned less with the nature of things, more with the nature of man. *For Whom the Bell Tolls* describes the deeds and thoughts of a man with a mission who fulfills his mission and dies. *The Old Man and the Sea* is a saga of sacrifice and endurance, of solidarity and transformation.

The Sun Also Rises is a parable of living with grace and dignity in spite of the tragedy and inevitability of death. It is typical of early Hemingway, fascinated with ritual and awestruck by the bullfight. In the process of developing these observations, Hemingway portrays his generation as one which saw no hope for change and hence were paralyzed by a sense of futility. "The sun also rises, and the sun goes down and hastens to the place where it arose. . . ."

Time constantly passes; events occur; things seem to happen; and yet all remains the same. In the face of this futility, the only meaning possible is an external meaning and a transitory meaning. This is realized by a rite or form which shows man to be man even though he is meant for dust.

This code becomes Hemingway's substitute for God at a time when faith is all but impossible. Later, in *A Farewell to Arms*, human love will become the substitute for God. At this stage, however, even love is impossible. Jake Barnes, the main protagonist, is impotent and incapable of a sexual expression of love; Robert Cohn can boast of his boxing victories or his sexual exploits, but he has not the inner strength necessary for genuine love; Georgette has reduced love to a simple monetary exchange.

In a world where God is dead, faith elusive, love impossible, men must devise some means of expressing who they are. The Hemingway code becomes the means they employ. Life must be reckoned with, and ritual is the only way men can do this. This is a time when men are incapable of expectation or nostalgia. They do what must be done as well as possible and die, with no capability of changing themselves or others. Religion is useless, at least for the moment, but this inability of religion to help is regretful.

. . . I was kneeling with my forehead on the wood in front of me, and was thinking of myself as praying. I was a little ashamed, and regretted that I was such a rotten Catholic; but realized there was nothing I could do about it, at least for a while, and maybe never, but that anyway it was a grand religion, and I only wished I felt religious and maybe I would the next time. . . .[167]

A *Farewell to Arms* is a more sophisticated literary creation than *The Sun Also Rises*. In this novel, the famous Hemingway style has reached a point of perfection. It is a novel of succinct speech and simple words. This style is an effective tool for the message Hemingway seeks to convey, a message which reminds us that we must live no longer in a world of abstractions or social conventions. Life must be made as elementary as possible. Otherwise, we shall confuse and be confused. The style, in its effort to be clear rather than nuanced, supports the fundamental epistemology of the book, telling us that truth, like simple words, depends more on the senses than on the mind.

The novel, of course, does more than this. It insists that a man who dies spiritually, whether he dies physically or not, is a defeated man.

A *Farewell to Arms* is the story of Frederick Henry, his love for Catherine, and their intention by their love, to make a "separate peace" in a time of war. In this way they hope to escape the terror and turmoil which surround them. The attempt fails. What matters more than the failure are the reasons for the failure.

Frederick left the field of battle for the sake of an easier life. In a powerful scene he runs from his captors and swims to safety across the Tagliamento River. The river is not only a physical body of water; it is a symbolic frontier bringing Frederick into a new life. Even the etymology of the river's name reinforces this interpretation.

The swimming of the river is a ritual, almost a baptismal rite, leaving on one side a life which is aimless, corrupt and death-dealing and seeking on the other side safety, salvation and serenity. Frederick's new world, however, does not bring him what he intended. It does not do this because he finds on the other side not peace but passivity.

There are no further tests, no place for courage, no revelation of glory or expression of grace under pressure. There is Catherine; there is love. But love is not enough unless real life is happening all around it. Frederick cannot give meaning to life by love alone because his love occurs in an artificial and inactive existence. In this sense he preserves his physical life but dies spiritually.

Frederick's escape from his execution is not merely a selfish concern with survival. He runs away because the new war which is being waged has little regard for gallantry. The Italian army is panic-stricken rather than valiant, desperate rather than disciplined. A man's virility or fortitude do not decide the contest, but impersonal machines and artillery do.

A soldier often dies, not because he was brave or even because his death was specifically intended, but merely because one faceless group of men fire a profusion of bullets at another faceless group of men until the soldier in question is killed. How he behaved before his death does not matter. How he met his death is unimportant. Sometimes no one knows of his death until he cannot be accounted for, and then no one can say precisely when he died or where his body might be.

In such a war, indeed, in such a life, manhood does not matter. Such an existence is pointless. It is chaotic, confused, aimless. It allows no sublimity.

I am always embarrassed by the words sacred, glorious, and sacrifice and the expression in vain. . . . Abstract words such as glory, honor, courage, or hallow were obscene words beside the concrete names of villages, the number of roads, the names of rivers, the number of regiments and the dates.[168]

Frederick reacts to his problem by running away with Catherine. He breaks the bonds of common cause with his fellowmen. Now there remains no opportunity for bravery nor even men for whose sake one might be brave. There are only Frederick and Catherine, their love, but also their aloneness.

Later, Robert Jordan in *For Whom the Bell Tolls* will face life in a way which permits a fuller salvation. He will love Maria but he will not cut himself off from mankind, his compatriots or his cause. He will love in the context of real life where men are put to the test by more than love, and where life responds by offering men not only challenges which ultimately undo them but the opportunity to know that one has served and died gloriously.

A Farewell to Arms is deceptively simple. Beneath the sparse words, there is power and a sophisticated symbolism which say more than the surface suggests. Hemingway once compared his writing to an iceberg, only one-eighth of which is visible.

THE SYMBOL OF RAIN

We have spoken already of the crossing of the Tagliamento. The symbol of water, in this case of rain, is seen by Catherine in a different context. In a significant exchange between Frederick and Catherine, she explains herself. Frederick speaks first.

"It's raining hard."
  "And you'll always love me, won't you?"
  "Yes."
  "And the rain won't make any difference?"
  "No."
  "That's good. Because I'm afraid of the rain. . . . I've always been afraid of the rain."
  "Why are you afraid of it?"
  "I don't know.
  "Tell me."
  "No."
  "Tell me."
  "All right. I'm afraid of the rain because sometimes I see me dead in it . . . and sometimes I see you dead in it. . . . It's all nonsense. It's only nonsense. I'm not afraid of the rain. Oh, oh, God, I wish I wasn't."
  She was crying. I comfort her and she stopped crying. But outside it kept on raining.[169]

Rain becomes a symbol of an all-pervasive evil, a symbol not unlike that of the rats and the plague in Albert Camus' famous novel or the dust in John Steinbeck's *The Grapes of Wrath*. One can do little about rain. He must accept it. Like the plague or a dust storm, it goes away when it chooses to go away, and it may at any moment and for no apparent reason return.

Hemingway is said to have rewritten the conclusion of *A Farewell to Arms* seventeen times. This is some indication of the care with which he must have chosen the final words of the novel and, therefore, of the significance of ending the novel on the word "rain." Frederick leaves the dead body of Catherine and explains: "After a while I went out and left the hospital and walked back to the hotel in the rain."[170]

The inability of the Hemingway code to give meaning to life in *A Farewell to Arms* makes matters desperate. There is no way for men to be men ritualistically when they are forced to fight machines. The failure of human love to serve as a means of interpreting life and giving it total significance adds to the confusion. One cannot struggle manfully in the modern world nor run away from the struggle and hope for peace. When religion also proves deficient, the wasteland of our modern era is complete.

In *The Sun Also Rises* and in *A Farewell to Arms*, there is a sense of disappointment rather than bitterness that religion could not have been of more help at a time when men were uncommonly helpless. Frederick sums it up when he admits that life "is never hopeless. But sometimes I cannot hope."[171] There may be reason for hoping, but men are hard put to discover the reason and, unfortunately, religion fares no better.

Yet Hemingway continues to wonder whether religion may have more to say about life than he has discovered. Frederick Henry is captivated, if not entirely convinced, by the hope the priest in the novel represents. Frederick cannot accept God, but neither can he accept a "hopeless" world. The relationship between the priest and Frederick remains friendly and inquisitive throughout the novel. The priest, noting that Frederick is in a foreign land and far from home, offers his home to Frederick. Frederick accepts but never acts on the offer.

THE SEARCH FOR FAITH

Frederick's search for love and the meaning of life do not permit him to give up completely on Christianity. His desire for identity, coupled with his fear of the rootless nothingness of life, the *nada* of living, compel him to affirm, not the formal acceptance of Christianity, but its residual forms and fundamental themes.

In a conversation with Count Greffi, Frederick admits to wondering about faith and life after death. The Count speaks first.

"We none of us know about the soul. Are you *Croyant?*"
"At night."
Count Greffi smiled and turned the glass with his fingers. "I had expected to become more devout as I grow older but somehow I haven't," he said. "It is a great pity."
"Would you like to live after death?" I asked and instantly felt a fool to mention death. But he did not mind the word.
"It would depend on the life. This life is very pleasant. I would like to live forever." He smiled "I very nearly have. . . ."
"I might become very devout," I said. "Anyway, I will pray for you."
"I had always expected to become devout. All my family died very devout. But somehow it does not come."
"It's too early."
"Maybe it is too late. Perhaps I have outlived my religious feelings."
"My own comes only at night."
"Then, too, you are in love. Do not forget that is a religious feeling."[172]

We shall consider later Hemingway's thesis on the relationship between human love and religious experience.

Earlier in the novel, Catherine had excluded a religious interpretation of their love. She and Frederick observe another couple sheltered in the protection of the Cathedral of Milan during a rain storm. Catherine refuses to enter the Cathedral.

There was a fog in the square and when we came close to the front of the Cathedral it was very big and the stone was wet.
"Would you like to go in?"
"No."
"They're like us."
"Nobody is like us," Catherine said. She did not mean it happily.

"I wish they had some place to go."
"It mightn't do them any good."
"I don't know. Everybody ought to have some place to go."[173]

Even though religion does not seem to be a viable option, Frederick yearns for something beyond his inquietude. His love for Catherine is an almost desperate effort to avoid chaos and *nada*. As he perceives the fact that life is impossible to conquer and that death is the ultimate consequence of his struggle, Frederick wonders if Christianity can help one accept defeat.

"It is in defeat that we become Christians. How would Our Lord have been if Peter had rescued him in the Garden?"
"I hoped for a long time for victory."
"Me, too."
"Now I don't know."
"It has to be one or the other."
"I don't believe in victory any more."
"I don't. . . . But I don't believe in defeat. Though it may be better."[174]

As the novel rushes to its conclusion, Frederick turns frequently but unsuccessfully to religion in his personal crisis. It is he who wishes his union with Catherine legitimized by a marriage ceremony. When he hears his child has been born dead, he wonders about Baptism. "I had no religion but I knew he ought to have been baptized. But what if he never breathed at all. He hadn't. He had never been alive."[175]

Soon after, Frederick surmises that Catherine may also die. He turns pleadingly to prayer. The answer to his prayer is Catherine's death, *nada*.

I knew she was going to die and I prayed that she would not. Don't let her die. Oh, God, please don't let her die. I'll do anything for you if you won't let her die. Please, please, please don't let her die. God please make her not die. I'll do anything you say if you don't let her die. You took the baby but don't let her die.

That was all right but don't let her die. Please, please dear God, don't let her die.[176]

The theme of alienation is interwoven throughout A *Farewell to Arms*. Frederick and Catherine are expatriates, unmarried, refugees from the war, without religious faith. Their isolation from society is complete.

Frederick tries often to find some meaning in existence. The world, as he sees it, offers none. Death awaits everyone, even the brave. Frederick tells Catherine:

"We won't fight."

"We mustn't. Because there's only us two, and in the world there's all the rest of them. . . ."

"They won't get us," I said. "Because you're too brave. Nothing ever happens to the brave."

"They die, of course."

"But only once."[177]

Death is most tragic when the issues involved in the person's life are misunderstood. This may be one reason why Hemingway was captivated by the death of Jesus of Nazareth. It is also the reason why he is revolted by the death of a soldier killed in fear and ignorance by a group of panic-stricken fellow soldiers who never knew where their bullets found their target.

He lay in the mud on the side of the embankment, his feet pointing downhill, breathing blood irregularly. The three of us squatted over him in the rain. He was hit low in the back of the neck and the bullet had ranged upward and come out under the right eye. He died while I was stopping up the two holes. . . . 'They were Italians that shot,' I said. 'They weren't Germans.' . . . He looked very dead. It was raining. I had liked him as well as any one I ever knew.[178]

It is life which kills. It kills the courageous most viciously and decisively. Once again, Jesus of Nazareth dies the type of death Hemingway most admired for the reason he most respected.

If people bring so much courage to this world, the world has to kill them to break them, so of course it kills them. The world breaks every one and afterward many are strong at the broken places. But those that will not break it kills. It kills the very good and the very gentle and the very brave impartially. If you are none of these, you can be sure it will kill you, too, but there will be no special hurry.[179]

Life kills.

Now Catherine would die. That was what you did. You died. You did not know what it was about. You never had time to learn. They threw you in and told you the rules and the first time they caught you off base they killed you . . . they killed you in the end. You could count on that. Stay around and they would kill you.[180]

When Catherine realizes she is about to die, she objects:

"I'm going to die. . . . I hate it. . . . I'm not afraid. I just hate it. . . . I'm not a bit afraid. It's just a dirty trick." . . . I went into the room and stayed with Catherine until she died. She was unconscious all the time, and it did not take her very long to die.[181]

There is no salvation. Even the effort to help sometimes complicates matters. In a famous scene, Frederick becomes aware of this as he watches ants swarming around a burning log and falling into the fire:

I remember thinking at the time that it was the end of the world and a splendid chance to be a messiah and lift the log off the fire and throw it out where the ants could get off onto the ground. But I did not do anything but throw a tin cup of water on the log, so that I could have the cup empty to put whisky in before I added water to it. I think the cup of water on the burning log only steamed the ants.[182]

A *Farewell to Arms* describes an attempt to make secular or human love a substitute for divine love. Catherine makes Frederick her religion. Toward the end of her life, Frederick asks her: "Do you want me to get a priest?" . . . "Just you," she said.[183] Frederick was once told by Count Greffi that love is a "religious feeling." Frederick's confusion even when things were supposedly going well with Catherine, coupled with Catherine's untimely death, show that such love does not provide universal or ultimate answers.

FOR WHOM THE BELL TOLLS

For Whom the Bell Tolls is the story of a man with a mission who fulfills his mission and dies. In order to write such a novel, a process of development had to take place in Hemingway's thought. The resulting literary effort was a blending of familiar and unfamiliar Hemingway themes.

One discovers again the commitment to duty which is an essential element in the Hemingway code. Pilar, the woman, questions Robert Jordan, who was given a mission to destroy a bridge: "And you have no fear?"

"Not to die," he said truly.

"But other fears?"

"Only of not doing my duty as I should."[184]

On an earlier occasion, we are reminded: "Neither you nor this old man is anything. You are instruments to do your duty."[185]

The code one must adhere to in order to be a man requires that one live his life in the "now." The past provides no further challenges; the future leads to *nada*. It is the present which demands discipline, dutiful living and ritualized courage.

You have it *now* and that is all your whole life is, now. There is nothing else than now. There is neither yesterday, certainly, nor is there any tomorrow. How old must you be before you know that? There is only now, and if now is only two days, then two days is your life and everything in it will be in proportion.[186]

These are familiar virtues in Hemingway's philosophy. *For Whom the Bell Tolls* differs from its predecessors, however, in its affirmation of mission and community rather than fortitude and individual glory. The title of the book suggests this new approach. It is taken from John Donne's devotions which speak of each man's involvement with mankind.

Hemingway portrays Robert Jordan as a man with a mission rather than as a man who performs a rite. Mission is made possible by a consideration of commitment and consecration lacking in Hemingway's earlier works. Jordan is capable of a more significant dedication to his fellowmen than Jake Barnes in *The Sun Also Rises*, who questions the value of any commitment, or Frederick Henry in *A Farewell to Arms*, who cannot give himself to anything other than his love for Catherine.

Jordan sacrifices himself for a cause, offering himself to a community of men, affirming by implication that relationships of this type must be maintained, choosing explicitly to love Maria only in the context of a more universal series of obligations. Jordan loves Maria deeply, but he does not make this love substitute for his responsibility to "the cause." He does not like war, but he refuses to make a "separate peace" while his fellowmen do battle. Jordan does not fight for his own fulfillment or under the urgency of an impersonal need to discharge his duty. ". . . you fought that summer and that fall for all the poor in the world, against all tyranny, for all the things that you believed. . . ."[187]

Jordan's sacrifice and death become an act of consecration to humanity. Such consecration demands "chastity of mind." "Who else kept that first chastity of mind about their work that young doctors, young priests, and young soldiers usually started with? The priests certainly kept it, or they got out. . . ."[188]

The act of consecration is ritualized. Jordan is sensitive to the holiness of creation and the deeper meaning involved in his death for others. Before he dies for the sake of his friends: ". . . he took a good long look at everything. . . . Then he looked up at the sky. . . . He touched the palm of his hand against the pine needles where he lay and he touched the bark of the pine trunk that he lay behind."[189]

Jordan's mission required a prior consecration to the transcending, saving quality of human relationships. Jordan believes in a love so universalized that a community issues from it.

He speaks in a way Frederick Henry could not. Reflecting on those with whom he has fought, he observes how much they have become a family for him: "Anselmo is my oldest friend . . . Agustin . . . is my brother and I never had a brother. Maria is my true love and my wife. I never had a true love. I never had a wife. She is also my sister, and I never had a sister, and my daughter; and I never will have a daughter."[190]

Jordan is not only at-one with his companions; he is identified with them. They are not collaborators; they are himself. This identity is, of course, most intense in the case of Maria. He begs Maria to run for safety as he prepares for death in words which express this reality. "Thou art me now. Thou art all there will be of me."[191]

Jordan asks her to go so that this much of him will not be lost and so that, to this extent, he might transcend his death.

In the person of Anselmo, this love for others extends beyond one's comrades and embraces even the enemy. Anselmo's hope is expressed in a secular prayer for universal brotherhood.

That we should win this war and shoot nobody. . . . That we should govern justly and that all should participate in the benefits according as they have striven for them. And that those who have fought against us should be educated to see their error. . . . That we should shoot none. Not even the leaders. That they should be reformed by work.[192]

Anselmo is convinced that an atonement or purification will be needed after the war to compensate for the killing.

I think that after the war there will have to be some great penance done for the killing. If we no longer have religion after the war, then I think there must be some form of civic penance organized that all may be cleansed from the killing, or else we will never have a true and human basis for living. . . . I wish I did not think about it so much. . . . I wish there was a penance for it that one could commence now because it is the only thing that I have done in all my life that makes me feel badly when I am alone. All the other things are forgiven or one had a chance to atone for them by kindness or in some decent way. But I think this of the killing must be a very great sin and I would like to fix it up.[193]

There is a deep kinship in the novel between Jordan and Anselmo. In great measure their understanding of human brotherhood unites them. In the grip of a strong conviction that men are brothers and that they must be purified of sin when they offend against this brotherhood, Anselmo touches the periphery of the God question. Jordan speaks first in the ensuing conversation:

"Yet you have killed."

"Yes. And will again. But if I live later, I will try to live in such a way, doing no harm to any one, that it will be forgiven."

"By whom?"

"Who knows? Since we do not have God here any more, neither His Son nor the Holy Ghost, who forgives? I do not know.

"You have not God any more?"

"No. Man. Certainly not. If there were God, never would He have permitted what I have seen with my eyes. Let *them* have God."

"They claim Him."

"Clearly I miss Him, having been brought up in religion."[194]

The transferral of divine love into secular or human love occurs in this novel as it did in *A Farewell to Arms*. Catherine made Frederick Henry her religion, as we have seen. Jordan likewise addresses Maria in words which, in another context, would have been suitable for religious or liturgical language.

I love thee as I love all that we have fought for. I love thee as I love liberty and dignity and the rights of all men to work and not be hungry. I love thee as I love Madrid that we have defended and as I love all my comrades that have died. And many have died. Many. Many. . . . But I love thee as I love what I love most in the world and I love thee more. I love thee very much. . . . More than I can tell thee.[195]

Though human relationships are profound, they cannot ultimately save Jordan. Maria must be sent away. His comrades in arms feel helpless as they leave Jordan, speaking some words of comfort, looking back in regret.

Jordan has known the world and loved it. He has lived with his fellowmen and treasured the experience. He found a cause worth dying for and now prepares to pay the price for this discovery. He has had everything but suddenly seems to have nothing. Jordan is alone, about to die, confused about the ultimate value of his sacrifice.

Salvation, for Jordan, was identified with the present, the concrete, the perceptible, especially the physically attainable in honor and effort for the sake of brotherhood and a transcendent cause. Now, however, the present is death-dealing; the concrete is the pain in his broken leg; the perceptible is the sense of enemy soldiers surrounding him; the physically attainable has been attained; the bridge has been destroyed cleanly, neatly, completely.

Jordan has done what he had to do. He has done it well. The friends on whom he relied had to leave, and the outcome of the cause for which he is about to die is uncertain. There is only "now" but "now" is *nada*.

Jordan hoped for much in life, even for meaning and salvation. His hopes are about to die with him. He prays as he is about to die although his prayer is not addressed to God.

How little we know of what there is to know. I wish that I were going to live a long time instead of going to die today. . . . I thought I knew about so many things that I know nothing of. I wish there were more time. . . . Each one does what he can. You can do nothing for yourself, but perhaps you can do something for another. . . . Every one has to do this once, one day or another. You are not afraid of it once you know you have to do it. . . . He looked down the hill slope again and he thought. . . . I hate to leave it very much and I hope I have done some good. . . . I have tried to do with what talent I had. . . . I have fought for what I believed in. . . . The world is a fine place and worth fighting for and I hate very much to leave it. . . . Dying is only bad when it takes a long time and hurts so much that it humiliates you.[196]

THE OLD MAN AND THE SEA

The Old Man and the Sea lends itself more easily to experience than explanation. One reads it and knows he has come in contact with something significant though it is difficult to verbalize reactions. The Old Man and the Sea is proof positive that Hemingway's writing was not as simple as it seemed. The Nobel Prize he was awarded, especially for this novel, is an indication that he dealt with universal concerns and the heart of man in his literary work.

The Old Man and the Sea is a story of redemption, told as a parable of an old man and the great fish he caught and lost. In sacrifice and endurance, Santiago redeems the weakness of his flesh and the infirmity of his age. His spirit transforms him. This transformation requires all his remaining physical strength and his manly courage. More than this, it necessitates a forceful spirit since the spirit prevails here where the body cannot. The redemptive meaning of The Old Man and the

Sea is underscored by its many Christological references as we shall see later.

We meet in this final work of Hemingway themes which have recurred before. There is loneliness, of course. The first words of the novel sound this note: "He was an old man who fished alone. . . . On the sea, "he was sorry for the birds . . . that were always flying and looking and almost never finding. . . ."[197]

And there is the code: "He was sleepy and the old man put his arm across his shoulders and said, 'I am sorry.'

'Que va,' the boy said. 'It is what a man must do.' "[198]

On the sea, Santiago is conscious of the struggle for existence, the wrestling with fate. "Take a good rest, small bird," he said. "Then go in and take your chance like any man or bird or fish."[199]

There is, too, admiration for human resources when they are summoned for a noble task and consecrated by disciplined courage. ". . . I will show him what a man can do and what a man endures . . . man is not made for defeat . . . a man can be destroyed but not defeated."[200]

There is finally the creed of solidarity with all life, human and animal, and a recognition of the universal interdependence of life upon life. But there is also more.

This is Hemingway's most subtle novel. It utilizes not only a refined symbolism but also a nuanced message. Redemption is consequent upon human relationships, not necessarily engaged in a common effort as in *For Whom the Bell Tolls* but simply for themselves.

Redemption, furthermore, depends upon faith, not faith in a cause but faith in meaning. Santiago's survival does not derive from what he does but more from the ability of the boy, Manolin, to understand this. Santiago's ritual, alone on the sea is crucial, but equally crucial is Manolin's appreciation of this.

The element of faith emerges clearly in *The Old Man and*

the Sea as part of the overall process of man's prevailing. This faith is especially important in the master-disciple relationship between Santiago and Manolin. Santiago is reassured by Manolin's faith and fidelity: "I know you did not leave me because you doubted."[201]

A little later Manolin comments: "He hasn't much faith."

"No," the old man said. "But we have. Haven't we?"[202]

Hemingway, we have noted, was haunted by the figure of Christ. One can say of Santiago what Hemingway's soldier said of Jesus in "Today is Friday": "He was pretty good in there today." In this, his final synthesis of faith and meaning, of bravery and redemption, of ritual and salvation, Hemingway creates an impressive variety of Christological symbols.

There is a faint suggestion of Jesus on the cross at noon, his forsakenness, and his conflict with Satan in Santiago's early description of the fish he has caught. "My choice was to go there to find him beyond all people. Beyond all people in the world. Now we are joined together and have been since noon. And no one to help either one of us."[203]

The symbolism, however, becomes more explicit. The redemptive suffering of Jesus on the cross provides a paradigm for the redemptive suffering of Santiago on the sea. Santiago feels the pain in his back: "Certainly his back cannot feel as badly as mine does."[204] His hands are wounded, first the right, and then, the left. "He felt the line carefully with his right hand and noticed his hand was bleeding."[205] Later, he notices that "his left hand was taking all the strain and cutting badly."[206]

The similarity between Jesus and Santiago is not restricted to the wounds they sustain as they are tested and transformed in their struggle. There is also a temporal concurrence. "The sun was rising for the third time since he had put to sea. . . ."[207] Santiago's destiny is accomplished in three days on the open sea. The number three is equally significant in the death and resurrection of Christ.

At one point in the novel, Hemingway becomes obvious lest the identification of Santiago with Jesus be lost. The fisherman senses the agony, almost the futility of his ordeal. "Ay," he said aloud. There is no translation for this word and perhaps it is a noise such as a man might make, involuntarily, feeling the nail go through his hands and into the wood."[208]

Santiago returns, without the fish. He leaves the boat and climbs the hill home, carrying the mast on his shoulder. He falls forsaken and exhausted in a cruciform position on his cot. "He started to climb again and at the top he fell and lay for some time with the mast across his shoulder . . . he slept face down on the newspaper with his arms straight and the palms of his hands up."[209]

Tennessee Williams

Tennessee Williams, like William Faulkner, is a Southern writer whose setting is the South but whose theme is the tragic condition of man rather than the analysis of a regional culture. Williams writes of the familiar existentialistic problems: alienation, our failure to communicate with one another, the loneliness of life. He sees tenderness and compassion as a source of healing for this distress. "Every artist has a basic premise. . . . For men the dominating premise has been the need for understanding and tenderness and fortitude among individuals trapped by circumstance."[210]

He writes of the South: its puritanism, its sense of tradition, its reaction against the vulgar materialism of the East and North, its resistance to the disintegration of gracious living caused by industrialism and pragmatism.

In addition, Williams has a sensitive religious instinct. His God is either nonexistent or helpless, but his religious convictions remain strong. He writes of moral responsibility dissipated in liquor, sex and violence; of guilt and retribution (*Suddenly, Last Summer*); of innocence and corruption

(*Sweet Bird of Youth*); of expectation (*The Glass Menagerie*); and finally, of faith (*The Night of the Iguana*).

In his major plays, Williams longs for salvation but distrusts its possibility and fears its arrival when it seems imminent. He searches for grace in a universe touched, it seems, by evil on every side. He desires a gracious God but suspects that God may be as brutal and destructive as men are. In the heart of man, and of God, if he exists, there is no saving mercy.

Without becoming forced or artificial, we can group the seven plays we shall consider into dominant themes. It so happens that these themes also follow the chronological order in which Williams published these plays. *The Glass Menagerie* and *A Streetcar Named Desire* are plays of advent or waiting. They are plays which consider what Tom in *The Glass Menagerie* calls "the long delayed but always expected something that we live for."[211] There is a hope for salvation in them and the creation of a world of illusion when that hope turns to despair. Laura assembles a menagerie of glass animals, brittle, beautiful and unreal. Blanche in *A Streetcar Named Desire* wears the clothing and adopts the manner of a way of life which once had its place but cannot survive in the present except at the price of sacrificing the present to the past.

Summer and Smoke and *Cat on a Hot Tin Roof* explore the demands of survival, granted that one intends to live in the present. They deal with the apparently unresolvable conflict between the spirit and the flesh, a conflict almost allegorized in the persons of Alma and John in *Summer and Smoke*. This tension between spirit and flesh must terminate in an affirmation of life or else the tension destroys.

Alma tries to become, first, too platonic, later, too hedonistic, and ends in failure. John begins as a selfish materialist but eventually maintains his balance. Likewise, Gooper and Mae in *Cat on a Hot Tin Roof* are sensualists and, therefore, inadequate for the demands life imposes on them. Brick is an idealist who symbolically longs for the moon and for perfect human friendships but surrenders himself to alcohol and self-hatred when he cannot find them. Margaret and Big Daddy Pollitt solve the tension; they recognize their sensual needs, but affirm life so strongly that they spiritualize their sense experiences.

Suddenly, Last Summer and *Sweet Bird of Youth* consider corruption and evil. In the first case, evil is horrible and savagely destructive; in the second, innocence is more subtly corrupted and there remains a possibility of rebirth, a possibility dramatized in the opening scene which occurs on Easter Sunday morning as church bells peal and an Alleluia chorus is sung. Finally, *The Night of the Iguana* wonders about God and sees the need for faith, at least in human goodness, perhaps in divine grace.

THE GLASS MENAGERIE AND
A STREETCAR NAMED DESIRE

The Glass Menagerie traces the slow and relentless disintegration of a family. It refers to a father who deserted his home and the crippled girl, Laura, who is too shy for life and whose delicacy is symbolized by the glass figurines she collects. The play's narrator is Laura's brother, Tom, who loves his sister but cannot help, partly because he himself is stifled in his life, partly because Laura needs a different type of love from that which he can offer.

Amanda, the mother of the family, does everything she can to hold her family together, but she fails. Her well-intentioned efforts, in fact, drive her children further apart. Tom leaves home at the end of the play and Laura has retreated forever inside herself after a halting and almost successful effort at recovery. Amanda wanted to save her children. Her tragedy and that of the play is the tragedy occasioned by the pain we inflict without having wanted to harm, indeed, having intended the opposite.

In his "Production Notes" to this play, Williams sums up its inner meaning. Speaking of the theme music for the staging of the story, he writes that it should be:

. . . the lightest, most delicate music in the world and perhaps the saddest. It expresses the surface vivacity of life with the underlying strain of immutable and inexpressible sorrow. When you look at a piece of delicately spun glass you think of two things: how beautiful it is and how easily it can be broken.[212]

The play is built on hope, a hope that someone will come from the world of reality to rescue the Wingfield family from its disaster and its illusions. The play expresses a desire for a savior who will not be another illusion but "an emissary from a world of reality." This desire is incarnated in the "gentleman caller" who, Tom explains, is "the most realistic character in the play."

The caller, Jim O'Connor, is more than the hoped-for answer to a specific need. He is a symbol of that "long delayed but always expected something that we live for."[213] The tragedy of the play is intensified because the gentleman caller's failure is not only a failure in terms of Laura but in terms of all those who are disappointed in their hope for a saving presence.

Amanda becomes the most heroic character in the story. She is gallant in the face of overwhelming odds. At times, she confesses: "I'm just bewildered—by life. . . ."[214] She also realizes that the only thing we have is one another. "In these trying times, all that we have to cling to is—each other. . . ."[215] She pleads with Tom to help her, but her pleading takes the form of nagging. She senses that Tom is her last hope as Jim O'Connor will be Laura's last hope. "I worry so much I don't sleep, it makes me nervous. . . . I've had to put

up a solitary battle all these years. But you're my right hand.
. . . Don't fall down, don't fail!"[216]

EXPECTATION AND ILLUSION

Amanda's life is a life of all expectation. Her expectations are
not selfish but for her children. Amanda reminds Tom at one
point of his sister's worsening condition. "She's older than
you, two years, and nothing has happened."[217] Immediately
before the gentleman caller arrives, Tom cautions: "Mother,
you mustn't expect too much of Laura."[218] In words which express her aspirations, she asks Laura to wish on the moon.

LAURA: What shall I wish for, Mother?

AMANDA: (her voice trembling and her eyes suddenly filling with
tears): Happiness! Good Fortune![219]

Williams' sympathy for Amanda is evident in his closing
explanatory notes. In the final scene, a pantomime between
Amanda and Laura occurs. The sometimes shrill words
Amanda uses cannot be heard. "Now that we cannot hear the
mother's speech, her silliness is gone, and she has dignity and
tragic beauty."[220]

Laura's beauty is of another kind. Her beauty is less sturdy,
less durable. It is a refined beauty for which the world should
have a place, but which the world will not allow to live.
When first she communicates with Jim, and love seems possible, Williams describes her as manifesting: "a fragile, un-
earthly prettiness . . . she is like a piece of translucent glass
touched by light, given a momentary radiance, not actual, not
lasting."[221]

Laura is the symbol of that which in human life does not
survive the harshness of reality. That which is lost might have
been preserved had there been more tenderness and compassion in life.

The problem is not only others. It is also ourselves. Laura

could not communicate her finer nature to her fellowmen, or she was unwilling, at least, or unable to bear the pain of expressing her sensitivity to a world which was harsher than she was. She created a world of illusions built not really on hope, which is made of sterner stuff, but on dreams, expectations and longings.

Laura lives in a world of glass, of figurines to whom she speaks but which can neither hear nor answer. She breaks as easily as they. When Jim holds one of the glass animals in his hand, he comments: "Unicorns, aren't they extinct in the modern world?"[222] Soon after, Jim accidentally shatters the glass. Laura gives him the broken pieces as a gift but also as a sign of what reality in the person of Jim has unwittingly done to her.

It is not Laura alone who is adrift in a world of illusion, although she most clearly suffers from this problem. Her father deserted his family looking for something life could not offer. Amanda, her mother, is handicapped by reveries of her lost youth and by groundless hopes for the future. Tom, her brother, goes to the movies compulsively because they have more adventure to them than his drab life permits. Even Jim, the gentleman caller, is captivated by the illusory American dream of success. He tells Laura that his life has not been what he wanted it to be but one day: ". . . Knowledge— Zzzzzp! Money—Zzzzzp!—Power! That's the cycle democracy is built on!"[223]

The Glass Menagerie is so artfully done that one can pay attention only to Laura's world of illusion, overlooking the illusory world of the others in the play and even his own illusory world which Laura dramatically expresses for him.

The ultimate purpose of our concern is theological, more specifically Christological. In the light of this, one wonders whether Christ should reveal to a Christian a life where hope is stronger than illusions, a life in which men pledge themselves, as Christ did, to the preservation of fragile beauty, the affirmation of innocence, and the commandment of compassionate love for one's fellow men. Christ is a Savior because he reveals a new way of living and offers his own life as grace and strength to support this vision and to purify it of all illusions by inspiring men with real hopes.

Christ can only be "an emissary from a world of reality" in a truly saving sense if he is not paralyzed, as we may be, by illusions which make us suppose life to be what it is not. These illusions lead us in the direction of pessimism when they convince us life has no meaning; they lead us in the direction of euphoria when they enchant us with promises different from those life gives. If Christ does not save us from such unreal attitudes, then the perpetuation of Christ may easily become the perpetuation of an illusion.

A *Streetcar Named Desire* is also concerned with illusions, especially those of Blanche. It dramatizes the pathos the death of all illusions instills, particularly in the case of Stella; it portrays the degradation which comes to a man when his illusions are no more inspiring than those of his material comfort and his animal nature as in the case of Stanley. Stanley's vision is limited to a world of sense experience and gratification. The contrast between Blanche and Stanley suggests the flesh-spirit tension which Williams will explore more directly in his later plays.

It is Blanche who holds center stage in the play and becomes one of the most striking characters Williams ever created. She is an anachronism; she knows it, but she will not compromise. She is herself a contradiction, playing for herself and for others the part of the Southern lady she wishes to be but is also caught treacherously in the prison of her own flesh, her economic indigence, her advancing age and her undisciplined sensuality.

When others are present, Blanche is constantly on stage. One suspects she plays this role, not because she is a hypocrite, but because she wants so desperately to believe her dreams that she seeks to convince others in the hope that their belief may reinforce her own. This leads her to admit: "I don't want realism. I want magic."[224] Her opening lines articulate the admixture of passion and dreams of paradise which engulfs her. "They told me to take a street-car named Desire, and then transfer to one called Cemeteries and ride six blocks and get off at Elysian Fields!"[225]

Blanche has been dismissed from her teaching position because of sexual misconduct and has become a scandal to the entire town. As the play begins, she arrives at her sister's home in New Orleans, affirming the spiritual in a manner which approaches angelism. She plays the part of a chaste Southern belle. Her sense of guilt, however, leads her to take baths of excessive length with ludicrous frequency.

Blanche requires more than freedom from guilt. She needs a world worth faith. Reality does not seem to provide such a world. She attempts, therefore, to create such a world by her speech and decorum and by finding someone, like her sister's husband Stanley, whom she can despise. Her effort at illusion is meticulous. She covers all the light bulbs in the apartment with lamp shades which allow a minimum of light and which, therefore, show her up best. She often cries out: "And turn that over-light off! Turn that off! I won't be looked at in this merciless glare!"[226]

Blanche's dreams make her lonely, but she will not give them up; conversely, her loneliness forces her more deeply into her dreams. Like Laura, she seeks a tenderness and a beauty of her own making. Unlike Laura, however, she is not merely a victim but a source of distress to others. When she discovered her husband was a homosexual, she refused to accept him and drove him to suicide. She relates that on the night of her discovery and his death, she told him of her revulsion: ". . . on the dance-floor—unable to stop myself—I'd suddenly said—"I saw! I know! You disgust me. . . ."[227]

Williams later used similar words to express Hannah's

refusal to reject someone whose sexual perversion, in this case fetishism, she encountered. She says in *The Night of the Iguana*: "Nothing human disgusts me unless it's unkind, violent."[228] Hannah is a different kind of idealist from Blanche. Her idealism does not injure; it heals.

Blanche is a weak but fundamentally good person. Her objections to Stanley's almost animal behavior are not unwarranted. Her unwillingness to reach him is more of a problem. Blanche, however, cannot come to terms with the world Stanley represents. She does not want to admit it exists, especially because she sees in Stanley something of herself. Caught between a world of the past and the present, she will not let go of the past and cannot make peace with the present. The end result is her destruction.

Like Laura, she hopes for a savior. Laura needed Jim O'Connor to save her, and he could not. Blanche needs Shep Huntley. He never arrives. There is no gentleman caller to deliver her from evil although she calls and cables, writes and reminisces. She believes that the physician who comes at the end of the play to take her to a mental institution is Shep Huntley, long awaited and at last arrived. When she discovers he is not Shep, she panics. She soon recovers and places herself in the doctor's care. Hoping she will be saved, she speaks the most tragic line of the play: "Whoever you are—I have always depended on the kindness of strangers."[229]

Blanche should not have held on to the past as tightly as she did. She did so because she wanted life at any cost, because the present was so depressing and because reality, if Stanley accurately reflected it, was so demeaning that this could not be called life.

Blanche's illusions were devised for the sake of life. She wanted life to be special so that there would be reason to adhere to a code, preserve a tradition and realize a sense of herself as gracious and pure. Her wish-world became a threat to Stanley because she made him feel less than almighty. In an orgy of violence, he smashes a radio she is listening to, persuades Mitch, Blanche's last hope, not to marry her and sexually assaults her on the evening his own wife is having a baby. By thus hastening her emotional collapse, Stanley proves to himself that his world of self-indulgence is more effective than Blanche's world of dreams and hopes.

Blanche cannot save herself. Nor is there any one to save her. Her inability to save herself derives from her failure to save her husband when he needed her. At that point she stopped believing in salvation. Since human salvation seemed to be the only salvation possible, she became desperate when she could neither communicate nor administer it. Referring to her husband, she comments: ". . . I loved him unendurably but without being able to help him or help myself."[230]

SUMMER AND SMOKE AND
CAT ON A HOT TIN ROOF

Summer and Smoke and *Cat on a Hot Tin Roof* are less concerned with a depiction of the illusions men make than with the reasons which force them to do this. These two plays confront the struggle of flesh and spirit which awaits those who decide to live in the present.

Summer and Smoke is an allegory vested in the simple story of Alma and John. The former is too "spiritual" to be real; the latter is too "material" to be noble. For Alma, the flesh offers no life; for John, the flesh is the only life we have. Eventually, Alma loses control of herself and forsakes the platonic. She fails to harmonize the spirit-flesh equation and meets an unfortunate end. John, on the other hand, softens his sensuality with moral responsibility and personal integrity. He balances the equation and achieves human success. The theme of the play is the reality of salvation which awaits those who forsake neither the transcendent nor the terrestrial in their acceptance of the world.

Alma's affirmation of the spiritual dimension of life is as cold and lifeless as the huge, stone angel around which much of the action of the play takes place. The angel fascinates Alma. Early in the story she reaches into the cold water of the fountain the statue forms to read with her fingers the inscription "Eternity" carved mutely, out of sight, indeed almost out of sense contact. The unreality of this nonmaterial spirituality is symbolized by the inscription and underscored by the quotation from Rilke which Williams cites in the frontispiece: "Who, if I were to cry out, would hear me among the angelic orders?"

The truths *Summer and Smoke* touche upon are truths difficult to prove or to accomplish. They are as elusive as summer or smoke. Yet such truths may be among the most profound and the most painful we must learn. It is less complicated to assert man's senses and ignore his heart, or to consider his ideals and overlook the harsh reality in which he must express them. It is less demanding to believe in God and not man, or to commit oneself to man and not God. Belief in both human and divine life is more creative and salvific. A God who remains God is less a problem than a God who becomes man. Such a God, however, encounters us less forcefully and saves us less effectively than a God whose humanity requires him to save himself as well as us.

Williams subtly suggests that there is a spiritual meaning more significant than those who distrust the material realize. This meaning is tentatively expressed by Alma but more convincingly affirmed by John whose eventual choice of the spiritual does not necessitate a distortion of reality. Alma's observation is nonetheless compelling, almost Chardinian:

How everything reaches up, how everything seems to be straining for something out of the reach of stone—or human—fingers? . . . The immense stained windows, the great arched doors that are five or six times the height of the tallest man—the vaulted ceiling and all the delicate spires—all reaching up to something beyond

attainment! To me—well, that is the secret, the principle back of
existence—the everlasting struggle and aspiration for more than
our human limits have placed in our reach. . . .[231]

Unfortunately, Alma responds to this intimation of the
transcendent by forsaking the real world in which she lives.
John explains this to her. "I'm more afraid of your soul than
you're afraid of my body. You'd have been as safe as the angel
of the fountain—because I wouldn't feel *decent* enough to
touch you. . . ."
Later, he tries to tell her he is happy and why this is so.
"It's best not to ask for too much. . . . I've settled with life
on fairly acceptable terms. Isn't that all a reasonable person
can ask for?"[232]
Since Alma could not do this, she loses touch with herself:
". . . the girl who said 'no,' she doesn't exist any more; she
died last summer—suffocated in smoke from something on
fire inside her."[233]
John is the one who articulates most persuasively the permanence of the spiritual when it is properly defined. Stanley's
triumph over Blanche in A *Streetcar Named Desire* was a
temporary victory, artificially won because Blanche's world
was as unreal as Stanley's. Alma's loss of the spiritual, likewise, is not really a loss of the spiritual but of the spiritualized
spiritual. John comes into possession of a spiritual kingdom
because he did not surrender the city of man. Indeed, he
comes into his inheritance by discovering the spirit not beyond
or above the walls of his own flesh but within them. He tells
Alma that a spirit or soul exists in the machinery of human
anatomy and organic structure.

But I've come around to your way of thinking, that something
else is in there, an immaterial something—as thin as smoke—
which all of those ugly machines combine to produce and that's
their whole reason for being . . . knowing it's there—why then
the whole thing—this—this unfathomable experience of ours—
takes on a new value.[234]

Cat on a Hot Tin Roof is a protest against death and sterility. Its theme is a theme of life, of life which refuses to be reconciled to death. Big Daddy, learning of his terminal cancer, cannot resign himself to death. The theme of life includes the will to create further life. Margaret will not accept Brick's unwillingness to love her physically. She probes for the reason and leads her husband to desire her sexually, not for the sake of sensual gratification, but for the sake of life, the life of their union and the life of the child they ought to have.

The play, as we have said, is a protest against death and sterility. This caused Williams to quote Dylan Thomas, the poet, in the frontispiece:

> Do not go gentle into that good night,
> Rage, rage against the dying of the light!

Big Daddy has a gargantuan desire for life which is as massive as his bulk. The source of his hunger for life is his capacity for love. There are, of course, those he cannot love but, for the most part, he covers his tenderness with bluster. Williams suggests that only in love does one become a force for life. In spite of his faults, Big Daddy is, as his name implies, a father in the fullest sense of that word. His fatherhood is best revealed in his relationship to his son, Brick. In his son, for whose life he is responsible, Big Daddy's love is made manifest.

Williams once wrote that "we come to each other, gradually, but with love."[235] Big Daddy is a bellowing gradualist whose patience is belied by his volume. His task is difficult He knows that Brick cannot live unless someone reaches him. Communication is not easy. "Why is it so damn hard for people to talk?" he demands.[236]

Communication is complicated because each partner in the dialogue brings his own problems to it. Big Daddy fears the truth as much as Brick does. The truth is essential for life, however, even though it sometimes gives life by seeming to take it away.

Williams sees human relationships as indispensable to life and love. He dramatizes in this play the worth of such relationships when they are based on truth. Truth is not symbolized by the cool, isolated, inert moon which Brick stares at so intently in the drama but by the fury and passion, the pain and surprise of a cat on a hot tin roof.

Brick cannot accept the truth about his friend Skipper, the truth of Margaret's love and Big Daddy's need for him, because he has made truth what he wants it to be rather than what it is. He has become, much as Holden Caulfield in *The Catcher in the Rye*, intolerant of ambiguity and evil, impatient with reality and people. Margaret complains to him: ". . . you asked too much of people, of me, of him, of all the unlucky poor damned sons of bitches that happen to love you. . . ."[237]

Big Daddy has Margaret as an ally in their common effort to bring Brick to life. Only in life is there possibility and hope, as Big Daddy sees it. Margaret insists that "my only point, the only point I'm making, is life has got to be allowed to continue even after the *dream* of life is—all—over. . . ."[238]

Cat on a Hot Tin Roof raises urgent questions and implies others. Granted the force for life in us which Margaret especially exemplifies, why do we seek to create? Why is our creation of life distinctly different from that of the animals? Why is it so dependent on our freedom that Brick can refuse to give life if he chooses?

Big Daddy's passion for life is the human heart's passion for life, a passion which turns to nostalgia as man feels his life slip away.

. . . But a man can't buy his life . . . he can't buy back his life . . . when his life has been spent . . . a man can't buy his life . . . he can't buy back his life when his life is finished . . . the human animal . . . buys and buys and buys and I think the reason he

buys everything he can buy is that in the back of his mind he has
the crazy hope that one of his purchases will be life everlasting.[239]

SUDDENLY, LAST SUMMER AND
SWEET BIRD OF YOUTH

If there be life and love in *Cat on a Hot Tin Roof*, there is
little of either in *Suddenly, Last Summer*. The play is a dis-
turbing portrayal of a universe penetrated with evil and
doomed to death. Sebastian Venable suffers a cannibalistic
death because he lives in a carnivorous universe presided over
by a savage God.

There is hardly a glimmer of hope in *Suddenly, Last Summer* except perhaps the possibility that the ritualistic destruction of Sebastian and his sacrificial compensation for evil
brings some order into the chaotic world he created.

The two main forces in the play never appear on stage.
The first of these in Sebastian Venable, a homosexual, who
uses his aging mother and later his girl friend, Catherine, to
solicit young men for himself. Sebastian is brutally murdered
by those he sexually exploits. He runs up a steep hill, is
exhausted by the effort and is killed on the top of the hill.
The murder takes place in the burning afternoon sun. His
flesh is torn and then eaten by his executioners.

Catherine witnesses this horror and admits "it's a hideous
story" but feels compelled to repeat it because "it's a true
story of our time and the world we live in. . . ."[240] Mrs.
Venable, Sebastian's mother, who was unaware of how her
son was using her, insists that a surgeon "cut this hideous
story out of her brain."[241] She seeks to save her son's reputa-
tion by sacrificing Catherine. Since the surgeon needs money
for his research and since Catherine is emotionally distraught
from her experience, there is every reason to believe the
lobotomy will be performed. In a more refined and sophisticated manner, cannibalism will occur a second time.

The second force in the play is the terrifying universe to which Sebastian sacrifices himself. There has seldom been a literary work which portrays more graphically the presence of evil in our lives. Even the stage directions for Scene One, a jungle-garden in the home of Mrs. Venable, set the mood for what is to follow:

The colors of the jungle-garden are violent. . . . There are massive tree-flowers that suggest organs of a body, torn out, still glistening with undried blood; there are harsh cries and sibilant hissings and thrashing sounds in the garden as if it were inhabited by beasts, serpents, and birds, all of a savage nature. . . .[242]

The cruelty of the universe is a reflection of the cruelty of God who set it in motion and demands savage sacrifice as the price one pays for life. In a startling image, Mrs. Venable describes what Sebastian discovered on his last trip with her before his death.

And the sand all alive, as the hatched sea-turtles made their dash for the sea, while the birds hovered and swooped to attack! They were diving down on hatched sea-turtles, turning them over to expose their soft undersides, tearing the undersides open and rending and eating their flesh . . . my son *was* looking for God, I mean for a clear image of him . . . he said, 'Well now I've seen Him,' and he meant God. . . . He meant that God shows a savage face to people and shouts some fierce things at them, it's all we see or hear of Him. . . .[243]

The following summer Sebastian is obsessed with his notion of God and with his conviction that he must be sacrificed to it. Catherine explains that she could not keep him from "completing—a sort of!—image!—he had of himself as a sort of!—*sacrifice* to a!—terrible sort of a . . . *cruel* (God)."[244] Catherine remembers the summer well because "suddenly, last summer, he wasn't young any more. . . ."[245]

It is not only the fate Sebastian suffers but the realization that she was helpless to save him which terrifies Catherine.

In such a world salvation is unattainable. Love happens but
not enough love to preclude Sebastian's murder. The one
hope for salvation may have been God. But God wears a
"savage face" and shouts "fierce things." This God cannot
save and has no intention of saving. Since God cannot help
us, we cannot help ourselves. If God be cruel, then life is
taken from us and in its absence love dies. "I loved him. . . .
Why wouldn't he let me save him? I tried to hold onto his
hand, but he struck me away and ran, ran, ran, in the wrong
direction."[246]

Sweet Bird of Youth considers corruption in a different
manner. It depicts the corruption of the human heart by age
and compromise rather than in the violent turbulence of *Suddenly, Last Summer*. It also differs from the former play in
the hope it offers.

Sweet Bird of Youth opens on Easter morning, with church
bells pealing, an Alleluia chorus, and the possibility of rebirth
which such a setting suggests. Chance Wayne is a symbol of
innocence lost. Since he trusted so much in time, he feels
hopeless when time takes its toll. "I couldn't go past my
youth," he confesses, "but I've gone past it."[247] Earlier, the
Princess had told him the same thing: "your time, your youth,
you've passed it. It's all you had, and you've had it."[248]
Chance's mistake is not a total absence of hope but its tragic
misplacement. He wanted to beat time. Since he could not
hope in anything more than beating time, he is defeated by
time. "Something's got to mean something, don't it Princess?
I mean like your life means nothing, except that you never
could make it, always, almost, never quite? Well, something's
still got to mean something."[249]

The meaning of life cannot be limited to youth, however.
Life itself matters more than one's age. The Princess longs
for life as ardently as Big Daddy in *Cat on a Hot Tin Roof*:
"It's life that I wish for, terribly, shamelessly, on any terms

whatsoever."[250] The Princess faces what Chance had to face: "I just wasn't young, not young, young. I just wasn't young anymore. . . ."[251] Her answer is not despair but a more profound search. "Well, sooner or later, at some point in your life, the thing you lived for is lost or abandoned, and then . . . you die, or find something else."[252]

Chance chooses to die, but the Princess affirms life and in the affirmation discovers the possibility of rebirth. In Christian theology Christ's choice of life even in death assures his resurrection. There is no point to rebirth for those who do not take seriously the consequences of their birth; there is no new life for those who refuse the life they have. Salvation is a process in which life continues because life was cherished. Salvation, unlike creation, is not the emergence of something from nothing. It is the reconstitution and reenforcement of something greater from something that already was.

Williams states explicitly that he sought to communicate a significant message in this play. "There is something much bigger in life and death than we become aware of . . . in our living and dying. . . . I would say that our serious theatre is a search for that something."[253]

The message of *Sweet Bird of Youth* is a promise of life, limited to those who always wanted life and to those who know that life is not life unless it leads us to love the life of others as well as our own. "That's the wonderful thing that happened to me. I felt something for someone besides myself. That means my heart's still alive, at least some part of it is. . . ."[254]

The "wonderful thing" we call Easter means more than the fact that Christ was alive. It means that the type of love for which his life was given prevailed. Salvation is not offered so that we might survive death but so that we might survive death in a certain way. Unless one has freely chosen life and freely loved, he has neither life nor love nor freedom to save.

THE NIGHT OF THE IGUANA

The Night of the Iguana is a synthesis of many Williams' themes with the first faint suggestion of a beneficent transcendence. It is a story of man's search for God and of the inadequacy of the substitute faith he prefers to belief in God. True faith is linked with "faith in essential . . . human . . . goodness!"[255] Yet this play seeks other aspects of faith, aspects which touch upon the mystery of God.

The Night of the Iguana is a relatively serene play. It has none of the anxiety of *Suddenly, Last Summer*. Its serenity is due, in part, to the type of universe it discovers.

Shannon, a dismissed cleric, now a tour guide, brings his party to a hotel managed by his friend Maxine. The guests at the hotel are in a desperate spiritual situation, except for Hannah whose destitution is only financial, and Nonno whose only infirmity is age. There is a minimum of action in the play. The drama occurs largely in dialogue, and most of the dialogue occurs between Shannon and Hannah.

Strapped into a hammock for his own safety, Shannon, verging on emotional collapse, is urged by Hannah not to choose the easier way. His problem is not suffering but lack of faith. He would like his life to be an atonement, but atonement requires faith more than suffering. "Who wouldn't like to suffer and atone for the sins of himself and the world if it could be done in a hammock with ropes instead of nails, on a hill that's so much lovelier than Golgotha, the Place of the Skull. . . ."[256]

Shannon must suffer more than this. He must suffer in faith and for faith, or else his suffering will be less redemptive for others and less creative for himself. Since suffering meant more to him than faith, he railed and screamed at his congregation the morning when their accusing faces revealed their awareness of his sexual misconduct. Hannah tells him he never noticed the faith in the "few old, very old faces,

looking up at you, as you begin your sermon, with eyes like
a piercing cry for something to still look up to, something
to still believe in."[257] Since Shannon's faith was confused,
he was more sensitive to his embarrassment and his congregation's indictment than he was of his responsibility in
faith to them..

HANNAH: Liquor isn't your problem, Mr. Shannon.
    SHANNON: What is my problem, Miss Jelkes?
    HANNAH: The oldest one in the world—the need to believe in
something or in someone—almost anyone—almost anything . . .
something.[258]

    Hannah, a portrait painter, has learned that belief in people
led her to some tentative affirmation of God.

HANNAH: I was . . . far from sure about God.
    SHANNON: You're still unsure about him?
    HANNAH: Not as unsure as I was. You see, in my profession I have
to look hard and close at human faces. . . .[259]

Hannah has come to believe in people so deeply that she
will not allow even their perversions or fetishisms to turn her
from them. "Nothing human disgusts me," she tells Shannon,
"unless it's unkind, violent."
    As Shannon and Hannah converse, they hear the scratching
of a lizard, an iguana, tied up for later use and struggling to
be free. Shannon decides to let it go "so that one of God's
creatures could scramble home safe and free . . . a little act of
grace."[260] He has become concerned with suffering other
than his own. It is not much, but it is a beginning.
    When the play opens, Shannon could not care about the
discomfort of his tour party whom he misled and cheated,
offended and, finally, forced to come to the hotel he wanted
to stay at even though they did not wish to do so. He steals
the key to the bus, insensitive to their reluctance to have a
vacation they have saved years to finance ruined. Now, later,

he is able to perform an "act of grace" for a tormented and bewildered creature. His conversion has begun.

As Hannah declares her faith and elicits the beginnings of faith in Shannon, Nonno dies. The closing words of the play are a plea for peace but also an expression of the peace that Hannah has found in the faith she keeps and communicates. "Oh, God, can't we stop now? Finally? Please let us. It's so quiet here, now."[261]

The Night of the Iguana has the tranquility of a prayer answered, a faith affirmed, a way discovered, leading not only out but up. Nonno, after an immense effort draining all his remaining physical and emotional strength, creates his last poem moments before he dies. Its final words beg Something beyond men to come to us with saving courage and dwell in our hearts.

> O Courage, could you not as well
> Select a second place to dwell,
> Not only in that golden tree
> But in the frightened heart of me?[262]

CONCLUSION

The plays of Tennessee Williams proceed from illusions to faith. *The Glass Menagerie* and *A Streetcar Named Desire* are filled with visions of what life could be, but their continuance requires a denial of life for the sake of glass figurines or impossible hopes. *Summer and Smoke* makes it clear that life occurs not in fantasy but in the flesh. It considers the spiritual dimensions of life in an incarnational rather than a Gnostic manner. *Cat on a Hot Tin Roof* builds its hope for life on life. It does not allow impossible burdens to be placed on human relationships or on the truth that must exist between people.

The world in which human relationships occur seems at times to be presided over by a savage God (*Suddenly, Last*

Summer) who gives no grace. At times this world tends to corrupt the innocent by the relentless destruction of their youth and ideals (*Sweet Bird of Youth*). Even granted this pessimism, rebirth is a possibility for those who remain faithful to life, to all life, to life at any cost.

Williams eventually considers faith in God. Such faith is given to those whose illusions are not the illusions which destroy life. It is a gift for those who accept their bodies as well as their hearts, human frailty as well as human love. It is a grace granted to those who believe in a saving God, a God who promises rebirth as long as nothing human disgusts us, and as long as we hold on to, or at least pray for, courage.

William Faulkner

William Faulkner may well be the most profound and the most religious writer our culture has produced. Few writers equal his power of allowing one to experience what he is reading; few artists reach more deeply into the substance of the human heart. When Faulkner accepted the 1950 Nobel Prize, he observed that literature must address itself to the "problems of the human heart in conflict with itself which alone make good writing because only that is worth writing about."

On the surface, Faulkner seems to be a writer whose work is a poetic elaboration of the "legend" of the South. In its essence, however, Faulkner's work explores the purpose of man's tenure on earth. His writing raises crucial questions. What is virtue? How do we deal with evil? Can we overcome the betrayal of our past? Will men learn compassion in deprivation and suffering?

The geographical vantage point from which Faulkner considers the problems of the human heart is the mythical county of Yoknapatawpha. It is an area where there once dwelt the Chickasaw chief Ikkemotubbe whose name in his own language means "The Man." It is an unfortunate kingdom where nature was despoiled and where men made slaves of other men. Because of this, there is a curse on the land of Yoknapatawpha and upon its inhabitants. In an observation which reminds one of the Christian doctrine of original sin, Quentin Compson declares: "There's a curse on us. It's not our fault."

Because of the way men behaved, evil was intensified and Flem Snopes achieved a position of malignant influence in Yoknapatawpha. Snopes is a Satanic figure, a symbol of rational materialism, and of the dehumanization of the modern world. Those who live in this territory, once a paradise, are men who inherit a guilt-ridden past which always rises up to defeat them. They are men trapped between an oppressive past and unattainable future. They are subjects of the curse of an original sin but not yet inheritors of redemption or freedom. In this world after the Fall and before the Atonement, Tommy is murdered, Goodwin burnt alive, Joe Christmas mutilated, Benjy castrated, Nancy devoured by vultures at the bottom of a ditch.

In the world described by William Faulkner no one has a future. Men are turned to the past and become victims who suffer far more than their misdeeds justify. Popeye, impotent and syphilitic, Sutpen, who tried to establish a dynasty only to meet murder and to have his mansion burned to the ground, Quentin, psychotic and eventually suicidal, are penalized far beyond the evil of their actions. They are punished because there is a curse upon them and no hope for a Redeemer. There is no future strong enough to deliver men from the guilt of their past.

Faulkner's writings are dominated by an awareness of guilt. No one can say exactly with whom the guilt began or where the decisive crimes were committed. All realize, however, that the guilt men bear arises not only from the evil of their own hearts but more precisely from their complicity in human history. Men inherit and then intensify the evil they never escape. Like Ingmar Bergman, Faulkner believes in original sin more passionately than he believes in divine love.

In spite of this, there is more than total darkness in Faulkner's world. Men are stronger than they think. Byron Bunch observes in *Light in August:* "I can bear a hill, a man can. It seems like a man can just about bear anything. He can even bear what he never done. He can even bear the thinking how some things is just more than he can bear." A type of salvation is possible, but it is reserved for those who participate. The human enterprise is a risk forever undertaken, an experience in which the true measure of greatness is not success but exposure.

Faulkner offers a glimmer of hope by setting some of his stories in a Christological framework, often during Easter week. *As I Lay Dying* describes a journey to Jefferson, the county seat of Yoknapatawpha where, as in Jerusalem, a mission is accomplished and a measure of peace is imparted. The crucifixion dominates the narration of Joe Christmas' murder. Christmas dies because he sets his face to Jefferson, returning freely to meet a fate he could have avoided.

A Fable is a retelling of the story of Christ in terms of a French corporal who tries to end a war by convincing men they are brothers who need not kill one another. Set in Easter week, *A Fable* describes the last supper, trial, innocence, execution, and subsequent "resurrection" of a soldier of peace whose twelve disciples seek to spread his message even though one in their number was a traitor.

Easter week is again the setting for Faulkner's masterpiece. *The Sound and the Fury,* which begins on Holy Saturday, shifts to Good Friday and reaches its conclusion on Easter Sunday when Dilsey weeps as a preacher reminds his congregation that Jesus is risen, salvation is possible and that no death comes to those who believe.

In effect, Faulkner envisions modern man as guilt-ridden, determined by his past, unsure of his future. There would be more of a future to hope in if men could believe in their salvation. With such a past, however, belief is difficult, almost impossible. Nancy in *Requiem for a Nun* speaks on behalf of modern man when she says: "Maybe what I need is to have to meet somebody. To believe. Not in anything; just to believe."

SANCTUARY AND ABSALOM, ABSALOM!

Sanctuary and *Absalom, Absalom!* deal with violation and subsequent destruction. In the former case, the violation is sexual; in the latter, it is racial. In both cases, death follows upon the respective desecration. In the former case, the violation is truly a violation. Temple Drake is sexually misused in a perverted and brutal manner. In the latter case, there is no real violation except in terms of those social conventions which choose to regard miscegenation as evil.

In the former case, Temple is violated by Popeye who is impotent, unable to love sexually, unwilling to love spiritually. In the latter case, Thomas Sutpen's efforts at building a dynasty collapse because he cannot love enough to accept his own family across racial lines. Temple Drake eventually accepts her violation and ratifies it by her subsequent lack of love. Thomas Sutpen never accepts the "violation" of his son's Negro blood which, since it is no violation, can only be viewed as such when men are blind to love.

Sanctuary is perhaps the most depressing story Faulkner ever told. Even *The Sound and the Fury* which described the disintegration of the Compson family ended with an Easter sermon and the endurance of Dilsey. Joe Christmas in *Light in August* dies brutally, but his death reveals the darkness in the hearts of men and, in this manner, accomplishes something. In *As I Lay Dying*, a family fulfills a promise, even though it may be for the wrong reasons.

Sanctuary, however, offers no hope. It does not mediate even a minimal meaning. Temple, the name is significant, is violated. Her only sanctuary is a brothel. Tommy, trying to protect Temple, is murdered. Goodwin, convicted on the false testimony of Temple, is burned by a lynching mob. Popeye, the sexually impotent, tormented, syphilitic figure, is sent to his death for a murder different from the one he performed. The innocent and evil die in a world where justice is lacking and where disorder prevails.

In *Sanctuary* nothing is right. Life is reduced to raw violence, senseless destruction, nihilism. Popeye gains a sense of life by destroying it. His fear of animals, his readiness to kill any man, his impotence manifest his total alienation from the mystery of life. Temple is fascinated with Popeye rather than with those whose innocence she once shared but whose innocence she no longer desires.

Sanctuary describes a cultural moment of madness when men are indifferent to their past, unconcerned about their future and irresponsible in the present. It is a moment when life no longer happens because men prefer death. Popeye cannot give life; nor can Temple offer life as a result of the perverted action she provokes and accepts. Temple finds sanctuary in a brothel which, since it is no sanctuary, denotes the absence of sanctuary, the loss of the sacred, and the impossibility of salvation in our modern age.

OF HUMAN DYNASTIES AND
UNFORGIVEN SINS

The theme of death and sterility occurs again in *Absalom, Absalom!* The opening lines of the novel set the mood. Miss Rosa Coldfield sits "in the eternal black" she had worn for many years and speaks to Quentin Compson of the rise and fall of Thomas Sutpen. She tells her story during a "long still hot weary dead September afternoon" in a "dim hot airless room with the blinds all closed and fastened for forty-three summers."[263]

Colonel Thomas Sutpen had dreamed of founding a dynasty. Miss Coldfield refers to him as "demon" who arrives in Jefferson one day with a horse and two pistols. No one knows anything of his past, but he soon builds a mansion on a large piece of land known as "Sutpen's Hundred." He marries a girl, Ellen Coldfield, by whom he has two children, Henry and Judith.

Sutpen is a calculating man who, filled with pride, has a "design" for living. He had married a girl before he married Ellen Coldfield. He deserted her, however, when he learned she had Negro blood and was, therefore, "unsuitable to his purpose." The son of this first union, Charles Bon, yearning for identity and his father, is refused both. Charles does not fit the "design" Sutpen has for the future.

Quentin Compson is the figure in this novel who wants most earnestly to uncover the story of Thomas Sutpen. He listens patiently to the story as it is related by different people implicated in the tragedy. Painstakingly, he adjusts mistakes, completes fragments, restores perspective, and, finally, discovers the whole truth. Quentin actually seeks in the rise and fall of Thomas Sutpen a knowledge of human history itself.

It is Sutpen's initial crime which dooms his progeny. This crime is rooted in a pride so monumental that it will not allow love or people to interfere with the design it envisions. At that moment when Sutpen seems to have achieved his destiny, his past intrudes upon him and undoes his work.

Suddenly Charles Bon comes to "Sutpen's Hundred." Charles, Sutpen's unrecognized son, is a college friend of Henry, Sutpen's recognized son. Charles intends to marry Judith, his half sister. This incestuous relationship would not have been considered had Colonel Sutpen received Charles Bon as his son from the beginning. Sutpen will not do this because he considers Charles to be "violated" with Negro blood.

Sutpen rules his life by reason. He is incapable of an act of faith in his son Charles as he was once incapable of an act of love toward his first wife once he realized she was Negro. Sutpen premises faith and love on his "design" rather than on brotherhood across racial barriers.

Henry, unable to bear the fact that Charles will "violate" Judith with Negro blood kills his own brother and announces the fact to Judith on the eve of her wedding. This fratricide also derives from Sutpen's primordial crime. Sutpen kept from his second son, Henry, the truth of his former life and by so doing left Henry no way to atone for the sinfulness of his father's past.

Henry, bearing the burden of his father's sins as well as the guilt of his own racial prejudice, murders his brother and destroys his sister by emotional trauma, announcing to her in her moment of happiness that he has just killed Charles.

"Now you can't marry him."
  "Why can't I marry him?"
  "Because he's dead."
  "Dead?"
  "Yes. I killed him."[264]

The tragedy of that moment is later described in greater detail.

. . . the sister facing him across the wedding dress which she was not to use, not even to finish, the two of them slashing at one another with twelve or fourteen words and most of these the same words repeated two or three times so that when you boiled it down they did it with eight or ten.[265]

In another version of the event, we are told that:

. . . Judith with just time to snatch up the unfinished dress and hold it before her as the door burst open upon her brother, the wild murderer whom she had not seen in four years and whom she believed to be . . . a thousand miles away; and then the two of them, the two accursed children on whom the first blow of their devil's heritage had but that moment fallen, looking at one another across the upraised and unfinished wedding dress.[266]

Thomas Sutpen's story is the story of man's fall from grace. "Sutpen's Hundred" began as a new Eden. Indeed, the beginning of the plantation is described in terms reminiscent of Genesis. Colonel Sutpen is portrayed as "creating the Sutpen's Hundred, the 'Be Sutpen's Hundred' like the oldtime 'Be Light.' "[267] The newness and innocence of this creation is violated by a crime against love for the sake of a prideful intent. People matter less than the building of this latter-day tower of babel.

Since Sutpen fails to love responsibly, he, the primal father, sets his children one against the other until Cain kills Abel once again. The evil which began with Sutpen is so complicated by the time his children come of age that "Sutpen's Hundred" is burned to the ground and the earth left barren.

As Quentin Compson uncovers the story of Thomas Sutpen, he discovers the story of the South which is burdened with the curse of its racial sins. He gains an insight, furthermore, into the story of man whose past mediates a guilt he cannot come to terms with unless he finds the proper Savior. In the biblical story, David weeps for his dead son Absalom, wishing that he might have died and Absalom live. In Sutpen's history, his son, Charles Bon, is not loved but forsaken. Sutpen wishes to replace his son, not like David so that his son might live, but so that he might be no more.

The refusal of Thomas Sutpen to recognize something of himself in the Negro blood of his son leads to the ultimate demise of the dynasty. Colonel Sutpen pretended he was not guilty, surmising his blood was free of what he thought was a curse. If Negro blood were a sign of guilt, then Sutpen had to recognize his guilt in that guilt. But Negro blood was, of course, no guilt at all except for those who devised a limited definition of reality and of man.

In the kingdom of Sutpen all the demonic fury and evil of lies and deception, of murder and rejection are unleashed. "Sutpen's Hundred" might have been paradise had Thomas Sutpen not sinned. Instead, "Sutpen's Hundred" was transformed into hell.

Those who lived on "Sutpen's Hundred" might have been saved had they had faith in one another and in their common destiny. Instead, they believed in prejudice and injustice, in their own schemes and their own plans. A series of tragedies results. Charles is murdered by his brother; Elihu Coldfield starves himself to death. Colonel Sutpen is killed by Wash Jones who also kills his fifteen-year-old granddaughter and the nameless baby she bore as Sutpen tried desperately to found a dynasty in the approaching collapse of "Sutpen's Hundred." When Wash Jones is pursued, he defiantly flings himself into death by running into instead of away from the guns and lanterns of his executioners. The inferno "Sutpen's Hundred" has become is complete when Henry, Sutpen's legitimate son, and Clytemnestra, his illegitimate daughter, perish in the fire which burns the mansion to the ground.

The story ends in fire as it had once begun in glory. In this fire, a ritualistic purgation for all the sins of Colonel Sutpen and his progeny is achieved. It is a purgation which leads, however, to the destruction of man together with his guilt. Had a different situation been possible, guilt might have died and Sutpen might have lived.

AS I LAY DYING

On the surface, As I Lay Dying is a simple story. It tell of Addie Bundren who dies while her son saws her coffin beneath

her window. It details the journey her family takes through
the back roads of Yoknapatawpha to redeem a promise they
had made to bury her in far-distant Jefferson. On the surface,
it is a simple story. In its essence, the journey described in
the book is a journey to redemption.

William Faulkner employs an artful technique in writing
this novel. The significance of the journey is described by
fifteen distinct characters who speak on sixty different
occasions. No one tells the whole story and no one is completely objective. The result is an epistemology implied in
presenting truth, not as an objectively discernible phenomenon, but as a subjective experience which fifteen people speak,
sense, feel and think. A further result of this technique is a
literary experience in which one participates in the drama of a
journey as it is lived by those for whom the journey has a
meaning. Faulkner suggests that human truth is not perceived
in objective data but in the subjective perception of an
experience in which one is involved and for which one has
sacrificed something.

More germane to our purposes, however, is not the implied
epistemology nor the literary experience but the insight into
life which the book provides. This insight is involved with the
personalities who make the journey as well as with the themes
which emerge as the journey continues.

Perhaps the most significant personality in the novel is
Darl. He speaks most frequently and serves as the sensitive,
identity-seeking individual with whom Faulkner is preoccupied. Critics have called Darl a Christ figure although he
possesses characteristics which militate against this attribution.
Like Benjy in *The Sound and the Fury*, Darl is instinctively
aware of truth he has not been given the opportunity to learn
in the usual manner. He has access to this prerogative because,
as Cora explains, he was "touched by God Himself": "When
the only sin she ever committed was being partial to Jewel that
never loved her and was its own punishment, in preference to

Darl that was touched by God Himself and considered queer by us mortals that did love her."[268]

Darl knows instinctively that his mother will die.

It was then, and then I saw Darl and he knew. He said he knew without the words like he told me that ma is going to die without the words, and I knew he knew because if he had said he knew with the words I would not have believed that he had been there and saw us. But he said he did know and I said 'Are you going to tell pa are you going to kill him? without the words I said it and he said Why?' without the words. . . .

"She is going to die," he says. . . .
"When is she going to die?" I say.
"Before we get back," he says.[269]

Darl is also intuitively aware that the father of his brother Jewel is not his mother's husband. "Jewel," I say, "whose son are you? . . . who was your father, Jewel . . . Jewel, I say, who was your father, Jewel?"[270]

Darl senses that his unmarried sister, Dewey Dell, is pregnant, even though no one else knows this. "And then I knew that I knew. I knew that as plain on that day as I knew about Dewey Dell on that day."[271]

Tull tells us that Darl read the hearts of others. "I always say it ain't never been what he done so much or said or anything so much as how he looks at you. It's like he had got into the inside of you, someway. Like somehow you was looking at yourself and your doings outen his eyes."[272]

Darl is convinced that one must not live life on safe grounds doing conventional things, but that one must be daring. In an introspective moment, he reflects: ". . . safe things are just the things that folks have been doing so long they have worn the edges off and there's nothing to the doing of them that leaves a man to say, That was not done before, and it cannot be done again."[273]

The designation of Darl as a Christ figure is due, no doubt, to those elements in his life which we have described. We are reminded in the closing words of the novel that "This world is not [Darl's] world; this life, his life."[274]

If Darl's intuitive knowledge reminds us of Benjy, his sensitive identity crisis recalls Quentin Compson in *The Sound and the Fury*. Like Quentin, Darl is too aware, and because of this cannot emerge as an harmonious personality. He is, like Quentin, a flittering consciousness with no substantial core of self-integration. Darl is contemplative, certainly kind, but ultimately schizoid. Sensing he is losing a grip on himself, he protests:

I don't know what I am; I don't know if I am or not. Jewel knows he is, because he does not know that he does not know whether he is or not. . . . I must be, or I could not empty myself for sleep in a strange room. And so if I am not emptied yet, I am is.[275]

Darl is a key figure in *As I Lay Dying*, speaking more often and appearing more frequently than anyone else. Faulkner was trying to say something significant through him.

In *The Sound and The Fury*, Benjy is a Christ figure who is impotent and helpless before the forces of disintegration. He is attuned to goodness but incapable of effecting its outcome. Quentin Compson, in the same novel, represents modern man in anguish and anxiety, a man whose identity is incomprehensible, whose need for innocence is frustrated, whose ultimate destiny is some form of self-destruction. Darl in *As I Lay Dying* is a combination of Benjy and Quentin. He is reminiscent of Christ and of modern man. He is intuitive, as Benjy, but also inquisitive as Quentin. The pressure is too much, and Darl loses touch with himself. He sets fire to a barn intending the burning of his mother's body, lapses into schizophrenia and is institutionalized. Darl is not an impotent Christ but a tormented Christ, someone whose essential goodness is distorted and undone by self-doubt and mistaken identity. Darl is a man who might have had a mission could he have settled in some reasonable way the problem of his own self-definition.

REALISM AND REDEMPTIVE SACRIFICE

Cash is the opposite of his brother Darl. He is logical, consistent, clear, matter-of-fact. He has solved the riddle of existence for himself. Cash is the realist who sees what must be done, proceeds to do it, and worries little about its ultimate meaning or its place in the schemes of things. It is Cash who builds a coffin and suffers a broken leg with no complaint. There is no sentiment in Cash, no romanticism, no idealism. His mother is dying, and a coffin must be built. So he builds it. In fact, he builds it in the most pragmatic manner possible. Cora describes why Addie, Cash's mother, watched her son carefully as he built her coffin:

Lying there with her head propped up so she could watch Cash building the coffin, having to watch him so he would not skimp on it, like as not, with those men not worrying about anything except if there was time to earn another three dollars before the rain come. . . .[276]

Cash's constant affirmation of the "real" allows him to become more effective than Darl. He is the one who does build the coffin; the one who does not slow down the journey even when his leg becomes inflamed with pain and infection; the one who tries to understand Darl although he sets fire to the barn. "Sometimes I ain't so sho who's got ere a right to say when a man is crazy and when he ain't. . . . It's like it ain't so much what a fellow does, but it's the way the majority of folks is looking at him when he does it."[277]

Cash finds his identity in his relationship to others rather than in convoluted self-appraisal. He is the only one who appreciates Darl. In a moment of crisis, he reaches out to another human being, his brother, quietly, gently, and in typical fashion, realistically.

If *As I Lay Dying* can be compared to a latter-day *Pilgrim's Progress*, one can see a need for Darl as well as for Cash in the cycle of man's living and dying. Darl is often too self-preoccupied to become a saving sign for others, even though his contemplative and intuitive approach to life is essential. Cash is able to place his talent and understanding at the disposal of others. In this, he is a more effective saving presence than Darl.

It is Jewel, however, who sacrifices *himself* and whose sacrifice becomes responsible for the fulfillment of the family's mission. Jewel's life is a realization of a prophecy made by his mother: "He is my cross and he will be my salvation. He will save me from the water and the fire. Even though I have laid down my life, he will save me."[278]

One must read *As I Lay Dying* to know how much Jewel identified himself with the horse he owned. He is so much attached to the horse that Darl declares: "Your mother was a horse. . . ."[279] Vardaman also observes: "But Jewel's mother is a horse."[280] When Jewel parts with his horse in order to secure Addie's burial, he rises to the heights of love. He does more than this. He saves Addie's body from the turbulent river which almost washes the coffin downstream. It is Jewel who runs into the burning barn and topples the coffin, end over end, to safety with "sparks raining on him" so that "he appears to be enclosed in a thin nimbus of fire."[281]

Jewel is not as self-preoccupied as Darl. Nor does he have existence figured out as completely as Cash does. He is capable of the soaring idealism of Darl and of the pragmatic decisiveness of Cash. At the proper moment, he is able to sacrifice everything. Jewel alone meets the challenge of the journey with a redemptive sacrifice. Three times he offers his life on behalf of others. He surrenders his horse, and later risks death in the raging river and burning barn. This sacrifice saves the family and Addie Bundren.

There is hardly a critic who does not find a Christ figure in

As I Lay Dying. Most identify Darl as the Christ figure. For the reasons given above, Jewel seems the more likely embodiment of those saving values which characterized Christ's life.

There are other personalities in *As I Lay Dying*, but the meaning of this novel is summed up most effectively in the three brothers Darl, Cash and Jewel. There is Vardaman, the very young boy in the family who searches for ways to deny his mother is dead. He bores holes in the coffin to let her breathe and claims that his mother lives on as a fish, an obvious Christian and resurrection symbol. There is Addie Bundren who elicits a promise from her husband that he will bury her in Jefferson. There is Dewey Dell, the girl in the family, who is completely absorbed in her own problems and uninterested in the significance of the journey. Dewey Dell, insensitive to the life she bears in her body, tries repeatedly to have an abortion.

In its ultimate meaning, *As I Lay Dying* is an elemental journey, a journey concerned with life and death. It describes a quest that must continue despite deluge and flood, water or fire. The journey of the Bundrens, like the journey of the Joads in *The Grapes of Wrath*, is the journey of man. It is a journey marked by selfishness (Dewey Dell), confusion (Darl), realism (Cash), sacrifice (Jewel). The journey is ritualized by the need to honor the recently dead, the urgency of keeping the promises one makes, the search for far-off Jefferson so that peace might be granted the dead who wished to be buried there.

Only in the context of ritual and promise, of quest and commitment does the journey of the Bundrens take on significance. Although Anse, Addie's husband, is not an admirable figure, he grasps the meaning of the journey. "I gave her my word. . . . It is sacred on me."[282] When Tull, a neighbor, tells Anse to postpone or at least delay the journey so as not to risk "the fire and the earth and the water," Anse repeats: "I give my promise. . . . She is counting on it."[283]

The journey is accomplished. In pragmatic terms, it makes no sense. Yet one perceives its significance in the scale of higher values. There is a salvation theme in the story, a salvation achieved in the strength of Jewel's love and sacrifice. If this salvation import may seem unimportant to some modern men, it may be due in part to what Addie understood when she observed that "people to whom sin is just a matter of words, to them salvation is just words, too."[284]

THE SOUND AND THE FURY

In the midst of the greenness of the April, on the day between the crucifixion of Jesus and the remembrance of his resurrection, thirty-three-year-old Benjy Compson recalls his sister Caddy, her innocence, and the sin which separated them. Benjy is mentally defective, castrated by his brother Jason, loved only by Caddy whom he lost and by Dilsey the Negro servant who brings him to church on Easter Sunday morning.

The Sound and the Fury is a story of the decline of the Compson family. It is told in four sections: first, by the idiot Benjy who forces us to grope for fragments as his undisciplined mind recalls events apart from their relationship to one another; secondly, by Quentin, the tormented brother of Benjy who went to Harvard and committed suicide there in June, delaying until June so that he might complete the academic year and thus get the full value of his paid-in-advance tuition; thirdly, by Jason who symbolizes evil and rejoices when others are punished; last of all, by Dilsey who lives by faith, who trusts in the rightness of things and who alone endures.

The Sound and the Fury tells how the Compson family came no longer to be. In the telling, however, Faulkner puts us into contact with the fall of the South and the confusion of modern man. The three Compson brothers are deeply influenced by their sister Caddy, a symbol of the South. Benjy knows he loved Caddy and was loved by her until that day when Caddy lost her innocence. Then, Benjy remembered only the loss of Caddy and the suffering this absence caused. Quentin loved in Caddy some concept of honor, as Faulkner himself tells us. When Caddy becomes pregnant outside of marriage, Quentin, no longer able to tolerate a world without honor, ends his life. Jason is most happy when he torments his sister Caddy and, later, when Caddy is dismissed from the house, Caddy's daughter. Had Caddy been faithful, Benjy would not have suffered, Quentin would have lived and Jason might not have despaired.

The Sound and The Fury is a highly complex novel, one perhaps best interpreted by a consideration of symbols (clocks and water), themes (order), and persons (Benjy, Quentin, Jason, Dilsey). The story line is simple, but it tells us little of what *The Sound and the Fury* seeks to say. It is not *what* happens to the Compsons which matters but *why* it happened and *how* it has affected them. *What* happens is quickly recounted. Caddy loses her virginity; Benjy is born an idiot; Quentin goes to Harvard and commits suicide; Jason becomes a clerk, plays the stock market, lives for revenge, and hates his fellowmen; Dilsey goes about her tasks, tries to keep the family at peace, affirms faith and hopes. The significance of this enormously significant novel is expressed not in the narrative but in symbols, themes and persons.

THE PROBLEM OF TIME

The symbol of clocks and the theme of time predominates in *The Sound and the Fury*. In the four sections into which the novel is divided, various reactions to time are recorded.

For Benjy, time simply is. There is no future, but there is a present which is indistinguishable from the past. He is not burdened by a past for which he feels guilty nor depressed by a future which holds no further promise. He knows neither

sin (past) nor despair (future). He lives in the present, react-
ing to it as it is given to him correlating it neither to significant
memories nor distant hopes. Benjy is the present, unadulter-
ated and unadorned. The present, divorced from the past and
unrelated to the future, has little meaning. It is true that
Benjy remembers Caddy, but it is less a memory of what she
was than a present sense of loss which characterizes his awareness of her. This may be why Faulkner commented in an
appendix to *The Sound and the Fury* written years after the
book was originally published that Benjy "could not remember
his sister but only the loss of her"[285] and, on another occasion,
that Benjy might not remember Caddy had she returned.

Time is a very different phenomenon for Quentin Compson. There is an ominous ticking throughout the Quentin
section, an awareness that man is enslaved by time, and time
is running out. The opening sentence of the Quentin section
makes this clear: "When the shadow of the sash appeared on
the curtains it was between seven and eight o'clock, and then
I was in time again, hearing the watch."[286] In an effort to
escape time's enslavement, Quentin smashes his watch into
"fragments of glass" and twists "the hands off."[287] Time,
however, continues and relentlessly destroys. Even Christ
could not withstand time. "Christ was not crucified; he was
worn away by a minute clicking of little wheels."[288]

For Quentin, time is torment. It is time which robs life of
its promise by burdening us with a past too heavy to bear.
If Benjy is present-preoccupied, Quentin is trapped by the
past so that he has no present and distrusts the future. Quentin
seeks a timeless land where alone redemption is possible.
When his effort to stop time by breaking his watch is unavailing, he commits suicide. Quentin cannot live in time.
Since an end to time is impossible, Quentin takes the only
alternative open to him, an end to living. "A quarter hour
yet. And then I'll not be . . . I was . . . I am not."[289]

Quentin remembers time as the medium in which honor

was lost. Once, in time, Caddy, his sister, was innocent, someone he could protect and worth protecting. Time made her
grow up, deprived her of sinlessness and changed her. Now
Caddy was no more. Time took her away. Living in time
means living in that which takes away and gives nothing.

Quentin is Faulkner's symbol of modern man. He inherits
a history from which there is no escape, a history of sin and
evil which predetermines him to live unredeemed, trapped in
time which not only kills but, worse, corrupts. There is no
exit. Quentin's father once gave him a watch hoping thereby
to give Quentin some relief from time: "I give it to you not
that you may remember time but that you might forget it
now and then for a moment and not spend all your breath
trying to conquer it."[290]

Jason views time differently. Like Benjy, he lives only for
the present. The present, however, is the time in which he
hates. He hates the past because it has deprived him of a
better present. He hates the present because people annoy
him. He hates the future because, like the present, it is going
nowhere. Completely immersed in the present, he makes
every minute count in terms of the money he can earn. Jason
uses the present to scheme and torment, to upset and over-
turn, to bemoan what was and distrust what will be.

Quentin had seen in the past a possibility for honor and
then an awareness of guilt from which he could not free himself. Jason sees the past as that which made him less able to
make money in the present. For Quentin, nothing in the
present can redeem the past. What is lost is lost forever. For
Jason, the present can redeem the past if he can become
wealthy. Jason has reduced time to a phenomenon which is
definable in terms of money alone. Thus, when his niece robs
him of his life savings, he is frantic because she has also robbed
him of time and value.

Quentin committed no sin and yet felt the guilt of a past
he shares with others. Jason's past is evil, but he feels no need

for regret or reform. His debasement is complete. When Caddy, his sister, longs to see her daughter whom she has not seen for years, she appeals to Jason on the only level he understands: "If you'll fix it so that I can see her a minute, I'll give you fifty dollars."[291]

Jason keeps the bargain literally. He holds the young girl in his arms and forces the driver of the carriage to hit the horses hard as he races past Caddy holding his niece to the window so that Caddy can see but neither touch nor speak to her daughter. He delights in this: "We went past her like a fire engine. . . . I could see her running after us through the back window . . . when we turned the corner she was still running. . . . I counted the money again that night and put it away."[292]

Dilsey alone knows how to live in time. She accepts its inevitability and works in time to bring about order and to offer compassion to others. She is all hope and no regret, all love and no fear. Dilsey believes in God, in the rightness of things, in an ultimate reckoning and an eventual salvation. Her name is written in the book, "writ out." Even though she cannot read, she trusts that one day she will be saved because "they'll read it for me. All I got to do is to say Ise here."[293]

Dilsey is proof that those who believe in another life are often more effective in this life. For Dilsey, eternity is the future, the past has been purified and the present is a time for faith and for hope, for labor and for love. It is she, Dilsey, who endures. She symbolizes the Negro community in the South which survives the general destruction as a believing remnant. She agrees with the preacher's Easter reminder of "de weepin and de cryin en de turnt-away face of God," but she also believes in his message that Christ "died dat dem what sees en believes shall never die."[294] For Dilsey, life is not for remembered guilt nor a limited present. It is meant for a redemptive, saving future. In faith, time never ends, never enslaves, never takes away life: "dem what sees en believes shall never die."

THE SYMBOL OF WATER

Time figures largely in the interpretation of *The Sound and the Fury*. Water is another symbol which recurs and which is perceived differently by the persons in the story. As with time, the symbol of water takes on meaning in terms of one's values. For Benjy and Caddy, water has a baptismal significance. Benjy wants Caddy to be innocent, to smell like trees, as he puts it.

When Caddy begins to express her love sexually though not to the point of losing her physical virginity, Benjy feels estranged from her. When Caddy washes, Benjy senses that her innocence has been restored. "I could hear the water . . . Caddy smelled like trees."[295] When, on another occasion, Charlie takes advantage of Caddy though not to the point of sexual intercourse, Benjy bellows in disapproval. "I won't," she said. I won't anymore, ever. Benjy. Benjy.' Then she was crying and I cried, and we held each other. . . . Caddy took the kitchen soap and washed her mouth at the sink, hard. Caddy smelled like trees."[296]

A time does come, however, when Caddy can no longer wash herself clean of guilt. She returns home after a sexual experience and can hardly face her brother. Benjy pushes her toward the bathroom so that she might wash and smell like trees. It is too late, however.

Caddy came to the door and stood there, looking at Father and Mother. Her eyes flew at me. . . . I began to cry. . . . Caddy came in and stood with her back to the wall, looking at me. I went toward her, crying, and she shrank against the wall . . . we went to the bathroom and she stood against the door, looking at me.[297]

For Quentin, water is not a symbol of innocence but of death. Quentin goes to the river, not to wash, but to end his life. His death by water is, in a sense, an attempt at purification. In a world of no innocence, death may have more meaning than life. It releases Quentin from time, from the guilt of the past and from the need of living on when purity of heart has become impossible. Quentin seeks purification in an act of despair.

The Jason section makes no mention of water. Jason has no sense of sin, no concern for purification, no faith in grace. He lives without reconciliation and without redemption.

In the Dilsey section, water is an action symbolizing grace. It is Easter morning and a light rain falls. Soon after this description, Dilsey is inspired by the sermon on the life, death and resurrection of Christ. The rain is a soft symbol of hope, a gift from above, an Easter grace. Since Dilsey is not paralyzed by Caddy's guilt nor Quentin's despair, water for her is a sign not of death but of life.

ORDER AS A CENTRAL THEME

The symbols of time and water are sacraments by which those who live on the Compson estate search for order and salvation. Benjy is upset whenever things are not as they should be. He moans when death comes to the Compsons, when Caddy loses innocence, when each day does not follow an ordered pattern. Benjy's sense of order is disturbed when love goes from his life in Caddy's departure, when water will no longer cleanse guilt, when his own castration leaves him disordered, mutilated.

When at the end of the novel, Benjy's carriage takes a wrong turn, he protests violently until its course is corrected. Then, in the closing words of the book "his eyes were . . . serene again." For, now he saw "post and tree, window and doorway, and signboard, each in its ordered place."[298]

Quentin is anxiety-ridden as he searches for a unifying principle beyond the loss he experiences in Caddy's surrendered innocence. When he cannot find a world of order or redemption, he ends his world. Nothing is right in the Quentin section. The clocks in the watch shop tell different times. The little girl he tries to help is neither his sister as he imagines nor assisted by what he does for her. Quentin's yearning for an ordered existence is pathetically expressed as he waits for the conclusion of the semester and then prepares for death by writing notes, brushing his teeth, tidying up his wardrobe. All the small things must be in order even if life is not. Quentin, modern man, encountering neither order nor redemption, commits suicide in a carefully planned and perfectly executed manner.

Dilsey is the only one who creates order from disorder. There is a religious dimension to her affirmation of order. For Dilsey, order is compassion and love, calling Benjy by his right name, allowing Caddy's daughter to learn of her mother, serving Mrs. Compson in spite of her hypochondria, worshipping God on Easter Sunday.

The Sound and the Fury must be interpreted, finally, in terms of the four persons who dominate each of its four sections: Benjy, Quentin, Jason, and Dilsey.

THE FOUR MAJOR PERSONALITIES

Benjy first tells the story of the Compson tragedy. Since he is mentally defective, the story is told incoherently and incompletely. Critics see in Benjy a Christ figure not only because of his age, thirty-three, but because of his innocence and his instinctive response to evil. If Benjy is a Christ figure, Christ is impotent in the modern world, able to descry evil but unable to resist it or undo it.

Benjy may also be a symbol of what has happened to the South. He has no future, and his present is doomed by a past for which he was not personally responsible but which has made him its victim nonetheless. Benjy delivers his monologue on Holy Saturday, the day when Christ is most helpless in the history of his life. He speaks at a time when Christ has been rejected and buried, not yet risen nor glorified. It is a time of no hope when the blackness of Friday and the bleakness of Saturday have not been transformed into the brilliance of Sunday. At such a moment idiots prevail, and the future lends itself to no interpretation.

Quentin next tells the Compson story. Since he is introspective and confused, the story is related in an agonized and tortured manner. The Quentin monologue is filled with references to shadows from the opening words of the section ("when the shadow of the sash appeared on the curtains . . .") until the suicide scene when Quentin sees his shadow in the water and leaps into the river to join it. Quentin, Faulkner's symbol of modern man, is as unsubstantial and ill-defined as a shadow. Like Darl in *As I Lay Dying*, he is a flittering consciousness with no inner consistency.

Quentin is concerned with moral issues, with "Jesus walking on Galilee and Washington not telling lies,"[299] with "good Saint Francis" who "never had a sister,"[300] with "the voice that breathed o'er Eden"[301] and the "dozen watches" with "a dozen different hours . . . contradicting one another."[302] Quentin is obsessed with the need for certitude in life. Instead, he comes upon his shadow at every turn and remembers his sister who deprived herself and him of honor. Quentin cannot cope with the problems of life since faith has been made impossible for him. His preoccupation with virginity is a preoccupation with discovering something pure and unspoiled so that he may believe. In place of redemption, he comes upon original sin: "there's a curse on us its not our fault is it our fault."[303] Finding no values to live by, nothing to have faith in, no one to love, and no hope for an ordered existence, he brushes his teeth, cleans his hat, puts his room in order and commits suicide.

Jason's memories are bitter. He knows the Compson world is doomed, but he is determined to gain from its destruction. He swindles his niece, deceives his mother, lies to his sister, hoards his money and makes everyone pay for the fact that his life has not gone as he wished. Jason is eager for money as Benjy was eager for innocence and Quentin for honor.

Each of the Compson brothers hoped in something less than the ultimate and were frustrated. Benjy's desire for innocence was involved with his sister who could not make a sinful world innocent. Quentin's need for honor was dependent upon Caddy who could not make a dishonorable world honorable. Jason measured meaning by money and was left valueless when his niece ran off with his life savings. Only Dilsey, who hopes in Christ and in Easter, endures.

Dilsey realizes better than anyone else in the novel that time gives and takes away, that water does not purify as deeply as God, that the order of existence does not depend on ourselves and that innocence or honor are possible as long as we know that sin and evil are also possible. Dilsey is the only one in the novel who forgives. She does not expect Caddy to be perfectly innocent nor Benjy to be intelligent nor Mrs. Compson to be well. She accepts life as she accepts time, with no compulsion to master them or to be mastered by them. Her faith in the rightness of things is a hope for salvation and redemption. On Easter Sunday she takes Benjy to church with her ("de good Lawd don't keer whether he smart er not")[304] and returns renewed and refreshed. Even though the Compson family is coming to an end, there is somehow more.

LIGHT IN AUGUST

Joe Christmas could never be sure if he was Negro or white. Since the culture in which Christmas found himself considered this distinction important, *Light in August* is more than a novel of racial identification. It is a novel of self-estrangement. In a manner characteristic of Faulkner, a story of the South's preoccupation with racial origins becomes a universal saga of the limitations and distortions society imposes on human conduct. *Light in August* reminds us that men are not free to choose their world or themselves.

The story line is simple. Joe Christmas grows up afraid he may be Negro, uncertain if he is white. He becomes the lover of a white woman, Joanna Burden, eventually kills her and is sought for her murder. The search for Christmas is made intensive when a friend of Christmas betrays him for a sum of money and accuses Christmas of being a Negro. There is a chance for Christmas to elude his captors, but he decides not to take it. For a reason known fully only to himself, Christmas walks back freely to Jefferson. There he is executed and then castrated as he lays dying.

There are a number of secondary narratives which are developed as the main story is constructed. Byron Bunch falls in love with Lena Grove, a symbol of enduring life. Rev. Gail Hightower, trapped in a world of delusions and past grandeur, becomes committed to the present for one moment as Christmas is about to be destroyed. Dr. Hines, Joe's grandfather, follows him as a malevolent deity and urges others to kill Christmas when he is finally captured.

The odds were against Christmas before he even came to be. The world into which he was born was a world which already had a guilty, unredeemed past. Christmas must die because of that past and because the present in which he finds himself has ratified the past with all its moral distortions. Society seeks a scapegoat for the guilt within itself. And Christmas, who makes society aware of its sins, is destroyed by that same society which imagines it can destroy its guilt by destroying him.

Christmas is a modern Christ. His name reminds us of the redemptive Christ though Christmas has no redemption to offer. Christmas can die, but his death has no healing power. He is a victim of society's sins but cannot serve as its savior. In a sense, his death intensifies the hatred and passions of his fellowmen. One value does emerge from Christmas' savage execution. Society is revealed in its sinfulness. Christmas' death lights up the darkness in the hearts of men, not so that this darkness may cede to light, but so that men might be made aware of the darkness within them. Joe's death is an act of defiance, a desperate acceptance of annihilation as a final freedom.

Joe Christmas begins his life as a stranger in the world, with no home to call his own. "There was something definitely rootless about him, as though no town nor city was his, no street, no walls, no square of earth his home."[305]

He is given a name not so much to identify him but to declare in some way what his role in life must be. Since he is found on the doorstep of an orphanage on Christmas day, he is named after the day men set aside to remember Christ's birth. Later, when Christmas comes of age, Byron Bunch, a co-worker, reflects on the meaning of the name Joe was given.

And that was the first time Byron remembered that he had ever thought how a man's name, which is supposed to be just the sound for who he is, can be somehow an augur of what he will do, if other men can only read the meaning in time. It seemed to him that none of them had looked especially at the stranger until they heard his name. But as soon as they heard it, it was as though there was something in the sound of it that was trying to tell them what to expect. . . .[306]

The second name Joseph Christmas bears is given to him as a result of circumstances as the second name of Jesus is a result of circumstance, a title given because of a belief he was the Christ, the Messiah. The first name of Joseph comes, as in the case of Jesus, from God. After the new baby is called Christmas, there is concern about a first name. Repeating a prophetic style, "old Doc Hines said, 'His name is Joseph,' and they quit laughing and they looked at old Doc Hines and the Jezebel said: 'How do you know?,' and old Doc Hines said 'The Lord says so' and then they laughed again, 'It is so in the Book: Christmas, the son of Joe,' Jesus, the son of Joseph."[307]

Since Christmas may be part Negro but easily passes for white, and since no one can say exactly who he is, he bears in himself the guilt of both blacks and whites. He belongs to no world, although he is victimized by two different racial worlds neither of which receives him as its own. Worse than this, even he has difficulty with his identity. In a manner not unlike that which can be harmonized with traditional Christology, as we shall see in a second book on this topic, Christmas spends his life striving toward the rudiments of consciousness.

THE MYSTERY OF CHRISTMAS

There is something in Christmas so perilous and yet so liberating that his full awareness of it means, as it may in the case of Christ, death and a new freedom. The developing consciousness of Christmas and Christ is not premised on the fact that no one knows who they are but on the fact that only God knows and that salvation is somehow involved with a revelation of this mystery. The correspondence, even on the theological level, of revelation with salvation has not been sufficiently explored. In a particularly painful point in the story, Christmas engages in a searching dialogue and a strange memory:

'I ain't a nigger,' and the nigger says, 'You are worse than that. You don't know what you are. And more than that, you won't never know. You'll live and you'll die and you won't never know . . . don't nobody but God know what you is. But God wasn't there to say because He had set His will to working . . . from that very first night, when He had chose His own Son's sacred anniversary to set it a-working on. . . .[308]

Little is known about Joe Christmas between his childhood and his early 30's. His three years of residence in Jefferson and his age, thirty-three, at the time of his death are known. The fact that he was tormented and that he was "turned in" for a sum of money by a friend, Joe Brown, to whom he revealed the truth about himself are also known. "He's got nigger blood in him. I knowed it when I first saw him. . . . One time he even admitted it, told me he was part nigger."[309]

The depth of the betrayal is significant. Brown reveals not a crime but the inner mystery of Christmas. Christmas, therefore, is condemned for who he is rather than for what he has done. It is the person of Christmas, his nature and identity, which leads to his execution. The issue in the life and death of Joseph Christmas is not the legality or the morality of his behavior but whether the world has a place for someone like himself.

The writers of the New Testament wondered why a man who went about doing good had to die. Christmas is also bewildered by the reasons men devise to destroy one another: "Just when do men that have different blood in them stop hating one another?"[310] Christ revealed a more universal definition of salvation and of man than Jew or Gentile. Christmas dies because men believed that black or white was a sufficient definition of salvation and of man. He returns to Jefferson as a final protest against a society which defined man so narrowly that it diminished all men. In such a world, Christmas could not live since he could not accept a definition of himself which made him his own enemy, part Negro, part white.

Light in August accepts that which traditional theology calls original sin. Christmas, like Christ, dies not only because of the resistance of his contemporaries but because of something done long ago which men continue to suffer from since they bear a common history. Past and present conspire to defeat each person whose character is flawed as a result of something he does not fully comprehend.

Remember this. Your grandfather and brother are lying there, murdered not by one white man but by the curse which God put on a whole race before your grandfather or your brother or me or you were even thought of. A race doomed and cursed to be forever and ever a part of the white man's doom and curse for its sins. Remember that. His doom and his curse. Forever and ever. . . .

I thought of all the children coming forever and ever into the world, white, with the black shadow already falling upon them before they drew breath, and I seemed to see the black shadow in the shape of a cross. And it seemed like the white babies were struggling even before they drew breath, to escape from the shadow that was not only upon them but beneath them, too, flung out like their arms were flung out, as if they were nailed to the cross. I saw all the little babies that would ever be in the world, the ones not yet born—a long line of them with their arms spread, on the black crosses. . . . What I wanted to tell them was that I must escape, get away from under the shadow, or I would die.[311]

THE TRIAL AND THE DEATH

It was on Friday that Christmas was captured. He was captured in Mottstown, not far from Jefferson. No one knew why he had returned, but all knew he must die. Perhaps Doc Hines summed up the sentiments of the crowd best when he screamed, "Kill him! Kill him!"[312] in a manner not unlike the former cry, "Crucify him. Crucify him."

Christmas denied nothing: "Ain't your name Christmas?" he was asked and "the nigger said it was."[313] During his trial, Christmas was buffeted but remained silent. "He had already hit the nigger a couple of times in the face, and the nigger acting like a nigger for the first time and taking it, not saying anything. . . ."[314]

Christmas had spent a lifetime longing for reassurance. Now as he met death he had a clear idea of what he must do and of who he was. He wondered "all his life without knowing it" about "God perhaps and me," seeking to convince himself that "God loves me, too," even in affliction.[315]

Faulkner changed key elements in the Christ story as he recounted the fate of Joe Christmas. The alterations say something about our culture's doubts and fears. In Joe Christmas, innocence is less possible than it was for Christ. *Light in August* offers little light and no redemption. When Christmas is dead, he is decisively dead. There is no Easter for Christmas. In a sense, Faulkner finds us less free, more burdened with guilt, too troubled by ambiguity to discover the Christ whose freedom is innocence and whose salvation seeks faith rather than perplexity.

Christmas died, but his death was less a reason for hope than an occasion for despair. Nothing could save men from meeting the same fate as Christmas met. Yet in perhaps a minimal way, Christmas' death serves a purpose. Though his death does not redeem, and though there is no resurrection from it, the very unattainability and incomprehensibility of his suffering impart a measure of healing.

For a long moment he looked up at them with peaceful and unfathomable and unbearable eyes. Then his face, body, all, seemed to collapse . . . the pent black blood . . . seemed to rise soaring into their memories forever and ever. They are not to lose it, in whatever peaceful villages, besides whatever placid and reassuring streams of old age, in the mirroring faces of whatever children they will contemplate old disasters and newer hopes. It will be there, musing, quiet, steadfast, not fading and not particularly threatful, but of itself alone serene, of itself alone triumphant.[316]

Christmas, like Christ, endures a ritualistic death. Like Christ, Christmas dies not alone on an empty road but in full view of his executioners and only after an entire society has become implicated in his death. Christmas, like Christ, dies less as a victim than as a martyr.

Christ's death reminds men that the world resists love. Christmas' death, since he is not totally innocent, shows men how the world punishes those it has decided beforehand are not worth love. Christmas' death had to be witnessed and remembered so that men might see in it something about themselves from which his death could not save them. When Jesus dies, however, he reveals to men something about themselves which counted less before God than the Easter life which cancelled out the death of Christ and the guilt of all his fellowmen.

A FABLE AND THE BEAR

It is strange that the most explicitly religious of all Faulkner's books is the one which is least religiously significant.

One Monday morning in May, during the First World War, a regiment of soldiers on the Western front refuses to attack the enemy. A foreign-born corporal in the French army, surrounded by twelve disciples, has convinced his fellow soldiers that they should lay down their arms. The corporal is executed for the message of peace he proclaimed.

More important than the novel is the intent Faulkner had in mind in writing it. Faulkner wanted A Fable to serve as a basis for the interpretation of his work. Christ may not be the Son of God for those who turn to him so often. It seems, however, that when men decide to write a truly profound work (Hemingway's, The Old Man and the Sea or Faulkner's A Fable), they frequently find in Christ a synthesis of those values which best express man.

Since so much about the life of Christ is transcendentally-oriented, one wonders if the fascination with Christ is due not so much to what he did and what he was for man but also due to his having made salvation believable. Grace from God is something man may want to accept. In the life of Christ, the reality of that grace is more difficult to deny than it is in the lives of lesser men. Christ may be a symbol of those virtues men know are most human. But he may also express, in a less defined manner, those truths men wish were true or, at least, more clear.

There is a stubborn conviction that man should somehow survive his death, that man is more important than the death which seizes him. The best sign, perhaps the only hope, that this conviction is neither dream nor fiction is the Christ story. The Christ figure in American literature is repeated so often because beneath the surface of our denials and doubts there is a longing to encounter a man such as he was and to be saved by the God in whom he believed.

Granting all this, we might ask why A Fable did not succeed. This is a book written by one of the finest writers of our time on a topic of profound significance at a time when he had the maturity and wisdom of a lifetime. Faulkner had won the Nobel Prize and wanted now to give a global view of those values and ideas he prized as a person and communicated as a writer.

One of the reasons why A Fable does not say more is because it tries to say too much. It so carefully parallels the life of Christ that one is left, not with a symbol of those vague religious feelings which stir the human heart, but with a too-conscious expression of those feelings in the life and history of Jesus of Nazareth. Man is made most aware of his religious nature when that nature is not graphically described. A Fable explains so much about religious man that as a result it categorizes him in an area of his life which eludes categories.

When Christ was a symbol in The Sound and the Fury and Light in August, or even in Hemingway's The Old Man and the Sea, men identified with him more easily than when Christ became a living man, a French corporal, accomplishing the limited objective of ending one battle in a global conflict. A Fable defines Christ more sharply than Catholic conciliar doctrine or creedal statements do. Implicit in Christological affirmations is the sense of mystery, the ineffable, the unattainable, the nondefinable. Thus, dogma says less about Christ than those who have not studied it may realize. The attempt to circumscribe Christ too logically weakens the literary fabric of A *Fable*. Those books of Faulkner which are more oblique in the Christ question are actually more to the point.

There is a further reason why A *Fable* disappoints. Faulkner details the Christ story so precisely that he is dominated by it. In other works, Faulkner wrote about man reaching through his history and beyond his heart to a Christ or salvation he missed and desired. In A *Fable*, Faulkner writes about Christ. He makes the Christ story more a myth than a reality because he merely reproduces its details in another setting without exploring those facets of man's personality which make the Christ story worth remembering. Faulkner, therefore, transposes the biographical data on Jesus of Nazareth into a modern situation giving us no further insight into that Jesus about whom men recorded their impressions nor into us modern men who may wonder whether there is an abiding significance in the life and death of Christ.

So closely does Faulkner follow the New Testament in telling his story, that, in effect, he rewrites it. A rewriting is valid only if it can offer us something the original text did not. A *Fable* does not. The fact that it is impossible to rewrite the Gospel effectively may tell us something about the religious significance of Scripture. Why cannot a more accomplished writer than the evangelists write more forcefully of Jesus than they did?

The Christological references in A *Fable* are concentrated. The corporal has a retinue of twelve men, one of whom betrays him, in spite of the fact that together they had formed a "brotherhood of . . . faith and hope."[317] He is captured on a Wednesday, celebrates a farewell supper in his jail cell on Thursday and is executed on a Friday with two other prisoners. As he dies, he falls into "a tangled mass of old barbed wire, a strand of which had looped up and around . . . the man's head,"[318] forming a crown of thorns.

The action takes place during a facsimile of Holy Week during which the corporal is tempted three times to give up his spiritual mission. He refuses, however, to purchase his freedom from death at the price it is offered. He is killed as a martyr to this cause and buried carefully on a Saturday by those who believed in him. On Sunday an intensive artillery barrage devastates the area where the corporal was buried. As some of his disciples look on, they behold a "vast pall of dust filled with red flashes" from "shell-bursts."[319] Marthe, one of those who accepted the corporal's message, runs to the place of burial after the firing is done and holds "in her hand a shard of the pale new unpainted wood which had been the coffin. . . . "That was Sunday. When the girl returned with the shovel, still running, they took turns with it, all that day until it was too dark to see. They found a few more shards and fragments of the coffin, but the body itself was gone."[320]

The Bear is the story of a group of Yoknapatawpha men and a young boy who keep a yearly rendezvous with a bear, Old Ben, whom they ritualistically pursue without intending to kill him. In the course of the hunt one year, Boon Hogganbeck kills the bear and is last seen sitting beneath a tree, his gun dismembered, and his mind disorganized by hysteria.

The young boy, Isaac McCaslin, is gradually initiated into the mystery and ritual of the hunt for Old Ben by Sam Fathers. The search for Old Ben requires more than ritualistic form. It demands personal virtue and surrender to a deep mystery. Isaac learns that to be a hunter in this manner can be given him "provided he in his turn were humble and enduring enough."[321]

He decides to make the sacrifice necessary to see the bear and strives for "humility through suffering" and "pride through the endurance which survived the suffering."[322] His hope is that one day, by means of this baptismal initiation, he might be counted worthy of "Sam and Old Ben and the mongrel Lion" who are "taintless and incorruptible."[323] The apprenticeship, however, is long and arduous. For it is no small thing to share the mystery of Old Ben and to behold him as he is.

In a way Isaac does not at first comprehend his apprenticeship will one day "prove him worthy" to participate on an almost supernatural level "in the yearly pageant-rite of the old bear's furious immortality."[324] In order to master his mission properly, he submits himself to the will of Sam Fathers. "He entered his novitiate to the true wilderness with Sam beside him as he had begun his apprenticeship . . . to manhood . . . with Sam beside him."[325]

Isaac first becomes aware of Old Ben in an extrasensory manner.

He only heard the drumming of the woodpecker stop short off, and knew that the bear was looking at him. He never saw it. He did not know whether it was facing him. . . . He did not move, holding the useless gun which he knew now he would never fire at it, now or ever. . . .[326]

As Isaac's awareness of mystery deepens, he perceives more clearly what must be done to become worthy of the great bear. He must give up those things men depend upon to give them direction in life. The reality he is now about to encounter cannot be met with those standards of measurement men use when they wish to be completely in control of their destinies.

He stood for a moment—a child, alien and lost in the green and soaring gloom of the markless wilderness. Then he relinquished completely to it. It was the watch and the compass. He was still tainted. He removed the linked chain of the one and the looped thong of the other from his overalls and hung them on a bush and leaned the stick beside them and entered it. . . . It seemed to him that something, he didn't know what, was beginning. . . . It was the beginning of the end of something; he didn't know what except that he would not grieve. He would be humble and proud that he had been found worthy to be a part of it, too, or even just to see it, too.[327]

Suddenly, the bear appears. Isaac has proved himself, been found worthy, not feared faith nor repelled mystery.

Then he saw the bear. It did not emerge, appear; it was just there, immobile, fixed in the green and windless noon's hot dappling, not as big as he had dreamed it but as big as he had expected, bigger, dimensionless against the dappling obscurity, looking at him.[328]

The Bear is the most hopeful story Faulkner ever wrote. Although much of his major writing was influenced by the problem of original sin, this short novel is his first venture into the world after the Incarnation. It is a world which has known guilt, a guilt Isaac discovers by leafing through the family records and finding there a description of the sins which stain his heritage. There is more, however. Before guilt, there was paradise, relative perfection and goodness. There was once a wilderness of innocence and beauty "which was bigger and older than any recorded deed."[329]

Sounding almost like F. Scott Fitzgerald, Faulkner sees the discovery of the new world as a final chance at Eden for the human family.

... men snarled over the gnawed bones of the old world's worthless evening until an accidental egg discovered to them a new hemisphere. . . . Dispossessed of Eden. Dispossessed of Canaan . . . blasphemous in His name until He used a simple egg to discover to them a new world where a nation of people could be founded in humility and pity and sufferance and pride of one to another.[330]

Faulkner, like Fitzgerald, vests the new world with a religious significance. America is established, not as a nation, but as a human experiment and a saving venture. The themes of hope and guilt, of expectation and providence, of pain and promise which characterize religious experience are present in the establishment of this new continent. Unfortunately the holiness of the new hemisphere is desecrated since the men who came to it were "already tainted even before any white man owned it by what Grandfather and his kind, his fathers, had brought into the new land which He had vouchsafed them out of pity and sufferance." It was as though the sails of the old world's ships were driven by a "tainted wind."[331]

Every gift of God is a new reason for hope and a new opportunity for sin. As man inhabits each new world, he says to himself: "What I want was not where I was, but it may be here since it must be somewhere." Human hope depends upon men always feeling they can find a new world. They are convinced that a place where hope is no longer disappointed must sooner or later appear. The discovery of America seemed to herald a turning point in human history. But the new reason for hope became also a new opportunity for sin. America, which thrilled and excited human hearts, could not, for all its power and apparent infinity, redeem those same hearts.

Don't you see? . . . Don't you see? This whole land, the whole South, is cursed, and all of us who derive from it, whom it ever suckled . . . lie under the curse . . . their descendants alone cannot resist it, not combat it—maybe just endure and outlast it until the curse is lifted.[332]

Who could now rescue man since America was God's redemptive gift and men had brought a curse upon it by their sin?

He had created them, upon this land this South for which He had done so much with woods for game and streams for fish and deep rich soil for seed and lush springs to sprout it and long summers to mature it and serene falls to harvest it and short mild winters for men and animals . . . where to East, North and West lay illimitable that whole hopeful continent dedicated as a refuge and sanctuary of liberty and freedom. . . . He had rescued them. . . .[333]

The wilderness was, of course, corrupted. Faulkner, however, dwells less on the guilt of our past in this story than on
our hope for the future. It is possible for a disciple, Isaac, to
be taught and formed by a charismatic, spiritual father, Sam.
Sam hands down a new way of being aware of innocence. Men
do not need further geography but consecration to a transcendent mystery. Faulkner has come upon a mystery larger
than guilt. More significant than our sinful history is the
human heart and its encounter with this saving mystery.
When God speaks, he speaks first to the heart of man.

The heart already knows. He didn't have His Book written to be
read by what must elect and choose, but by the heart, not by the
wise of the earth because maybe they don't need it or maybe the
wise no longer have any heart, but by the doomed and lowly of the
earth who have nothing else to read with but the heart. Because,
the men who wrote his Book for Him were writing about truth and
there is only one truth and it covers all things that touch the heart.
. . . They were trying to write down the heart's truth out of the
heart's driving complexity, for all the complex and troubled hearts
which would beat after them.[334]

Salvation, then, is not a question of another continent nor
further human wisdom. They are healed by a saving mystery
who surrender themselves in faith and hope to something the
heart best comprehends. The heart, however, does not learn
as quickly as the mind. Humility and endurance, patience and
sacrifice are needed for the heart to sense that one mystery
which surpasses even its own mystery.

Isaac cannot come upon Old Ben all of a sudden. Fathers
must reveal to him what he must do. Isaac must summon
the grace and courage of his heart to set aside his stick and
rifle, his watch and compass and enter the wilderness alone.
The risk in the great encounter between Isaac and Old Ben is
mutual. Old Ben, like God, becomes concrete only by emptying
himself of something. When God, like Old Ben, becomes

visible, he also becomes vulnerable. Isaac sees Old Ben. Soon
after, Old Ben is killed by Boon Hogganbeck.

The Bear recounts the story of how Isaac McCaslin learned
those lessons men seldom learn properly. The Bear has none
of the pessimism of Sanctuary nor the massive guilt of
Absalom, Absalom! It functions on a level deeper than that
of the ritual and pilgrimage in As I Lay Dying. It does not
describe the demise of a family as does The Sound and the
Fury, nor the martyrdom of a man who was killed, not for his
sins, but because he made men aware of something about
themselves they could not abide (Light in August).

The Bear tells of hope and salvation. Although Old Ben
dies, Isaac makes himself worthy of him. And Isaac, the
Mississippi huntsman, becomes a messenger of peace and
faith to his fellowmen. As long as he is alive, men would have
someone to tell them of a lost innocence which, since it was
greater than their guilt, was not really lost for those who wish
to regain it. Isaac ends his days emulating Jesus of Nazareth,
becoming a carpenter to imitate him most perfectly and
reasoning that "if the Nazarene had found carpentering good
. . . it would be all right for Isaac McCaslin."[335]

John Steinbeck

"In utter loneliness a writer tries to explain the inexplicable."
That is how John Steinbeck described himself in a letter written during his work on East of Eden. It says much more about
the loftiness and universality of his intention as an author.
Steinbeck's writing is, therefore, replete with symbols and
allegories, visions, hopes, and intimations. He tirelessly seeks
the right word in the right place so that the wordless will be
at least felt if not described.

There is a mystic tendency in Steinbeck. It leads him away
from materialism in such books as The Pearl, East of Eden,
The Winter of Our Discontent. So pervasive is this mysticism

that one might say he constructs a religious system from it. It is not a religious system built on belief in what we would call God. It derives from nature, although there is a transcendent quality to Steinbeck's natural mysticism.

Steinbeck is not concerned with a passive sense of reverence before nature but with an active obligation on man's part to establish bonds with the created order. He is like Hemingway in his perception of the holiness of creation. He is unlike him in the fact that Steinbeck attributes to creation a healing and sanctifying power apart from any need to struggle with the created order in ritualized courage. There is a serenity to Steinbeck's view of creation; Hemingway is more emphatic about nobility and its demands upon us. When Steinbeck wrote *The Red Pony*, he said that one of his objectives was "to put down the way 'afternoon felt.'" Hemingway was less contemplative about creation.

Steinbeck's mystic tendency leads him in the direction of a transcendent unity, a unity which is not God nor personal but certainly beyond man. In this, there is an openness to faith even if not an affirmation of it. In *The Pearl*, he writes of "an aching chord that caught the throat, saying this is safety, this is warmth, this is the *Whole*."[336] On another occasion, he explained

And it is a strange thing that most of the feeling we call religious, most of the mystical outcrying which is one of the most prized and used and desired reactions of our species, is really the understanding and the attempt to say that man is related to the whole thing, related inextricably to all reality, known and unknowable.

Steinbeck reaches heights of poetic intensity when he describes the wonder of nature in *The Red Pony, The Pearl, Of Mice and Men*. But Steinbeck has further dimensions. When he was awarded the Nobel Prize in 1962, attention was called to his interest in the disinherited, the helpless, the exploited. Steinbeck often links the saga of man's oppression with his perennial yearning for homecoming and a promised land. He does this most effectively in *Of Mice and Men* and *The Grapes of Wrath*.

Steinbeck is committed to the myth of the natural man. If man is mystically attuned to creation, and if he is not broken by the artificiality of modern life or the inhumanity of his fellow men, he is as near to perfection as it is possible to be. There is, of course, death with which man must contend, and there is little sense of ultimate purpose in life. But these are questions outside Steinbeck's scope.

We said above that Steinbeck sought "to explain the inexplicable." Hence, he reached at times the outer limits of his natural mysticism and wrote of man's ethical aspirations in *East of Eden* and of his concern with a revelatory light and a moral redeemer in *The Winter of Our Discontent*. His allegory of good and evil in *East of Eden* and his anguish in *The Winter of Our Discontent* at the thought that men would one day consider their evil tendencies to be virtues reach biblical and cosmic proportions. In the former work, salvation from evil lies in man's use of freedom; in the latter book, salvation depends upon a preservation of inherited and traditional wisdom.

As did Hemingway, Steinbeck ends his career with a recognition of man's need to prevail over his own weakness by faith and moral sensitivity. Santiago in *The Old Man and the Sea* transfigures his flesh by the power of his spirit. Ethan Hawley in *The Winter of Our Discontent* rises from the cave where he was about to commit suicide to a new life. In a moment of revelation, he comes to believe that the light will ultimately prevail.

Steinbeck considers in his work a range of religious questions: mysticism and universal wholeness, guilt and salvation, human bondage and moral freedom, pilgrimage and the promised land, the clash of good and evil, the need to win a victory in faith over our own brittleness. He is further indica-

tion that Americans are involved in the struggle for salvation
and that they seek a salvation which transcends secular salvation.

THE RED PONY AND THE PEARL

Both *The Red Pony* and *The Pearl* are concerned with moral
awareness. In the former book, a young boy, Jody, becomes
aware of the ethical dimensions of life and of his own obligation to assume moral responsibility for life. In the latter book,
a young man, Kino, confronts the problem of evil in its stark-
ness. He is beguiled for a time, indeed, obsessed. He eventually
sees what he must do and summons from himself the strength
to part with the pearl.

The Red Pony is a novel of uncommon power and beauty
and warmth. It is divided into four parts: "The Gift," "The
Great Mountains," "The Promise," and "The Leader of the
People." Each of these sections brings Jody face to face with
the fact that loss and death, sometimes violence, occur in life.
He comes to perceive the fallibility and limitations of human
nature.

In "The Gift," Jody learns that even Billy Buck, the ranchhand whom he trusts completely, cannot justify all the hope
Jody has in him. One day, Billy leaves a red pony which Jody
prized out in the rain after he had promised he would not.
Billy was detained elsewhere by a storm. As a result, the pony
dies. Jody is never the same again. He has experienced life as
tragedy for the first time, and he sees that all men must be
fallible if even Billy Buck can fail him.

Jody understands something further. He gains an insight
into his own fallibility, indeed, into the fallibility of life itself.
One night he sleeps while looking after the ailing pony. The
pony, unguarded, wanders into the chill and darkness. When
Jody retrieves him, the pony's condition worsens, and he dies
soon after. Jody was born with a need to sleep. This need con-

tains within itself the possibility of the pony's death. And Jody has no control over this need.

Jody realizes that no one can protect anyone all the time. Life itself is unable to make life totally safe. For life has within it the weakness of its own mortality and limitation. The essential imperfection of life itself makes tragedy inevitable.

Jody achieves maturity from this experience. He accepts his own fallibility, and although he can never consider Billy Buck in the same light again, he forgives Billy and learns to relate to him in a new way.

In "The Great Mountains," Jody meets death, not as a violent experience, but as a mellow end to life. Gitano, an old man, returns to the area of the Great Mountains where he was born so that he may die. Jody befriends him and asks him about the Great Mountains which Jody can see from the ranch but which he has never visited. The day after his arrival the old man rides off alone to the mystery of the mountains and of his death.

Jody learns that death is not merely an accident (as with the pony) but an inevitable part of life. And he becomes compassionate in the process. In "The Gift," Jody forgave Billy his fallibility; in "The Great Mountains," Jody comforts an old man about to die, a man who feels his aloneness and who does not comprehend what is about to happen to him.

"The Promise" allows Jody to see that death is not the end of life but that new life often comes from death. Billy Buck promises Jody that he will do everything possible to assure the safe birth of a colt Jody awaits. Billy feels the pressure of his responsibility since he knows he must not disappoint Jody a second time.

When it becomes evident to Billy that the birth is going all wrong, he senses his inability to disillusion Jody again. He acts against his natural instincts, kills the mare and tears from her the colt, alive and unharmed. In exhaustion and confusion, covered with blood and shaken by the experience, he puts the newly born colt into Jody's arms. The promise has been kept. Sometimes death itself is required for the fulfillment of a promise. There are times when only death assures life.

Jody now views death in a new light. Death need not always be, as it was with the red pony, something which happens when life is taken away. Nor is death the outcome one awaits when life has exhausted its resources, as it was with Gitano. Death may be an occasion for new life.

The final section of The Red Pony is entitled "The Leader of the People." Here, Jody rises to the heights of compassion and moral awareness. He feels sensitively the insult his grandfather suffers when Jody's father is overheard complaining that the old man has outlived his time and that he annoys others by endlessly repeating the same stories. Jody senses the shattering pain the old man has suffered. Although he knows he may be punished for his action, he asks his grandfather to "tell about Indians" once more.

When at the end of the section his grandfather confides to Jody the fact that his father may be right and that time has passed him by, Jody yearns to help. He leaves the porch and asks his mother to make a lemonade for his grandfather. His mother suspects that this is Jody's way of getting a lemonade for himself. But Jody refuses. He wants this to be a gift, a pure gift, to his grandfather, a gift in which Jody gains nothing for himself, a gift which will be total giving. Jody gives as totally as a boy can give and as simply as a boy can give. The gift of an almost worthless glass of lemonade is a symbol of the compassion and selflessness Jody has acquired.

Jody has come of age. His action of grace on behalf of his grandfather required, however, that he suffer first. "A longing caressed him, and it was so sharp that he wanted to cry to get it out of his breast. He lay down in the green grass. . . . He covered his eyes with his crossed arms and lay there, a long time, and he was full of a nameless sorrow."[337]

The Pearl is a parable of paradise and sin, of love and salvation. It is a simple story. Kino, the young husband of Juana and the father of Coyotito, finds a great pearl, the pearl of the world. He dreams of the hope and healing it will bring him. Unfortunately, the pearl, despite its unsurpassed beauty, brings only evil. It leads Kino to beat his wife, to lose touch with his people, to kill his enemies, to leave his village and finally to witness the shooting of his child.

By contrast, the description of life in the opening pages of *The Pearl* is idyllic. Eden has happened. Kino is brave and strong; Juana is faithful and loving; the morning on which the story begins is "perfect among mornings."[338] On such a day, however, Kino will come upon the pearl which will cause him to fall from grace. As Kino hopes desperately in the pearl to bring him salvation, he finds that it envelops him more deeply in illusion, despair and tragedy. Gradually, he becomes a slave of evil. "This thing is evil," [Juana] cried harshly. "This pearl is like a sin! It will destroy us. . . . Throw it away, Kino. Let us break it between stones. Let us bury it and forget the place. Let us throw it back into the sea. It has brought evil. Kino, my husband, it will destroy us."[339]

Kino persists. He has become so identified with the pearl that surrendering it would be equivalent to ending his life. "This pearl has become my soul . . . if I give it up, I shall lose my soul."[340] Only when Coyotito is killed does Kino come to his senses. Death allows him to achieve a measure of redemption. He hurls the pearl, a symbol of salvation by an object rather than by life, into the sea.

EAST OF EDEN

The question of morality which Steinbeck poses in *The Red Pony* and *The Pearl* was given classic expression in *East of*

Eden. Taking as his theme the recurring history of Cain and Abel, he explores the problem of good and evil through two generations. The Cain and Abel story occurs in the lives of Charles and Adam Trask and then again in Adam's sons, Caleb and Aron. In the course of its development, Steinbeck reaches two pivotal conclusions.

He affirms strongly that, although the human family is beset by evil forces, it is human freedom rather than fate which makes evil continue. And he suggests subtly that evil may be lessened as time goes its way, and human love is multiplied. Charles Trask, the true Cain of the novel, is far more ruthless than his nephew Caleb whose moral situation is made less malicious and somewhat ambiguous by his father's love.

There are further themes in the novel, themes which are oblique but urgent, nonetheless. Steinbeck makes it clear, for example, that evil is not overcome unless it is recognized as evil. This is an insight he takes up again in *The Winter of Our Discontent.*

In *East of Eden,* Adam is not able to escape the influences of his wife, Cathy, the symbol of demonic hatred in the novel, until he recognizes her as evil. As long as Adam considers evil impossible, he is trapped by it. When Adam confronts the reality of Cathy in all her perversity, he is near redemption. When he realizes that Eden cannot happen again and that what Cathy represents will always be part of life, Adam recovers his balance. Adam learns one of the most difficult of all lessons: goodness does not emerge from a denial of evil but from a victory over evil. This truth is crucially important in the construction of a Christian doctrine of original sin.

Steinbeck also intimates that evil is lessened when genuine fatherhood is found. This happens to Caleb when his father accepts him, forgives him and reminds him of his freedom. Adam does not make life easy for Caleb, but he does give him a chance to live. He offers him a choice. There is salvation from evil because there is fatherhood. This truth is essential in the articulation of a Christian doctrine of redemption, moral freedom and divine Fatherhood.

East of Eden is a story of evil as well as of love. Every attempt to explain salvation requires both. Moral evil has a more personal and interior quality to it in *East of Eden* than in *The Grapes of Wrath*. In the latter novel, it is the situation or civilization or societal structures which bring evil. In the former novel, evil derives from something more intimate to man than his environment.

Young Adam, for example, escapes evil not by fleeing an evil system or fighting it as do the Joads in *The Grapes of Wrath* but by silencing the evil of his own heart. "[Adam] contributed to the quiet he wished for by offering no violence, no contention, and to do this he had to retire into secretness, since there is some violence in everyone."[341]

It is only when Caleb, at the end of the novel, comes to his father, crushed by guilt and fully conscious of his evil choices, that he is redeemed by love and acceptance. Aron, his brother, on the other hand, in a strange reversal of the Cain-Abel story, cuts himself off from life because he would not admit or forgive evil. Unable to recognize evil, Araon consequently handles goodness improperly.

The presence of this evil in the midst of life makes it difficult for men to affirm faith in God. Steinbeck links this faith with moral awareness and with confidence in one's own worth.

But I think that because they trusted themselves and respected themselves as individuals, because they knew beyond doubt that they were valuable and potentially moral units—because of this they could give God their own courage and unity and then receive it back. Such things have disappeared perhaps because men do not trust themselves any more. . . .[342]

Steinbeck's comments on the existence of God are pointed. God is bound up with the sense of life. "The proofs that God does not exist are very strong, but in lots of people they are not as strong as the feeling that he does exist."[343]

The presence of evil in our hearts and insensitivity to our moral nature lead us away, not only from God, but from one another.

A child may ask, 'What is the world's story about?' . . . I believe that there is one story in the world, and only one. . . . Humans are caught—in their lives, in their thoughts, in their hungers and ambitions, in their avarice and cruelty, and in their kindness and generosity, too—in a net of good and evil. . . . In uncertainty I am certain that underneath the topmost layers of frailty men want to be good and want to be loved. Indeed, most of their vices are attempted short cuts to love. When a man comes to die, no matter what his talents and influence and genius, if he dies unloved, his life must be a failure to him, and his dying a cold horror.[344]

Indeed, Steinbeck presents the problem of original sin in traditional Christian terms. Original sin is related to the Cain-Abel story. And men feel in their own lives the reality and truth of both stories.

Two stories have haunted us and followed us from our beginning . . . the story of original sin and the story of Cain and Abel. And I don't understand them at all but I feel them in myself. . . . No story has power nor will it last, unless we feel in ourselves that it is true and true of us. What a great burden of guilt men have! . . . The human is the only guilty animal.[345]

Caleb admits his guilt and accepts his freedom. Therefore, he is forgiven and redeemed. Lee, the Chinese servant, teaches him that the final choice of good or evil is made by the person alone even though all men have evil in their ancestry. Moral responsibility in life does not require our knowing why there is evil or what purpose it serves. It is there. But so is freedom. And we must decide how we shall act and whether evil will take hold of us.

When Caleb understands this, his conversion begins with a prayer: "Dear Lord . . . let me be like Aron. Don't make me mean. . . . I don't want to be mean. I don't want to be lonely. For Jesus' sake. Amen."[346]

In the powerful closing scene of the novel, Adam is dying and Caleb pleads for recognition and forgiveness. Lee acts as intercessor and tries to reach Adam through the semiconscious state which has overcome him. "Adam, give him your blessing. Don't leave him alone with his guilt. Adam, can you hear me? Give him your blessing."[347]

Only Adam, Caleb's true father, can make him innocent again. Adam, Caleb's only father, must accept his son before his son can accept himself.

The novel ends on a ringing note of forgiveness and saving fatherhood. Adam speaks but one word to Caleb, a word reminding him of his freedom. In the power of this pardon and grace, redemption comes to Caleb. Lee reminds Caleb that the promise of redemption is never denied us. "Cal, listen to me. Can you think that whatever made us—would stop trying?"[348]

East of Eden reminds us that there is rather more to life than its heartaches or even its joys, more than its victories and temptations, more than its ventures and frustrations. There is also the experience of innocence, a suggestion of the sacred, the wonder of belonging to a reality which exceeds us. There is undiminished hope, unexpected forgiveness, a father's blessing, the healing influence of our responsibility for one another. There is also this conviction that tomorrow will always come, and that it will bring with it the redemption we hunger after.

OF MICE AND MEN

In a letter to his publisher in the year following the publication of *Of Mice and Men*, Steinbeck explained: "My whole work drive has been aimed at making people understand each other." Steinbeck pursued this objective by considering in some depth the moral nature of men and by writing forcefully of the dreams and aspirations which inspire us.

The works of Steinbeck we have discussed thus far, *The Red Pony*, *The Pearl* and *East of Eden* explore questions of moral awareness and moral choices. In *Of Mice and Men* and *The Grapes of Wrath* Steinbeck directs his attention to the longing for homeland and paradise which are an essential part of what it means to be a human being.

Of Mice and Men is a story of human hope and human helplessness. It is a drama of human brotherhood in which George believes he can arrive at a harbor of safety if he can help Lennie, the mentally retarded friend with whom he wanders from job to job, reach it with him. Homecoming for George would not be homecoming unless there was someone with whom he could share the experience. "A guy needs somebody—to be near him. . . . A guy goes nuts if he ain't got nobody. Don't make no difference who the guy is, long's he's with you. I tell ya . . . I tell ya a guy gets too lonely an' he gets sick."[349]

Of Mice and Men returns frequently to the theme of irremedial loss in human life and of the healing power of human sympathy to sustain us in those moments. Curley's wife in the novel is inadvertently killed by Lennie who is unaware of his great strength. She flirted with Lennie as she did with almost all the men on the ranch. It is clear as she dies, however, that she was beset by loneliness, a loneliness which sent her walking around the ranch, looking constantly for something she could not find. It was not sex she sought or even a demonstration of her ability to tease men. She needed understanding and insight into her own sense of emptiness and futility. Steinbeck describes her face tenderly as she lies dead: "Curley's wife lay with a half-covering of yellow hay. And the meanness and the plannings and the discontent and the ache for attention were all gone from her face. She was very pretty and simple, and her face was sweet and young."[350]

We said above that the theme of longing is central to *Of Mice and Men*. This longing transcends the longing we have for one another and for mutual understanding. It extends to a longing for a distant homeland we never seem to reach, a longing for belonging to life more deeply than we do.

When Candy, who planned to join George and Lennie on the dream farm they spoke of so often, sees that Curley's wife is dead and that Lennie is responsible for it, he is gripped by anxiety and disappointment.

Now Candy spoke his greatest fear. "You an' me can get that little place, can't we George? You an' me can go there an' live nice, can't we, George? Can't we?"

Before George answered, Candy dropped his head and looked down at the hay. He knew.

George said softly,—"I think I knowed from the very first. I think I knowed we'd never do her. He usta like to hear about it so much I got to thinking maybe we would."[351]

Steinbeck's intention was to present the deep longing for the apparently unattainable in life. He wrote on one occasion that Lennie was meant to be a symbol of "the unarticulate and powerful yearning of all men." This dream is so universal that George and Lennie attract other men to it. In a ritualistic fashion, they recite a formula hoping for the land they will one day possess.

The ritual is so well known that even Lennie who has trouble remembering anything learns and shouts out the refrain of the story whenever George begins to tell it: "An' live on the fatta the lan.'" George and Lennie believe in their hope so ardently and repeat the ritual expressing this hope so often that others are drawn into the dream.

Candy, the old man, and Crooks, the Negro ranchhand, ask

if they can share the dream and work the farms. Before Lennie kills Curley's wife, the number captivated by the dream is doubled to four, representing different ages, races and levels of intelligence. The hope for Eden, paradise, homecoming, belonging is thus shown to be universal.

The dream is destroyed by human weakness and by this alone. Lennie is not evil, only imperfect. He does "bad things" as he calls them, not because he wishes to harm or hurt but because his efforts at love are awkward. Reflecting the pathos of the human dilemma, Lennie, after he has killed Curley's wife and run away, gives voice to his instinctive goodness and his innate weakness: "I tried . . . I tried and tried. I couldn't help it . . . I tried . . . I tried and tried."[352]

Of Mice and Men is a story of salvation in which men hope for more understanding among themselves and for a port of safety beyond the horizon. Meanwhile, men go on dreaming, restless for home, anxious to be rescued, sensing we are lost, not quite where we ought to be. Whether or not we believe we shall one day overcome our homelessness is the difference between faith and despair.

THE GRAPES OF WRATH

The moral themes Steinbeck considered in The Red Pony and The Pearl were given classic expression in East of Eden. In a similar manner, Of Mice and Men developed the theme of pilgrimage to a promised land, a theme which was set in classic form in The Grapes of Wrath.

The Grapes of Wrath consciously intends to be an epic. The novel opens on a universal scale, introducing no specific people but describing the timeless struggle against the elements for survival. Dust is the symbol of that force which resists life and destroys man. The dust is so oppressive that at night "the stars could not pierce the dust to get down."[353]

During the day, women battle the dust, children are obliged to play in it and men's faces are hardened by it.

The omnipresent dust serves as the symbol of spiritual and physical death. Hemingway used the symbol of rain; Camus, of bubonic plague. In each case, however, one is dealing with a frightening reality over which men have no control. Dust, rain or disease come upon man all of a sudden. Steinbeck places his story in this tradition from its opening chapter to its last words.

The Grapes of Wrath is not a work of social protest or a literary description of the trials of the Joad family. It is rather the story of man. It is an allegory of humanity's history of dispossession, wandering, struggle, defeat, hope, victory, sacrifice and salvation. It is a tribute to all men of good will who inherit the earth and come home to a promised land because of their stubborn loyalty to life against the forces which seek to break the human spirit.

The vastness of the theme Steinbeck has chosen leads him to link his story with the Old Testament and the New. The saga of the Joad family is the saga of Israel retold. There are twelve Joads, similar to the tribes of Israel, who flee from the bondage of those capitalists who oppress them. Route 66 becomes the scene of another Exodus and California, the Promised Land. Like Israel, the Joads drive on against adversity until their hope becomes reality in a new homeland.

The Grapes of Wrath is written in the American cultural idiom. The Joads seek the promised land along Route 66 in an old Hudson in need of tires. They are inspired not only by this promised land but by the fulfillment of the American dream. In a typical American fashion, they go West, yearning for peace and hope, for freedom and an unspoiled Eden. Their values are pragmatic and their ethical decisions derive from personal reasoning rather than from tradition or authority. The Joads are undauntedly optimistic. On one occasion, Ma

warns sternly: "You ain't got the right to be discouraged. . . .
You jus' ain't got the right."[354]

The salvation the Joads seek is a secular salvation, and yet
Steinbeck never allows us to forget that there are profound
religious implications in what he seeks to say. The Reverend
Jim Casy is, for example, an obvious Christ figure. He joins the
twelve Joads and becomes their moral leader. While he is
with them, he preaches a message of love and brotherhood.
Casy speaks of a new world and of a time when the spirit will
prevail over institutions. His initials identify him with Christ
and his death completes the symbolism. Casy dies as a martyr
for his cause, leaving Tom Joad in his place as a disciple, telling his executioners: "Listen . . . you fellas don' know what
you're doin'. . . . You don' know what you're a-doin'."[355]

Tom Joad takes up Casy's cause. Ma understands that her
Tom was called to be a prophet from the beginning. "Ever'-
thing you do is more'n you. When they sent you to prison I
knowed it. You're spoke for."[356] Tom confesses his faith in a
passage which makes the spiritual meaning of *The Grapes of
Wrath* unmistakable. When Ma tells of her fears that Tom
may be killed, he says:

Then it don' matter. Then I'll be all aroun' in the dark. I'll be
ever'where—whenever you look. Whenever they's a fight so hungry
people can eat, I'll be there. Whenever they's a cop beaten' up a
guy, I'll be there. If Casy knowed, why, I'll be in the way guys yell
when they're mad an'—I'll be in the way kids laugh when they're
hungry an' they know supper's ready. An' when our folks eat the
stuff they raise an' live in the houses they build—why, I'll be
there.[357]

The Grapes of Wrath is a novel of conversion and salvation. It tells the story of men who left one world and who,
although they have not reached the promised land, are on the
way, hopeful they will arrive and that in their arrival they
shall be welcomed home.

THE WINTER OF OUR DISCONTENT

In *The Winter of Our Discontent*, Steinbeck returns to his concern with the question of good and evil. His analysis, however, is not set in a classic framework as it was in *East of Eden*. The setting is contemporary, and the literary form this time is not allegory. Steinbeck, in all probability, won the Nobel Prize for this work as much as for any other.

A number of familiar Steinbeck themes recur in this novel. He directs his attention anew to the mystery and sublimity of man. "What a frightening thing is the human, a mass of gauges and dials and registers, and we can read only a few and those perhaps not accurately."[358]

The obvious problem is the need to discover what can help us read rightly that which must be read. In this context, revelation takes on meaning for a Christian.

Steinbeck rejects a pragmatic view of man as a legitimate way to interpret human experience. "The what's-he-getting-out-of-it? attitude must be particularly strong in men who play their lives like a poker hand."[359] He is more sensitive to the ill-defined but ever-present mystic tendencies in human life. "Like most modern people, I don't believe in prophecy or magic and then spend half my time practicing it."[360]

This sensitivity keeps us aware of the enigmatic nature of man. "It's hard to know how simple or complicated a man is. When you become too sure, you're usually wrong."[361]

This is one reason why Steinbeck rejects an excessively scientific approach to human aspirations.

I guess we're all, or most of us, the wards of that nineteenth-century science which denied existence to anything it could not measure or explain. The things we couldn't explain went right on but surely not with our blessing. We did not see what we couldn't explain, and meanwhile a great part of the world was abandoned to children, insane people, fools, and mystics, who were more interested in what is than in why it is.[362]

Steinbeck is concerned in *The Winter of Our Discontent* with a religious definition of man as well as with his moral conduct. The novel is an inversion of the Gospel acted out in modern dress. The story is a portrayal of the Kingdom of Satan established in the Long Island village of New Baytown. The action occurs in the time between Good Friday and July Fourth, an obvious blending of the religious and the secular, the sacred and the patriotic which is not unusual for Americans. Life in New Baytown differs considerably from life in *East of Eden*. Men have now become servants of evil in the name of virtue. In this realm, the Prince of Darkness reigns, but he wears the raiment of light and sweet reasonableness, of gentle compromise and clever planning.

Corruption has rules in New Baytown, a certain style, one might say, a new set of commandments. "Like never take the first offer, and like, if somebody wants to sell, he's got a reason, and like, a thing is only as valuable as who wants it."[363]

In this inverted world, a refusal to go along is vice; honesty is deemed worthy of social excommunication and unrelenting ridicule. Ethan Hawley, the protagonist of the story, is made to feel sinful because he is committed to integrity. Eventually, he agrees that his pursuit of moral goodness is rooted in the past and, therefore, an obstacle to his involvement with the present. Ethical behavior is an anachronism. Worse than this, it is selfish since it prevents one from sharing life with his contemporaries.

It is Good Friday as *The Winter of Our Discontent* opens. It is a strange Good Friday, and Ethan Hawley is fascinated with the day. "Do you remember it's Good Friday?," he asks repeatedly. "Why do they call it Good Friday?"

Ethan goes to his grocery store where he preaches a sermon to the canned goods and prays over them in Latin. The life and death of Jesus have no more impact on New Baytown than they do on the groceries to which Ethan proclaims the good news. Jesus is no savior in New Baytown since, without faith, he is powerless to help. Ethan is preoccupied with the thought that Jesus died on this day. "Good God," he comments, "it took him a long time to die—a dreadful long time."[364] He continues: ". . . Good Friday has always troubled me. Even as a child I was deep taken with sorrow, not at the agony of the crucifixion, but feeling the blighting loneliness of the Crucified. And I have never lost the sorrow. . . ."[365]

When Joey Morphy suggests to Ethan that he become part of a "deal," Ethan reacts in anger. Morphy explains that what Ethan calls dishonesty is, in reality, integrity. Although Ethan is not persuaded, he regrets his hostility. "I didn't mean it. Honest to God I didn't, Joey . . . this is a dreadful holiday— dreadful . . . every year, ever since I was a kid . . . it gets worse because—maybe I know more what it means, I hear those lonely 'lama sabach thani' words."[366]

Hawley plays two roles in this reenactment of the Good Friday narrative: Jesus and Judas. This is a typical Steinbeck technique. No man, he reasons, is all good or all evil. As we have seen, even the Cain-Abel story is told ambiguously.

The Christ symbolism in Hawley's life is intentional. He struggles with temptations which involve not merely a misdeed but, as in the case of Christ, the mission and meaning of life itself. "Can a man," Hawley asks, "think out his life, or must he just tag along?"[367] The question reminds one of the messianic temptations of Christ, but it also reflects the force of public opinion on American ethics. It suggests the pressure an outer-directed culture exerts on a man seeking to devise a self-definition. Hawley confronts the problem of his temptations and self-identity in Holy Week. He is called a "savior" frequently during the course of the book, and as we shall see later, emerges from the tomb where he was about to die with new life.

Hawley discovers, however, that there is no place for the words or deeds of Christ in New Baytown. In this world of darkness, Christ is not only impotent to help; he is "evil."

Christ is excluded in the name of virtue and human values, in the name of life and for the sake of constructing a more effective "faith" and a viable "moral" system.

COMPROMISE AND BETRAYAL

Hawley is shaken by this realization. In despair and bewilderment, he seeks for some way to belong to this new world. On the Saturday recalling the burial of Jesus, Ethan questions the need for honesty and decides that all moral values are relative. He plays the part of Judas and betrays his friend, Danny, for a sum of money. Then he reports his trusting employer, Mr. Marullo, to the civil authorities as an illegal immigrant so that he may get ahead at Marullo's expense.

Marullo regarded Ethan as the only honest man he had met. After the capture of Marullo, Ethan learns that the ownership of the store had been transferred to him by Marullo in gratitude for his honesty. Marullo never learns who reported him. He does not suspect Ethan, but he sees in his betrayer the honest man he wanted to be when he believed in the message of the Statue of Liberty.

The title of the book is taken from Shakespeare's *Richard III*. In that play, Richard speaks lines which Ethan sings while cleaning the grocery store. "Now is the winter of our discontent. Made glorious by this sun of York."[368]

The artistry of *The Winter of Our Discontent* is evident in subtle blending of American themes, New Testament allusions and Shakespearean references. In *Richard III*, Richard is physically deformed. He is disillusioned as he learns that courage and manhood do not count at court. Flattery and deception are judged far more important and useful.

Ethan finds that he is morally "deformed" by New Baytown standards. He is confused when ethical behavior, faith in God, trust in people are deemed disadvantages. Gimmicks, deals and hypocrisy make the difference in life. One must never be open, sincere, too obvious. One must speak to few men and never honestly. Every man is a potential enemy, and all men are competitors. The moral man in the modern age is un- armed and ill-prepared to cope with life.

At this point in the story, Hawley wonders about the larger issues in living. He recognizes that there are larger issues, but he does not know how to acknowledge their validity and re- main part of the present. The pragmatic tasks he is asked to perform seem to go counter to the transcendental values he is anxious to affirm. He senses that whatever his culture has achieved, it has not earned much happiness. "It does seem to me that nearly everyone I see is nervous and restless and a little loud. . . ."[369] In words reminiscent of the doctrine of original sin, he asks why we fail. "If it's that simple, why don't more people do it? Why does nearly everyone make the same mis- takes and over and over. Is there always something forgot- ten?"[370]

Ethan worries about his inability to have faith in life after death. Once, while watching his wife Mary sleep, he looks for a reason why she has less trouble sleeping than he does.

I have thought the difference might be that my Mary knows she will live forever, that she will step from the living into another life as easily as she slips from sleep to wakefulness. She knows this with her whole body, so completely that she does not think of it any more than she thinks to breathe. . . . On the other hand, I know in my bones and my tissue that I will one day, soon or late, stop living and so I fight against sleep. . . .[371]

Ethan hopes for salvation from his predicament by turning to prayer and to faith in the mystical dimension of life. He retires often to a cave by the sea which he calls "The Place" where he turns his heart to something like prayer. "I call what- ever happens in the Place 'taking stock.' Some others might call it prayer, and maybe it would be the same thing. I don't believe it's thought."[372]

Ethan returns to the Place at crucial moments in his life.

I spent night-tide there before I went in the service, and the night-tide before I married my Mary, and part of the night Ellen was born that hurt her so bad. . . . Now, sitting in the Place, out of the wind, seeing under the guardian lights the tide creep in, black from the dark sky, I wondered whether all men have a Place or need a Place, or want one and have none.[373]

DESPAIR AND REBIRTH

Hawley begins to feel life is no longer worth living when he sees that his entire family has gone the way of darkness. Mary, his wife, is preoccupied with money; Ellen seems at times no different from the other children of New Baytown; Allen is caught cheating in a national "I love America" contest. When Allen shows no repentence, Ethan is shaken. "I raised Allen. I could not find his early face, the face of joy and excitement that made me sure of the perfectibility of man."[374]

In despair, Ethan takes razor blades and goes out to "The Place" to commit suicide. In his reflective prayer before death, he remembers Ellen who, although influenced by her contemporaries, has a mystical tendency. One night he saw Ellen hold fast the family talisman which was a symbol of the family's inheritance of morality and wisdom. In Ellen, he reasons, there may be reason for hope. "Maybe it is Ellen who will carry and pass on whatever is immortal in me."[375]

Ethan has already learned that suffering must be part of life: "to be alive at all is to have scars."[376] Now the combination of suffering and hope count in his favor. He becomes aware as death presses in on him that each man must bear in his own heart light for the world. "It isn't true that there's a community of light, a bonfire of the world. Everyone carries his own, his lonely own."[377]

This light must be borne on behalf of one's fellowmen and for the sake of their salvation. Ethan had come to the realization during Holy Week that "my guilt comes because I am my brother's keeper and I have not saved him."[378] Now he understands that saving his brothers depends upon the light he brings into the world and the revelation he offers them.

When Marullo made a gift of his store to Ethan, he saw this as "his down payment, kind of, so the light won't go out."[379] As Ethan is about to end his life, he complains: "My light is out. There's nothing blacker than a wick."[380]

In the final scene of the novel, Ethan approximates Holden Caulfield. Holden wanted to be a catcher in the rye; Ethan knows he should be a light for others. Holden decided that innocence must be preserved and saw himself standing in a field of rye, catching children who might fall off the cliff into hypocrisy. Ethan reaches a similar decision. No more lights must go out in the world. "It's so much darker when a light goes out than it would have been if it had never shone."[381]

Ethan rejects suicide and rushes from the "tomb" into new life as the surging sea floods the cave. It is Ethan's Easter, the day when he understands what Good Friday was for, the moment when "the winter of our discontent" is "made glorious by the sun of York. I had to get back—had to return the talisman to its new owner. Else another light might go out."[382]

REFLECTIONS ON THE THEME
OF SALVATION

By almost every significant category we can consider, it appears that modern man is a creature aspiring toward salvation. His philosophy is often an effort at asking why he has not yet been saved or an attempt at analyzing how he might be saved in his humanity. Arthur Schopenhauer wondered whether the demands of the transcendent were so imperative that man's only salvation lay in relinquishing this life. His thinking is characteristic of Eastern thought and traces of this approach are manifest in many world religions.

Western man, for the most part, tends to be more active and more immanent than Schopenhauer or Eastern religions in the quest for salvation. Auguste Comte, perhaps, went the furthest in fusing religion and science. The result was at times bizarre, on occasion almost humorous but, in any case, it emerged from a sincere desire to achieve a total redemption for man. This redemption would bind ritual and reason, the secular and the sacred. The end product was, however, so contrived and forced that neither religion nor science survived intact. Comte is of interest to us, not because of the viability of his project, but because of its attestation to a perennial longing for salvation.

John Stuart Mill was less doctrinal in his salvation concern. He opted for ethics, an ethic built on rational categories and pragmatically productive of the greatest qualitative happiness for the greatest number. Karl Marx and Sigmund Freud were destined to influence modern man most incisively in their respective theories concerning an exclusively secular salvation brought about by human resources and presided over by the community of man. The fact that neither Marx nor Freud is accepted today without serious qualification is an indication of man's need for the mystical.

Marx and Freud are too pat, too deterministic, too scientific, too rational to suit contemporary man. Although the former is optimistic and the latter pessimistic, each lacked sensitivity to those dimensions of man which lead him to ask about God and to pause in wonder before the mystery of himself and the mystery of reality even after these have been understood and explained. The fact that anything *is* a mystery too large for words, too elusive for reason, too awesome for philosophical solution.

The reciprocity between the mystery all around us and our instinctive responsiveness to the sacred has caused man to create religions and to invest more time, energy and devotion in religion than in any other experience he has encountered.

Man expresses himself in religion, not only because he is filled with awe, but more because he senses that he must be rescued from himself, from the complexities and insufficiencies of his own relationships, from his maladjustment to the objective order.

Man seeks to be saved although his religion is often a tortured way of saying that he does not know how this must be done. Nonetheless, he hopes salvation will come to pass. And so he prays and sacrifices, believes and celebrates. He sings and dances, ritualizes and reasons through his religious feeling. In all of this, he is trying to declare that he knows he is not everything, that something more must be said about him and done for him. His plea is fundamentally a plea for God to reveal to him how he should proceed, a prayer that he may be gifted with grace and strength to accomplish what man must accomplish. Man's most ardent dream is that God may stand by his side in some incarnational form, as Krishna or Buddha, as Christ or at least as a prophet who might help us appreciate what it means to be a human being and to discover a God worth worship.

The search for salvation continues in the context of American culture. A people disinclined to the transcendent and passionate about the secular managed to become a people sensitive to God. Americans might possess all that the human spirit could wish to possess. And yet they feel that they must be saved not merely in the secular order which they prize but in those areas of life where their humanity is at issue and where they sense a hunger for God and a spiritual poverty despite the affluence and largeness in which they live.

Americans are pragmatic and experimental about religion. They prefer action to doctrine, public consensus to authority. Present utility is more urgent than preserved tradition. Yet Americans wonder why they are not enchanted in this new Eden or who might save them or at least what is missing.

F. Scott Fitzgerald made it clear that the religious aspirations of Americans were often trivialized by a culture which offered only secular objects for religious devotion. In this milieu it was easy to become confused since one knew neither the place for the secular nor the correct definition of the sacred. As a result, the American could be tormented by both and consoled by neither.

Ernest Hemingway tried a different approach to salvation. He admitted the wasteland and lostness described by Fitzgerald. He wanted, however, to find a measure of redemption from the *nada* or nothingness in which we live. He considered in turn ritual and courage, grace under pressure and romantic love as possible saving realities. When these failed, he spoke of brotherhood in a common cause and then, finally, of the human spirit, the healing power of pain and the haunting figure of Christ.

For Tennessee Williams, the inability of man to make life more beneficent led us to devise worlds of illusions in which we hoped for the salvation we would never be given. Sometimes our viciousness with one another became so stark that symbolic cannibalism was the only way to describe it. Sometimes God seemed so distant that destruction of life appeared to be the sole reality which could reach him. Eventually Williams becomes hopeful and begins to write of Easter and rebirth, of faith and grace and of a saving God who could redeem men when they did not despair of his power to do so.

Both William Faulkner and John Steinbeck devoted their attention more immediately to moral awareness and its relationship to salvation. In both cases tradition was taken seriously. For Faulkner, tradition or the past was oppressive. We are unsaved because the guilt of our former sins, personal sins or the original sin of the race itself always rises up to defeat us. Most of Faulkner's victims are punished for sins other than their own and far in excess of the malice of their misdeeds.

Only in A *Fable* and *The Bear* do some measure of hope or

redemption seem possible. In *The Sound and The Fury*, *Sanctuary* and *Absalom, Absalom!* there is a sense of doom and despair. The world has no savior, life no redeemer, the future no potential to overcome the past. *Light in August* touches on the theme of a suffering Christ figure and the power of pain itself to serve in some way the process of redemption. *The Bear* considers the possibility of a transcendent revelation or vision for those who sensitize themselves to the mystical and spiritual realities of life. Revelation is active in our midst. If we see nothing, it is not because there is nothing to see but because our eyes are closed.

John Steinbeck was more immediately attuned to human nature than to its past sins. No man was immune from the force of evil. Every man had to be redeemed in hope and suffering. Even Aron, the Abel of *East of Eden*, became proud in his innocence and resentful in his idealism. Even Aron stood in need of the redemption he resisted.

When George and Lennie dream of a day when they can "live on the fatta the lan'," or when the Joads press on to a new life in a new world, Steinbeck is telling us that the human heart will not rest until it comes home. The fact that we have not yet experienced homecoming is, perhaps, not as significant as the fact that we refuse to stop dreaming of this.

We will not be dissuaded from the conviction that somehow, some way the whole race will be saved and healed, recognized, called by name and welcomed home. Although the entire salvation enterprise may seem a mirage at times, the winter of our discontent is continually made glorious by the sun of a saving light which never goes out and which keeps us aware that because we have been made for more we shall receive it.

Notes

1. Salvation Themes in Modern Philosophy

1. Cf. *The Estranged God* (New York: Sheed and Ward, 1966), where I have developed these themes more fully.

2. Karl Marx, *Gesamtausgabe* (Berlin: Marx-Engels Institut, 1932), I: 3. The quote is from the essay "Alienated Labor" (1844) which appears in this collection.

3. Karl Marx, *Capital*, trans. C. H. Kerr (Chicago: Random House, 1909), I: 83.

4. Karl Marx, *The Communist Manifesto* (New York: Random House, 1932), p. 323ff.

5. John Dewey, *Freedom and Culture* (New York: Putnam's, 1936), p. 78.

6. I am indebted to Dr. Louis Dupre, *Philosophical Foundations of Marxism* (New York: Harcourt, Brace, and World Inc., 1966) for some of the ideas in this critique.

7. Ignace Lepp, *From Karl Marx to Jesus Christ* (New York: Sheed and Ward, 1958).

8. George H. Hampsch, *The Theory of Communism* (New York: Citadel, 1965), pp. 43–44.

9. An interesting position paper in this area is Roger Garaudy's, *From Anathema to Dialogue* (New York: Herder and Herder, 1966).

10. *Mater et Magistra* (Washington, D.C.: U.S.C.C., 1961), 255.

11. Cf. *The Estranged God* (New York: Sheed and Ward, 1966), where I sought to give an interpretation of Camus' thought.

12. I am considerably indebted in this section to John F. McMahon for his article, "What does Christianity Add to Atheistic Humanism?", *Cross Currents*, XVIII, n.2 (Spring, 1968), pp. 129–150.

13. Ernest Jones, *The Life and Works of Sigmund Freud*, Vol. 1, 1953; Vol. 2, 1955; Vol. 3, 1957 (New York: Basic Books, Inc.), III: 383.

14. *Ibid.*

15. *Ibid.*, I: 157–8.

16. *Ibid.*, III: 279.

17. *Ibid.*, 42.

18. Sigmund Freud, *Beyond the Pleasure Principle*, p. 67.

19. W. F. Albright, *From the Stone Age to Christianity* (Baltimore: The Johns Hopkins Press, 1946), pp. 74–75.

20. Sigmund Freud, "Obsessive Acts and Religious Practices" in *Collected Papers* (London: Hogarth Press, 1924), II: 34.

21. Sigmund Freud, *The Future of an Illusion*, trans. W. D. Robson-Scott, p. 51; used with permission of Liveright, publishers, New York.

22. *Ibid.*, p.52.

23. *Ibid.*, p. 53.

24. *Ibid.*

25. *Ibid.*, pp. 56–57.

26. *Ibid.*, p. 57.

27. *Ibid.*, p. 58.

28. Ernest Jones, *op. cit.*, III: 359.

29. *Ibid.*

30. *Ibid.*

31. Sigmund Freud, *An Autobiographical Study*, trans. James Strachey (London: Hogarth Press, 1935), pp. 124–5.

32. *Ibid.*, p. 125.

33. Ernest Jones, *op. cit.*, III: 354.

34. Sigmund Freud, *Totem and Taboo*, trans. A. A. Brill, p. 213; copyright W. W. Norton & Co., Inc.; used with permission.

35. *Ibid.*, p. 207.

36. Sigmund Freud, *Civilization and Its Discontents* (London: Hogarth Press, 1946), p. 118.

37. Ernest Jones, *op. cit.*, III: 365.

38. *Ibid.*

39. *Ibid.*

40. *Ibid.*

41. *Ibid.*, p. 353.

42. *Ibid.*, p. 357.

43. Theodor Reik, *From Thirty Years with Freud* (London: Hogarth Press, 1942), p. 123.

44. cf. *The Estranged God* where I considered these philosophers in more detail.

45. Helen Walker Puner, *Freud* (London: Grey Walls Press, 1949), p. 220.

46. Sigmund Freud, *Totem and Taboo, op. cit.*, p. 196.

47. *Ibid.*, p. 205.

48. A. A. Goldenweiser, "Totemism and Analytical Study," *Journal of American Folklore*, XXIII, pp. 179–293.

49. A. L. Kroeber, *Anthropology* rev. ed. (New York: Harcourt, Brace & World, Inc., 1948), pp. 616–617; reprinted with permission.

50. Sigmund Freud, *New Introductory Lectures on Psychoanalysis* (New York: W. W. Norton, 1933), p. 228.

51. Otto Rank, *Will Therapy and Truth and Reality* (New York: Knopf, 1950).

52. *Ibid.*, p. 239.

53. Sigmund Freud, *Civilization and Its Discontents* (London: Hogarth Press, 1946), p. 85; reprinted by permission of W. W. Norton & Co., Inc., New York.

54. Herbert Spencer, *First Principles* (London: Harrison & Sons, 1863).

55. Sigmund Freud, *An Outline of Psychoanalysis* (New York: W. W. Norton, 1949), p. 106.

2. The Religious Phenomenon

56. Mircea Eliade, *The Myth of the Eternal Return*, trans. Willard R. Trask (New York: Bollingen Series XLVI, 1954); by permission of Princeton University Press, p. 101.

57. Mircea Eliade, *The Sacred and the Profane* trans. Willard R. Trask (New York: Harper Torchbooks, Harper & Row, 1959), p. 127.

58. *Declaration on the Relationship of the Church to Non-Christian Religions*, (Washington, D.C.: U.S.C.C., 1965), p. 2.

59. *Ibid.*

60. *Dogmatic Constitution on the Church*, c.2, n. 16.

61. *Declaration on the Relationship of the Church to Non-Christian Religions*, 3.

62. Eliade, *The Sacred and the Profane, op. cit.*, p. 23.

63. *Ibid.*, p. 213.

64. Eliade, *Cosmos and History, op. cit.*, p. 104.

65. Peter L. Berger, *A Rumor of Angels* (Garden City, New York: Doubleday & Company, Inc., 1969), pp. 112–114; copyright © 1969 by Peter L. Berger; reprinted by permission.

3. The American Experiment

66. George Santayana, *Character and Opinion in the United States* (New York: W. W. Norton Co. Inc., 1967), p. 168.

67. *Ibid.*, p. 169.

68. Henry Steele Commager, *The American Mind* (New Haven: Yale University Press, 1950), pp. 90, 97.

69. Alexis de Tocqueville, *Democracy in America*, ed. Richard D. Heffner (New York: The New American Library, 1956), p. 144; used with permission.

70. *Ibid.*, p. 143.

71. Henry Steele Commager, *op. cit.*, p. 162.

72. Alexis de Tocqueville, *op. cit.*, p. 163.

73. *Ibid.*, p. 164.

74. *Ibid.*, p. 158.

75. *Ibid.*, p. 163.

76. Jacques Maritain, *Reflections on America* (New York: Charles Scribner's Sons, 1958), pp. 54–55; copyright © 1958 Jacques Maritain; reprinted with permission.

77. Harvey Cox *The Secular City* (New York: The Macmillan Company, 1965), p. 51.

78. Henry Steele Commager, *op. cit.*, p. 162.

79. *Ibid.*, pp. 410–411.

80. George Santayana, *op. cit.*, pp. 144, 213.

81. Henry Steele Commager, *op. cit.*, p. 164.

82. Alexis de Tocqueville, *op. cit.*, pp. 148, 154–155.

83. George Santayana, *op. cit.*, p. 5.

84. Henry Steele Commager, *op. cit.*, p. 421.

85. George Santayana, *op. cit.*, pp. 196–197.

86. Jacques Maritain, *op. cit.*, p. 43.

87. George Santayana, *op. cit.*, pp. 210–212.

88. Alexis de Tocqueville, *op. cit.*, p. 212.

89. *Ibid.*, pp. 212–213.

90. George Santayana, *op. cit.*, p. 198.

91. Jacques Maritain, *op. cit.*, p. 15.

92. Margaret Mead, *New Lives for Old* (New York: William Morrow, 1956). The quotation is from Jacques Maritain, *op. cit.*, p. 40.

93. Alexis de Tocqueville, *op. cit.*, p. 155.

94. *Ibid.*, p. 216.

95. *Ibid.*, p. 235.

96. George Santayana, *op. cit.*, p. 5.

97. Henry Steele Commager, *op. cit.*, p. 166.

98. Will Herberg, *Protestant, Catholic, Jew* (Garden City, New York: Doubleday, 1955), p. 3.

99. George Santayana, *op. cit.*, pp. 178–179.

100. *Ibid.*, pp. 174–176, 196.

101. Will Herberg, *op. cit.*, p. 3.

102. *Ibid.*, p. 84.

103. *Ibid.*, p. 265.

104. *Ibid.*, p. 260.

105. *Ibid.*, p.: 272. Herberg is quoting Norman Thomas.

106. Jacques Maritain, *op. cit.*, p. 24.

107. *Ibid.*, p. 25.

108. Martin Marty, *Varieties of Unbelief* (Garden City, New York: Doubleday, 1966), p. 80.

109. Jacques Maritain, *op. cit.*, p. 27.

110. Albert Ellery Bergh, ed., *The Writings of Thomas Jefferson* (Washington, D.C.; Jefferson Memorial Association, 1903), XV; 273–274.

111. *Ibid.*, p. 276.

112. *Ibid.*, p. 203.

113. *Ibid.*, p. 109.

114. Albert Ellery Bergh, *op. cit.*, XVI: 118–119.

115. William James, *Collected Essays and Reviews* (New York: Longmans-Green, 1920), p. 413.

116. *Ibid.*, p. 412.

117. William James, *Pragmatism: A New Name for Some Old Ways of Thinking* (New York: Longmans-Green, 1921), p. 201.

118. John Dewey, *Experience and Nature* (New York: W. W. Norton, 1929), p. 222.

119. John Dewey, *Creative Intelligence: Essays in the Pragmatic Attitude* (New York: Holt, Rinehart & Winston, Inc., 1956), p. 144.

120. John Dewey, *The Quest for Certainty* (New York: Minton, Balch, 1929), p. 255.

121. John Dewey, *A Common Faith* (New Haven: Yale University Press, 1934), p. 6.

122. *Ibid.*, p. 7.

123. *Ibid.*, pp. 8–9.

124. *Ibid.*, p. 9.
125. *Ibid.*, p. 15.
126. *Ibid.*, pp. 23, 19, 26.
127. *Ibid.*, p. 26.
128. *Ibid.*, p. 42.
129. George Santayana, *op. cit.*, p. 159.
130. John Dewey, *A Common Faith, op. cit.*, pp. 31–32.
131. *Ibid.*, p. 44.
132. *Ibid.*, p. 50.
133. *Ibid., passim*, pp. 77–78.
134. *Ibid.*, pp. 84, 87.
135. Thornton Wilder, *Three Plays* (New York: Harper & Row, Publishers, 1958), pp. 61–62; copyright Harper & Row; used with permission.
136. *Ibid.*, p. 8.
137. *Ibid.*, p. 62.
138. *Ibid.*, p. 15.
139. *Ibid.*, p. 21.
140. *Ibid.*, p. 31.
141. *Ibid.*, Preface, p. xi.
142. *Ibid.*, p. 52.
143. Arthur Miller, *Death of a Salesman* (New York: The Viking Press, 1949), p. 51; copyright 1949 by Arthur Miller; reprinted by permission of the Viking Press, Inc.
144. *Ibid.*, p. 24.
145. *Ibid.*, p. 85.
146. *Ibid.*, p. 33.
147. *Ibid.*, p. 36.
148. *Ibid.*, p. 98.
149. *Ibid.*, p. 86.
150. *Ibid.*, p. 132.
151. *Ibid.*, p. 138.
152. *Ibid.*, p. 52.

4. Salvation Themes in American Literature

153. F. Scott Fitzgerald, *The Great Gatsby* (New York: Charles Scribner's Sons, 1925), p. 2; copyright 1925 Charles Scribner's Sons; renewal copyright 1953, Frances Scott Fitzgerald Lanahan; reprinted with permission.
154. *Ibid.*, p. 48.

Notes

155. *Ibid.*, p. 2.
156. *Ibid.*, pp. 21–22.
157. F. Scott Fitzgerald, *Tender is the Night* (New York: Charles Scribner's Sons, 1933), p. 75.
158. *The Great Gatsby, op. cit.*, p. 149.
159. *Ibid.*, p. 112.
160. *Ibid.*, p. 69.
161. *Ibid.*, p. 181.
162. *Ibid.*, p. 182.
163. "A Clean, Well-lighted Place" in *The Short Stories of Ernest Hemingway* (New York: Charles Scribner's Sons, 1938), p. 481.
164. Ernest Hemingway, *The Old Man and the Sea* (New York: Charles Scribner's Sons, 1952), p. 114; copyright 1952 Ernest Hemingway; reprinted with permission of Charles Scribner's Sons.
165. Ernest Hemingway, *A Farewell to Arms* (New York: Charles Scribner's Sons, 1929), p. 324; copyright 1929 Charles Scribner's Sons; renewal copyright © 1957 Ernest Hemingway; reprinted with permission of Charles Scribner's Sons, 1926), p. 97.
166. *The Old Man and the Sea, op. cit.*, pp. 139–140.
167. Ernest Hemingway, *The Sun Also Rises* (New York: Charles Scribner's Sons, 1926), p. 97.
168. *A Farewell to Arms, op. cit.*, pp. 184–185.
169. *Ibid.*, pp. 125–126.
170. *Ibid.*, p. 332.
171. *Ibid.*, p. 71.
172. *Ibid.*, pp. 261, 263.
173. *Ibid.*, p. 147.
174. *Ibid.*, pp. 178–179.
175. *Ibid.*, p. 327.
176. *Ibid.*, p. 330.
177. *Ibid.*, p. 139.
178. *Ibid.*, pp. 213–214.
179. *Ibid.*, p. 249.
180. *Ibid.*, p. 327.
181. *Ibid.*, pp. 330–331.
182. *Ibid.*, p. 328.
183. *Ibid.*, p. 330.
184. Ernest Hemingway, *For Whom the Bell Tolls* (New York: Charles Scribner's Sons, 1940), p. 91; copyright 1940 Ernest Hemingway; renewal copyright © 1968 Mary Hemingway; reprinted with permission of Charles Scribner's Sons.

185. *Ibid.*, p. 43.
186. *Ibid.*, p. 169.
187. *Ibid.*, p. 236.
188. *Ibid.*, p. 239.
189. *Ibid.*, p. 471.
190. *Ibid.*, p. 381.
191. *Ibid.*, p. 464.
192. *Ibid.*, pp. 196, 198.
193. *Ibid.*
194. *Ibid.*, p. 41.
195. *Ibid.*, p. 348.
196. *Ibid.*, pp. 380, 466–468.
197. *The Old Man and the Sea, op. cit.*, p. 32.
198. *Ibid.*, p. 28.
199. *Ibid.*, p. 61.
200. *Ibid.*, pp. 73, 114.
201. *Ibid.*, p. 10.
202. *Ibid.*, p. 11.
203. *Ibid.*, p. 55.
204. *Ibid.*, p. 58.
205. *Ibid.*, p. 61.
206. *Ibid.*, p. 90.
207. *Ibid.*, p. 94.
208. *Ibid.*, p. 118.
209. *Ibid.*, p. 134.
210. Lincoln Barnett, "Tennessee Williams," *Life*, XXIV (Feb. 16, 1948), p. 113.
211. Tennessee Williams, "The Glass Menagerie" in *Six Modern American Plays*, p. 439; copyright © 1945 by Tennessee Williams and Edwina D. Williams (New York: Random House, 1951).
212. *Ibid.*, p. 511.
213. *Ibid.*, p. 439.
214. *Ibid.*, p. 446.
215. *Ibid.*, p. 460.
216. *Ibid.*, p. 459.
217. *Ibid.*, p. 462.
218. *Ibid.*, p. 471.
219. *Ibid.*, p. 473.
220. *Ibid.*, p. 508.
221. *Ibid.*, p. 475.
222. *Ibid.*, p. 498.

223. *Ibid.*, p. 498.
224. Tennessee Williams, A *Streetcar Named Desire* (New York: The New American Library, 1947), p. 117.
225. *Ibid.*, p. 15.
226. *Ibid.*, p. 19.
227. *Ibid.*, p. 96.
228. Tennessee Williams, *The Night of the Iguana* (New York: The New American Library, 1964), p. 117.
229. A *Streetcar Named Desire*, *op. cit.*, p. 142.
230. *Ibid.*, p. 95.
231. Tennessee Williams, *Summer and Smoke* (New York: The New American Library, 1961), p. 77; copyright © 1948 by Tennessee Williams; reprinted by permission of New Directions Publishing Corporation.
232. *Ibid.*, pp. 114, 115.
233. *Ibid.*, p. 116.
234. *Ibid.*, p. 117.
235. Tennessee Williams, *Cat on a Hot Tin Roof* (New York: New Directions Publishing Corp., 1955), p. ix; copyright 1955 by Tennessee Williams; reprinted by permission.
236. *Ibid.*
237. *Ibid.*, p. 43.
238. *Ibid.*, p. 44.
239. *Ibid.*, p. 65.
240. Tennessee Williams, *Suddenly, Last Summer* (New York: New Directions Publishing Corp., 1958), p. 47; copyright © 1958 by Tennessee Williams; reprinted with permission.
241. *Ibid.*, p. 93.
242. *Ibid.*, p. 9.
243. *Ibid.*, pp. 16–20, *passim*.
244. *Ibid.*, p. 64.
245. *Ibid.*, p. 77.
246. *Ibid.*, pp. 38–39.
247. Tennessee Williams, *Sweet Bird of Youth* (New York: The New American Library, 1962), p. 122; copyright © 1959 by Two Rivers Enterprises, Inc.; reprinted by permission of New Directions Publishing Corporation.
248. *Ibid.*, p. 120.
249. *Ibid.*, p. 122.
250. *Ibid.*, p. 47.
251. *Ibid.*, p. 37.

252. *Ibid.*, p. 39.
253. *Ibid.*, p. xii.
254. *Ibid.*, p. 98.
255. Tennessee Williams, *The Night of the Iguana* (New York: The New American Library, 1964), p. 26; copyright © 1961 by Two Rivers Enterprises, Inc.; reprinted by permission of New Directions Publishing Corporation.
256. *Ibid.*, p. 99.
257. *Ibid.*, p. 61.
258. *Ibid.*, p. 106.
259. *Ibid.*, p. 109.
260. *Ibid.*, p. 126.
261. *Ibid.*, p. 127.
262. *Ibid.*, p. 124.
263. William Faulkner, *Absalom, Absalom!* (New York: Random House, Inc., 1936), p. 7.
264. *Ibid.*, p. 172.
265. *Ibid.*, p. 174.
266. *Ibid.*, p. 135.
267. *Ibid.*, p. 9.
268. William Faulkner, *As I Lay Dying* (New York: Vintage Books, Random House, Inc., 1930), p. 159.
269. *Ibid.*, pp. 26–27.
270. *Ibid.*, pp. 202–203.
271. *Ibid.*, p. 129.
272. *Ibid.*, p. 119.
273. *Ibid.*, p. 125.
274. *Ibid.*, p. 250.
275. *Ibid.*, p. 76.
276. *Ibid.*, pp. 22–23.
277. *Ibid.*, p. 223.
278. *Ibid.*, p. 160.
279. *Ibid.*, p. 202.
280. *Ibid.*, p. 187.
281. *Ibid.*, p. 212.
282. *Ibid.*, p. 133.
283. *Ibid.*
284. *Ibid.*, p. 168.
285. William Faulkner, *The Sound and the Fury* (New York: Vintage Books, Random House, Inc., 1929), p. 423.
286. *Ibid.*, p. 93.

287. *Ibid.*, p. 98.
288. *Ibid.*, p. 94.
289. *Ibid.*, p. 216.
290. *Ibid.*, p. 93.
291. *Ibid.*, p. 252.
292. *Ibid.*, p. 255.
293. *Ibid.*, p. 71.
294. *Ibid.*, p. 370.
295. *Ibid.*, p. 50.
296. *Ibid.*, p. 58.
297. *Ibid.*, pp. 84–85.
298. *Ibid.*, p. 401.
299. *Ibid.*, p. 99.
300. *Ibid.*, p. 94.
301. *Ibid.*, p. 100.
302. *Ibid.*, p. 104.
303. *Ibid.*, p. 196.
304. *Ibid.*, p. 362.
305. William Faulkner, *Light in August* (New York: The Modern Library, Random House, Inc., 1932), p. 27.
306. *Ibid.*, p. 29.
307. *Ibid.*, p. 337.
308. *Ibid.*, p. 336.
309. *Ibid.*, p. 85.
310. *Ibid.*, p. 218.
311. *Ibid.*, pp. 221–222.
312. *Ibid.*, p. 302.
313. *Ibid.*, p. 306.
314. *Ibid.*, p. 307.
315. *Ibid.*, p. 91.
316. *Ibid.*, p. 407.
317. William Faulkner, *A Fable* (New York: Random House, Inc., 1966), p. 346.
318. *Ibid.*, p. 385.
319. *Ibid.*, p. 400.
320. *Ibid.*, pp. 400–401.
321. William Faulkner, *Three Famous Short Novels* (New York: Vintage Books, Random House, Inc., 1963), p. 187.
322. *Ibid.*, p. 283.
323. *Ibid.*, p. 185.
324. *Ibid.*, p. 188.

325. *Ibid.*, p. 189.
326. *Ibid.*, p. 196.
327. *Ibid.*, pp. 201, 218.
328. *Ibid.*, p. 202.
329. *Ibid.*, p. 245.
330. *Ibid.*, p. 248.
331. *Ibid.*, p. 249.
332. *Ibid.*, p. 267.
333. *Ibid.*, pp. 272–273.
334. *Ibid.*, p. 250.
335. *Ibid.*, p. 296.
336. John Steinbeck, *The Pearl* (New York: Bantam Books, Inc., 1956), p. 4.
337. John Steinbeck, *The Red Pony* (New York: Bantam Books, Inc., 1948), pp. 51–52; © 1933, 1938; © renewed 1961, 1966 by John Steinbeck; reprinted by permission of The Viking Press, Inc.
338. *The Pearl, op. cit.*, p. 4.
339. *Ibid.*, p. 50.
340. *Ibid.*, p. 87.
341. John Steinbeck, *East of Eden* (New York: Bantam Books, Inc., 1955), p. 16; © 1952 by John Steinbeck; reprinted by permission of The Viking Press, Inc.
342. *Ibid.*, p. 10.
343. *Ibid.*, p. 61.
344. *Ibid.*, pp. 366–367.
345. *Ibid.*, pp. 236–240.
346. *Ibid.*, p. 338.
347. *Ibid.*, p. 533.
348. *Ibid.*, p. 532.
349. John Steinbeck, *Of Mice and Men* (New York: Bantam Books, Inc., 1954), p. 80; © 1937; © renewed 1965 by John Steinbeck; reprinted by permission of The Viking Press, Inc.
350. *Ibid.*, p. 101.
351. *Ibid.*, p. 103.
352. *Ibid.*, p. 111.
353. John Steinbeck, *The Grapes of Wrath* (New York: Bantam Books, Inc., 1954), p. 2; © 1939; © renewed 1967 by John Steinbeck; reprinted by permission of The Viking Press, Inc.
354. *Ibid.*, p. 312.
355. *Ibid.*, p. 344.
356. *Ibid.*, p. 314.

357. *Ibid.*, p. 374.
358. John Steinbeck, *The Winter of Our Discontent* (New York: Bantam Books, Inc., 1962), p. 82; © 1961 by John Steinbeck; all rights reserved; reprinted by permission of The Viking Press, Inc.

359. *Ibid.*, p. 146.
360. *Ibid.*, p. 266.
361. *Ibid.*, p. 150.
362. *Ibid.*, p. 75.
363. *Ibid.*, p. 60.
364. *Ibid.*, p. 13.
365. *Ibid.*, p. 39.
366. *Ibid.*, p. 29.
367. *Ibid.*, p. 39.
368. *Ibid.*, p. 169.
369. *Ibid.*, p. 166.
370. *Ibid.*, pp. 60–61.
371. *Ibid.*, p. 38.
372. *Ibid.*, p. 49.
373. *Ibid.*, pp. 47–48.
374. *Ibid.*, p. 206.
375. *Ibid.*
376. *Ibid.*, p. 99.
377. *Ibid.*, p. 297.
378. *Ibid.*, p. 45.
379. *Ibid.*, p. 243.
380. *Ibid.*, p. 298.
381. *Ibid.*
382. *Ibid.*

Subject Index

Absolute Reality: in Hegel—8.
Alienation:
  in Hegel—30.
  in Marx—31f., 47f.
  and despair in Hemingway—
    188.
Aloneness of man, the: in Hem-
    ingway—177f.
American character: in Riesman
    —141f.
American culture—161, 163f.,
    168, 172.
  contemporary concerns—140f.
  fundamental weaknesses—171f.
American Experiment, the—98f.
  classic features—101f.
  observations by de Tocqueville
    —101f., 110f.
  observations by Maritain—104,
    107, 109.
  observations by Santayana—
    105f., 114f.
American Religiosity—115f.
Antithesis between flesh and
    spirit: in Williams—170.

Art: in Schopenhauer—10.
Asceticism: in Schopenhauer—10.
Atheistic humanism—54.

Biography:
  of Freud—58f.
  of Marx—29f.
  of Mill—22f.
  of Schopenhauer—7f.
Boredom—149f.

Capitalism: in Marx—31f.
Christ as a symbol: in Faulkner
    —251f.
Commitment to duty: in Hem-
    ingway—190.
Common Faith, A: in Dewey—
    127f., 135f.
Compromise and Betrayal—277f.
Critique:
  of Comte—20f.

Name Index

Abel—226, 265f., 276, 284.
Absalom, Absalom!—222f., 258, 284.
Absalom—226.
Albright, W. F.—62.
Allah—93f.
Alma (*Summer and Smoke*)—170, 199, 207f.
Amida—92.
Anselmo (*For Whom The Bell Tolls*)—192f.
Arrowsmith—153.
Arrowsmith, Martin—153.
As I Lay Dying—221f., 227f., 242, 258.
Auguste Comte and Positivism—22.
Autobiographical Study, An—66.

Babbitt—153.
Babbitt, George F.—153.
Barban, Tom—167, 170.

Barkley, Catherine—176, 178f., 181f., 186f., 194.
Barnes, Jake—180, 191.
Bear, The—250, 253, 255, 258, 284.
Being and Time—31.
Bentham, Jeremy—22.
Berger, Peter—97.
Bergman, Ingmar—221.
Bhagavad-Gita—89.
Bhakti—89.
Bodhisattva—92.
Bon, Charles—224f.
Bonhoeffer, Dietrich—71.
Brahman-Atman—88f.
Breuer, Joseph—58f.
Buchanan, Daisy—164f., 170f.
Buchanan, Thomas—164f., 170.
Buck, Billy—261f.
Buddha—91, 282.
Buddha, Celestial—92.
Buddhist—91f.
Bundren, Addie—227, 231f.
Bundren, Anse—233.